Aerin Zor

The Bi-Entity Fusion Uprising on Velan-7

Nia Mahmoud

ISBN: 9781779694607
Imprint: Fern Herder Press
Copyright © 2024 Nia Mahmoud.
All Rights Reserved.

Contents

Chapter 1: From Stardust to Activism   **1**
Section 1: A Galactic Birth   1
Section 2: Interstellar Education   14
Section 3: The Journey to Velan-7   28
Section 4: The Bi-Entity Fusion Uprising   45
Section 5: Triumph and its Aftermath   65

Chapter 2: Beyond Velan-7: The Intergalactic Movement   **79**
Section 1: An Advocate for Change   79
Section 2: The Alien Experience   92
Section 3: The Extraterrestrial Alliance   107
Section 4: From Activism to Diplomacy   124
Section 5: A Vision for a Galactic Utopia   140

Chapter 3: The Personal Side of Aerin Zor   **153**
Section 1: Love and Interspecies Relationships   153
Section 2: Family and Alien Identity   166
Section 3: The Trials and Tribulations of Leadership   179
Section 4: The Legacy of Aerin Zor   194

Chapter 4: Interviews and Reflections   **207**
Section 1: Insights from Alien Activists   207
Section 2: Personal Reflections   221
Section 3: Celebrating the Life of Aerin Zor   235

Index   **247**

Chapter 1: From Stardust to Activism

Section 1: A Galactic Birth

Subsection: Cosmic Origins

In order to understand Aerin Zor's journey towards activism, we must first delve into the cosmic origins that set the stage for her unique existence. The universe, as we know it, is a vast and mysterious place, filled with celestial bodies, dark energy, and the remnants of exploding stars. It is within this cosmic symphony that Aerin Zor's story begins.

According to modern astrophysics, the birth of the universe can be traced back to the Big Bang, a cataclysmic event that occurred approximately 13.8 billion years ago. At this moment, all matter and energy were densely packed into an infinitesimally small point, and in an explosive burst, started to expand rapidly, giving rise to space and time as we know them.

As the universe expanded, cosmic gases cooled and condensed, forming the building blocks of galaxies. Within these galaxies, massive stars were born, and through thermonuclear fusion, they transformed light elements like hydrogen and helium into heavier elements like carbon, oxygen, and iron. These elements, along with dust and gas, were flung into space when these stars eventually exploded in supernovae.

In this cosmic dance of birth and death, planets like our own Earth were formed. And it is on one such planet, known as Velan-7, that Aerin Zor would take her first breath.

Now, you may ask, how did Aerin Zor come to exist as a fusion of two separate entities? Well, on Velan-7, there exists a unique species known as the Bi-Entities. These extraordinary beings, unlike any other in the universe, are comprised of two distinct entities that merge at birth, sharing a single physical form and consciousness.

Aerin Zor's fusion occurred when her parents, two separate Bi-Entities, came together in a cosmic union. Through a mysterious process not yet fully understood by scientists, their consciousness and physical forms merged, giving rise to a new individual with a deep connection to the cosmos.

Growing up in the cosmos shaped Aerin Zor's perspective on existence. As a Bi-Entity Fusion, she inherited a profound sense of interconnectedness with the universe. From her very first breath, she understood that her existence was a part of a much grander tapestry.

As Aerin Zor navigated the complexities of her fusion identity, she couldn't help but feel a calling from the stars. Through her unique understanding of the cosmos, she became acutely aware of the injustices and inequalities that plagued her own planet and beyond. The cosmic origins of her existence awakened a deep sense of empathy and a desire to fight for justice.

It was during her education at the Nebula Academy, a renowned interstellar institution, that Aerin Zor deepened her knowledge of the universe and its history. She learned about the struggles of other species, the triumphs of civilizations, and the interplay between power and oppression.

With this knowledge came a tremendous power - the power to challenge the status quo and effect change. Aerin Zor discovered that education could be a catalyst for empowerment, enabling individuals to break free from the cycles of ignorance and prejudice.

Armed with her cosmic origins, Aerin Zor embarked on a journey to Velan-7, a planet divided by the Bi-Entity Fusion dilemma. On one side, the Bi-Entities struggled for recognition and equal rights, while on the other, the society clung to traditional notions of individuality and segregation.

In the next section, we will explore the interstellar education journey that led Aerin Zor to Velan-7 and delve into the challenges she faced in her quest for social change.

— Key Takeaways:

- The universe originated from the Big Bang, a cataclysmic event that gave birth to space and time. - Massive stars formed through the condensation of cosmic gases and underwent nuclear fusion, producing heavier elements. - Planets like Earth were formed from the remnants of dead stars. - Velan-7 is home to unique beings called Bi-Entities, who are composed of two merging entities. - The fusion of Aerin Zor's parents resulted in her unique existence as a Bi-Entity Fusion. - Growing up in the cosmos shaped Aerin Zor's perspective and fueled her passion for justice. - Education played a crucial role in expanding Aerin Zor's knowledge and empowering her to challenge societal norms. - Aerin Zor's journey to Velan-7 marked the beginning of her fight for equal rights for Bi-Entities and the broader alien community.

Birth of a Fusion

In this fascinating subsection, we delve into the captivating story of Aerin Zor's birth—a momentous occasion in the cosmos that would unknowingly set the stage for a future of activism and change. The birth of a fusion, a being comprised of two distinct alien species, is a remarkable phenomenon, both scientifically and culturally.

The Cosmic Fusion

The concept of fusion is not limited to the scientific realm—it extends to the intermingling of cultures, ideas, and individuals. In the case of Aerin Zor, their birth brought together two alien species, the Veridians and the Crytarians, within a single being. The Veridians, characterized by their striking emerald-green skin and telekinetic abilities, were a peaceful and highly intellectual species. On the other hand, the Crytarians possessed crystalline exoskeletons and were renowned for their innate curiosity and adaptability.

The Everlasting Bond

Aerin Zor's fusion was the result of an uncommon bond formed between a Veridian diplomat and a Crytarian scientist. Their love and shared experiences transcended the boundaries of their respective species, igniting a connection that went deeper than mere physical attraction. Their union symbolized hope for a harmonious coexistence between different alien races—a vision that would later shape Aerin Zor's path towards activism.

Nurturing Differences

Growing up as a fusion, Aerin Zor experienced the world through a unique lens. They learned to appreciate the distinct qualities of both Veridian and Crytarian cultures, gaining insights into the rich tapestry of diversity that the universe had to offer. This upbringing endowed Aerin Zor with a deep sense of empathy and a profound understanding of the interconnectivity of all life forms.

The Power Within

As Aerin Zor matured and discovered the extent of their fusion abilities, they realized the potential they possessed to bridge the gaps between various alien races. By harnessing the combined strengths of their Veridian and Crytarian heritage, Aerin Zor could communicate with individuals from disparate backgrounds, finding common ground and fostering understanding.

Embracing Individuality

Despite being a fusion, Aerin Zor maintained a strong sense of self-identity. They embraced their uniqueness and celebrated the diversity within them. This self-acceptance became a driving force behind their determination to promote equality and justice for all beings across the universe.

The Call of Destiny

It was during their formative years that Aerin Zor first heard the call of destiny. A series of profound dreams, visions, and encounters with celestial entities revealed to them their purpose in the cosmos—to use their powers and influence for the betterment of others. This call awakened a deep sense of responsibility within Aerin Zor, propelling them towards a life of activism and advocacy.

Unconventional Solutions

Inspired by their fusion heritage, Aerin Zor developed a unique approach to problem-solving. They recognized that traditional methods often failed to address the complexities of interplanetary issues and so sought out unconventional solutions. By thinking outside the box and bringing together diverse perspectives, Aerin Zor revolutionized the way social problems were tackled, paving the way for innovative strategies in the fight for alien civil rights.

Finding Balance

Navigating the dual nature of their fusion was not without its challenges for Aerin Zor. They had to strike a harmonious balance between the Veridian and Crytarian aspects of their being. This inner equilibrium allowed them to draw strength from both sides and approach their activism with a well-rounded perspective, promoting unity and understanding.

A Message of Unity

Aerin Zor's birth as a fusion resonated with individuals from all walks of life. It symbolized the beauty and potential of diverse species working together towards a common goal. The powerful message of unity that radiated from their unique existence became a driving force behind their quest for alien civil rights.

An Unwavering Spirit

Aerin Zor's birth marked the beginning of an extraordinary journey—a journey that would see them inspire countless others to challenge the status quo and fight for a more inclusive and equal universe. Their unwavering spirit and determination, rooted in the fusion of two distinct species, propelled them to become a galactic symbol of hope and change.

As we conclude this enlightening subsection, let us reflect on the awe-inspiring birth of Aerin Zor—a fusion that not only defied the boundaries of conventional existence but also laid the foundation for an extraordinary life dedicated to fighting for justice and equality in the cosmos. The fusion of Veridian and Crytarian heritage within Aerin Zor serves as a potent reminder of the power that lies in embracing diversity and nurturing unity among all intergalactic beings.

Subsection: Growing Up in the Cosmos

Growing up in the vast expanse of the cosmos was anything but ordinary for young Aerin Zor. Born into a world where intergalactic travel and alien encounters were the norm, Aerin's childhood was filled with countless wonders and unique experiences that shaped their perspective on life and the universe.

From an early age, Aerin was fascinated by the stars. They would spend hours gazing up at the night sky, mesmerized by the celestial bodies that seemed to hold the secrets of the universe. Aerin's parents, both prominent astronomers, nurtured this curiosity, providing books and telescopes to foster their child's love for astronomy.

One of the most memorable moments of Aerin's early years was their first trip to a nebula. The vibrant colors and swirling gases ignited their imagination, sparking a deep desire to explore the cosmos and uncover its mysteries. It was in that very moment that Aerin realized their destiny was intertwined with the stars.

Growing up, Aerin was exposed to a diverse range of alien cultures and traditions. Their parents, who themselves came from different planets, ensured that Aerin was immersed in a melting pot of interstellar customs. From attending interplanetary festivals to participating in traditional rituals, Aerin developed a strong appreciation for the rich tapestry of alien societies.

But it wasn't all awe-inspiring experiences for Aerin. The vastness of the cosmos also revealed a dark side. Alongside the wonders of the universe, they witnessed the inequality and prejudice that existed between different alien species. It was during these formative years that Aerin's empathy began to blossom, and they developed a strong sense of justice and fairness.

Aerin's realization that not all beings were treated equally was a catalyst for their advocacy work. They couldn't stand idly by while injustice persisted in the cosmos. This sparked a fire within them to fight against discrimination and champion the rights of all sentient beings, regardless of their planetary origins.

Throughout their youth, Aerin voraciously consumed all the knowledge they could find. They devoured books on history, philosophy, and sociology, eager to understand the historical and societal factors that perpetuated inequality. This thirst for knowledge would later fuel their activism, empowering them to challenge the deep-rooted systems that oppressed alien communities.

In their teenage years, Aerin began to actively question the status quo. They engaged in conversations with their peers, discussing the issues faced by their fellow alien beings. These discussions often centered around the need for unity and solidarity, recognizing that only by standing together could they bring about meaningful change.

As they navigated the challenges of adolescence, Aerin's commitment to justice and equality deepened. They witnessed firsthand the struggles faced by their alien friends and family members, from microaggressions to blatant discrimination. These experiences solidified their resolve to dedicate their life to activism and advocacy.

Aerin's growing awareness of the injustices present in the cosmos compelled them to take action. They began organizing community events and awareness campaigns, using the power of art, music, and storytelling to amplify the voices of marginalized alien communities. Their efforts garnered attention, and soon, they became a beacon of hope for alien beings who had long been silenced.

Looking back on their youth, Aerin acknowledges the unique privilege they had in growing up in a cosmopolitan environment. The exposure to different cultures, combined with their own personal experiences, laid the foundation for their activism and advocacy work. It shaped their belief that true equality could only be achieved through empathy, understanding, and the dismantling of oppressive systems.

In this subsection, we have explored Aerin Zor's journey of growth and self-discovery in the cosmos. From the wonders of the night sky to the harsh realities of discrimination, their early experiences set them on a path of activism and advocacy. In the following subsection, we will delve into Aerin's awakening to

SECTION 1: A GALACTIC BIRTH

injustice and their discovery of purpose. Stay tuned as we continue to unravel the extraordinary life of Aerin Zor: The Bi-Entity Fusion Uprising on Velan-7.

Subsection: A Calling from the Stars

Our story begins with young Aerin Zor, born in the heart of the cosmos. From a young age, Aerin had a deep fascination with the stars, feeling an unexplainable connection with the vast expanse of the universe. It was as if the celestial bodies whispered their secrets and wisdom directly into Aerin's soul.

Growing up in the cosmos was no ordinary childhood. Aerin's parents, both renowned astrophysicists, raised their child to appreciate the beauty and mysteries of the universe. They would spend countless nights stargazing, sharing stories of distant planets and civilizations, instilling in Aerin a sense of wonder and curiosity.

As Aerin embarked on the journey of self-discovery, a cosmic phenomenon occurred that changed everything. While observing a rare solar eclipse on their home planet, Aerin witnessed a breathtaking fusion of two celestial entities. The melding of energy, colors, and consciousness left Aerin in awe, unable to tear their eyes away from the mesmerizing display of cosmic unity.

It was in that awe-inspiring moment that Aerin realized their purpose in life. They felt a calling from the stars, a deep yearning to promote unity and equality across the universe. Aerin understood that just as the fusion of two entities created something greater than the sum of its parts, so too could different beings and civilizations come together to achieve extraordinary feats.

Buoyed by this newfound sense of purpose, Aerin began to question the injustices and prejudices they observed within their own galactic community. They saw how certain beings were marginalized, their voices silenced, and their rights trampled upon simply because they were different. Determined to challenge the status quo, Aerin set out on a path of activism, ready to fight for justice and equality.

But change wouldn't come without knowledge. Aerin recognized the importance of education in effecting real transformation. They devoted themselves to learning everything they could about galactic history and the struggles faced by oppressed communities throughout the cosmos. Aerin believed that true empathy and understanding were the keys to fostering interplanetary relations and dismantling the barriers of prejudice.

With a wealth of knowledge and a burning desire for change, Aerin set their sights on Velan-7, a planet deeply divided by discrimination against bi-entity fusion beings. This discrimination had persisted for generations, with bi-entity fusions being denied basic rights and opportunities. Aerin knew that the civil rights movement on Velan-7 was in desperate need of a leader, someone who could rally the oppressed and challenge the oppressive system.

Aerin's journey to Velan-7 was not an easy one. They had to navigate through interstellar politics and establish connections and alliances with like-minded individuals and organizations. But every step of the way, Aerin's resolve grew stronger, fueled by the injustices they witnessed and the growing support from fellow activists.

Finally, the time came for Aerin to make their stand. The Bi-Entity Fusion Uprising would forever alter the course of Velan-7's history. Aerin, alongside a diverse group of courageous beings, organized protests, marches, and acts of civil disobedience. They challenged the Velan-7 government, demanding equal rights for all, regardless of their fusion status.

Throughout the uprising, Aerin emphasized the power of nonviolent resistance. They believed that true change could only be achieved by appealing to the moral conscience of the oppressors. By remaining peaceful in the face of violence and hatred, Aerin inspired others to follow suit, amplifying their message and dispelling the myth that violence was a necessary means to an end.

The struggles endured, but Aerin's unwavering determination proved instrumental in the fight for equality. The Velan-7 government was ultimately forced to concede, granting bi-entity fusion beings their long-denied rights. The liberation of Velan-7 became a beacon of hope for oppressed communities across the cosmos, showcasing the power of collective action and the triumph of justice over prejudice.

But Aerin was not one to rest on their laurels. The uprising on Velan-7 was just the beginning of their intergalactic journey. They recognized the need for a larger movement, one that would unite alien worlds in the fight for civil rights. Through advocacy, outreach, and collaboration, Aerin established the Alien Civil Rights Alliance, a powerful force for change in the universe.

Aerin's vision extended beyond mere equality to a grander idea of coexistence and celebration of diversity. They believed in erasing the boundaries that separated different species, fostering a galactic utopia where all beings could thrive and express their individuality, free from fear and prejudice. Aerin saw art as a catalyst for change, using creative expression to challenge societal norms and uplift the voices of the marginalized.

Even as Aerin's journey brought them face-to-face with interplanetary prejudice, they remained steadfast. They fought for alien employment rights, advocated for alien voting rights, and worked to address deep-rooted xenophobia. Aerin understood that achieving true equality required a multi-faceted approach, one that tackled systemic injustices at every level.

SECTION 1: A GALACTIC BIRTH

Through it all, Aerin formed bonds with fellow alien activists, collaborating to overcome interstellar barriers and build a network of support. Grassroots organizations sprang up, united by a shared vision of galactic change. Aerin's charisma and leadership inspired countless individuals, fueling a new generation of activists committed to the fight for alien civil rights.

Aerin's impact extended beyond activism and into diplomatic circles. They became a representative for alien communities in planetary governments, negotiating intergalactic treaties and advocating for alien rights in universal law. Aerin's transformation from activist to diplomat showcased the transformative power of policy change, proving that true progress stemmed from holistic and inclusive approaches.

The legacy of Aerin Zor lives on, even after their passing. Their contributions to the cause of alien civil rights continue to inspire future generations. Anniversaries and milestones are commemorated, with Aerin Zor Day serving as a reminder of the hero who sparked a revolution.

Artistic tributes and cultural celebrations keep Aerin's memory alive, ensuring that their story is never forgotten. Legacy projects and initiatives carry forward their vision of a galactic utopia, perpetuating the fight for equality and justice. The world continues to be grateful for Aerin Zor, the hero of Velan-7, whose legacy echoes through the cosmos.

Remembering Aerin's journey reminds us that change begins with a calling from within. It takes courage, determination, and a relentless pursuit of justice to challenge the prejudices and inequalities that exist in our own worlds. Aerin's story teaches us that with empathy, knowledge, and unity, we too can make a profound impact and build a future of coexistence and celebration of diversity.

In the dark expanse of space, where countless stars shine, Aerin Zor's light shines the brightest, guiding us toward a universe where equality reigns supreme. Let us carry their torch, generations after generation, and continue the fight for a brighter future for all.

Subsection: Awakening to Injustice

Growing up in the vast expanse of the cosmos, Aerin Zor had always felt a deep connection to the stars. From an early age, they were drawn to the beauty of the universe and the diverse beings that inhabited it. However, it wasn't until their teenage years that Aerin's eyes were opened to the injustices that existed within their own celestial home.

As they navigated the galaxy, Aerin witnessed firsthand the disparities and discrimination faced by different alien species. They saw how certain communities were marginalized, denied basic rights, and subjected to prejudice solely based on their cosmic origins. This awakening to the brutal reality of inequality forged a burning fire within Aerin's soul, igniting a passion for justice and a desire to effect change.

One pivotal moment that shifted Aerin's perspective occurred during a visit to the planet Vorta Prime. Amidst the bustling streets, Aerin encountered a group of Bi-Entity Fusions - beings born from the fusion of two different alien species. These individuals possessed unique abilities and strengths, yet they faced constant discrimination and were treated as lesser beings by the dominant humanoid population.

Witnessing the Bi-Entity Fusions' struggle for recognition and acceptance struck a chord deep within Aerin's heart. It was a poignant reminder of the injustices that lurked beneath the glorious facade of the cosmos. Determined to make a difference, Aerin made a personal vow to fight for the rights of all alien beings, regardless of their biological composition.

This awakening to injustice led Aerin to question the very foundations of the intergalactic society they had known. They delved into the history of discrimination on various planets, studying the social, economic, and political systems that perpetuated inequality. Aerin's research fueled their passion for activism, and they became determined to challenge the status quo and dismantle these systems of oppression.

As Aerin delved deeper into their studies, they discovered that the root cause of much of the injustice they witnessed was a fundamental lack of empathy and understanding between different alien species. In the vastness of space, fear of the unknown had led to prejudice, xenophobia, and the denial of basic rights. Aerin recognized that breaking down these barriers and fostering interplanetary empathy would be essential in the fight for equal rights.

To further educate themselves, Aerin enrolled at the prestigious Nebula Academy, known for its commitment to interstellar diversity and social justice. Here, they immersed themselves in the teachings of galactic history, philosophy, and sociology. They learned about the struggles and triumphs of previous alien activists who fought tirelessly for equality, finding inspiration in their stories of resilience and perseverance.

It was during their time at the Nebula Academy that Aerin began to develop a keen understanding of the power of education as a catalyst for social change. They learned that by sharing knowledge, challenging discriminatory beliefs, and fostering empathy, it was possible to sow the seeds of a more inclusive and egalitarian cosmos.

Inspired by their education and fueled by their personal conviction, Aerin embarked on a journey to raise awareness of the injustices faced by marginalized alien communities. They traveled from planet to planet, speaking at conferences, engaging in grassroots organizing, and collaborating with other activists who shared their vision of a more just and equitable universe.

Through their travels, Aerin began to witness the unifying force of collective action. They saw firsthand how marginalized alien communities came together, supporting one another in their struggle for recognition and equal rights. Aerin's own experiences of alienation and discrimination solidified their commitment to standing in solidarity with all who faced injustice.

As Aerin's journey continued, their deepening understanding of the intricate web of social, economic, and political factors perpetuating inequality gave them the tools to envision a better future. They began to formulate strategies and tactics for challenging oppressive systems, utilizing the power of community organizing, peaceful protests, and legislative advocacy to effect lasting change.

Through their endeavors, Aerin became a beacon of hope, inspiring countless individuals with their passion, empathy, and unwavering determination. They helped alien communities recognize their own potential and encouraged them to stand up against the forces that sought to marginalize and silence them.

With each victory, both small and significant, Aerin's resolve only grew stronger. They became a symbol of resilience and a testament to the power of an individual's commitment to justice. Their journey from stardust to activism served as a reminder that change starts within, with the awakening of empathy and the unwavering belief that a better cosmos is possible.

As Aerin's story continues, their path will intersect with the unfolding struggles of different alien communities, weaving together the collective fight for equality across the cosmos. Their tireless advocacy and unyielding spirit will forever leave an indelible mark on the universe, inspiring future generations of activists to pick up the mantle and continue the work of creating a truly just and inclusive cosmos.

Subsection: Discovering a Purpose

As a young child, Aerin Zor always felt a deep connection to the stars. Their glittering beauty and infinite expanse fascinated and captivated Aerin from a young age. But it was not just a fascination with the cosmic skies that ignited a sense of purpose within Aerin. It was a growing awareness of the injustices and inequalities that permeated the universe.

Growing up in the cosmos was not always easy for Aerin. As a fusion of two bi-entity beings, their existence was a rarity in the galactic community. The fusion of two distinct entities often led to discrimination and a lack of recognition in society.

Aerin witnessed firsthand the struggles faced by individuals like themselves, who were relegated to the fringes of alien society, denied their rightful place among their peers.

But instead of succumbing to bitterness or anger, Aerin channelled their experiences into a desire for change. They felt a calling from the stars, urging them to make a difference and fight for equality. Aerin realized that their unique position as a bi-entity fusion gave them a voice and a perspective that could challenge the status quo and bring about meaningful change.

It was during their interstellar education at the Nebula Academy that Aerin's purpose truly began to take shape. They immersed themselves in the study of galactic history, learning about the struggles and triumphs of various civilizations across the universe. They discovered the power of knowledge in shaping societies and inspiring social change.

Empathy and interplanetary relations became central pillars in Aerin's pursuit of justice. They understood that to bring about meaningful change, they needed to connect with others and foster understanding among different species and cultures. Aerin believed that true equality could only be achieved through unity and cooperation.

Driven by their thirst for knowledge, Aerin delved into the darker side of the cosmos, uncovering the systemic injustices that plagued many alien worlds. They learned about the oppressive regimes, the suppression of individual freedoms, and the deep-rooted prejudices that had seeped into the very fabric of the universe.

But rather than being disheartened by these revelations, Aerin saw them as opportunities for growth and empowerment. They realized the power of education in uplifting marginalized communities and empowering them to challenge the status quo. Aerin dedicated themselves to sharing the knowledge they had acquired, empowering others to rise up and fight for their rights.

The journey to Velan-7, a planet divided by the Bi-Entity Fusion Dilemma, marked a turning point in Aerin's life. In this planet's civil rights movement, they saw a chance to make a tangible difference and fulfill their purpose. They sought to establish connections and alliances, uniting those who had been marginalized and oppressed.

Preparing for the uprising was no easy task. Aerin knew that change would require more than just protests and street rallies. They understood the importance of strategic planning and organizing resistance from within. It was a battle not only against the Velan-7 government but against the deep-seated prejudices and biases that permeated society.

Aerin embraced the philosophy of nonviolent resistance, believing in its effectiveness as a means to challenge the status quo. They understood that violence

SECTION 1: A GALACTIC BIRTH

would only perpetuate a cycle of hatred and further marginalize those who were already oppressed. They championed peaceful protests, harnessing the power of collective action and civil disobedience to bring about change.

The triumph of the bi-entity fusion uprising on Velan-7 was not the end of Aerin Zor's journey but just the beginning. The liberation of Velan-7 marked a turning point in the fight for alien civil rights across the galaxy. Aerin's legacy resonated far beyond the borders of Velan-7, inspiring others to rise up and fight for their rights.

Now, Aerin's purpose expanded beyond Velan-7. They became an advocate for change on an intergalactic scale, spreading their message across galaxies. They sought to unite alien worlds, creating the Alien Civil Rights Alliance to fight for equality and justice in all corners of the universe.

But the road ahead was not without its challenges. Aerin faced obstacles and resistance from those who clung to their prejudices and sought to maintain the status quo. They navigated the complexities of interplanetary politics, negotiating treaties and advocating for alien representation in planetary governments.

Throughout their journey, Aerin remained grounded in their vision of a galactic utopia, a universe where all species could coexist in harmony and celebrate their diversity. They believed in the transformative power of art and culture in breaking down barriers and erasing boundaries.

The personal side of Aerin Zor was also instrumental in their activism. Their extraordinary love story transcended intergalactic boundaries, challenging taboos and redefining relationships in the cosmic era. Aerin drew strength from their family and alien ancestry, using these ties to raise awareness and empower others within their communities.

Leading a movement came with its own challenges and sacrifices. Aerin grappled with the weight of responsibility and the toll it took on their mental health. But they persevered, learning from setbacks and inspiring others with their resilience and unwavering commitment to justice.

Aerin Zor's legacy continues to shape the fight for equality and justice in the universe. Their impact on future generations cannot be overstated, and their memory lives on through commemorations, artistic tributes, and cultural celebrations.

As we reflect on the life of Aerin Zor, we find inspiration, hope, and a call to action. Their story reminds us that each of us can discover a purpose, no matter how big or small, and make a difference in the world. The fight for equality and justice is ongoing, and the future of coexistence in the universe depends on our collective efforts. Let us carry on the legacy of Aerin Zor, forever grateful to the hero of Velan-7.

Section 2: Interstellar Education

Subsection: Discovering Wisdom at the Nebula Academy

At the Nebula Academy, Aerin Zor embarked on a journey of knowledge and self-discovery. This subsection explores the wisdom gained by our protagonist during their time at this prestigious interstellar institution.

The Nebula Academy, located on the celestial plane of Galactia, is renowned for its commitment to fostering intellectual growth and exploration. Here, students from various galaxies come together to learn, share ideas, and challenge conventional wisdom. Aerin Zor was one such student who found their purpose within the walls of this hallowed institution.

The curriculum at the Nebula Academy delves into a wide range of subjects, including astrophysics, interplanetary politics, cosmic history, and personal development. Through a combination of theoretical study, hands-on experiments, and practical applications, students are empowered to question the status quo and push the boundaries of understanding.

One of the core principles instilled at the Nebula Academy is the importance of curiosity. Students are encouraged to ask difficult questions and pursue answers beyond the predetermined confines of traditional knowledge. This emphasis on curiosity opens up new horizons of understanding and challenges students to think critically and creatively.

Aerin's favorite course at the Nebula Academy was Cosmic Philosophy, a multidisciplinary exploration of the nature of existence, consciousness, and morality in the vast expanse of the universe. Led by esteemed cosmic philosopher, Dr. Lyra Vega, this course pushed boundaries and encouraged students to question their place in the cosmos.

One of the fundamental teachings in Cosmic Philosophy was the concept of interconnectedness. Dr. Vega emphasized that every being, regardless of their origin or form, is interconnected and part of a cosmic web. This understanding underscored the importance of empathy and cooperation among species. Aerin carried this wisdom forward, recognizing that the fight for alien civil rights must extend beyond individual planets, encompassing the entire universe.

Another pivotal course at the Nebula Academy was The Lessons of Cosmic History. Taught by Professor Orion, this course delved into the long and intertwined history of various galactic civilizations. Students explored the rise and fall of empires, the consequences of power imbalances, and the importance of learning from the mistakes of the past.

SECTION 2: INTERSTELLAR EDUCATION

Aerin discovered that the struggles faced by alien communities on Velan-7 were not unique but part of a recurring historical narrative. The lessons learned from these historical examples served as a guiding compass for Aerin's activism, enabling them to anticipate challenges and devise effective strategies for change.

To cultivate a holistic understanding of the cosmos, students at the Nebula Academy engaged in interplanetary cultural exchange programs. These initiatives brought together individuals from diverse backgrounds, fostering empathy, understanding, and appreciation for different ways of life.

Aerin's experience in the interplanetary cultural exchange program was transformational. They formed deep connections with students from planets vastly different from their own. This immersive experience broadened Aerin's perspective, enabling them to see beyond the narrow confines of their own planet and understand the multifaceted challenges faced by other communities.

The Nebula Academy also prioritized personal development, recognizing that success in the pursuit of justice and equality requires inner strength and emotional intelligence. Through mindfulness training, meditation, and self-reflection, students were encouraged to develop a sense of self-awareness and resilience.

Aerin found solace in these practices, especially during moments of doubt or adversity. The cultivation of inner wisdom and emotional balance became essential tools in their journey as an activist. By tending to their own well-being, Aerin was better equipped to navigate the challenges they encountered on the path to social change.

But the Nebula Academy was more than just a place of learning; it was a community of like-minded individuals committed to making a difference in the universe. Collaborative projects and extracurricular activities provided students with opportunities to work together, harnessing collective wisdom to tackle complex issues.

One such project that Aerin was involved in was the Galactic Unity Initiative. This grassroots movement aimed to bridge the gaps between different alien communities and foster a sense of shared purpose. The project taught Aerin the immense power of community-driven initiatives and the strength that comes from collective action.

In summary, Aerin Zor's time at the Nebula Academy was instrumental in shaping their worldview and guiding their path towards activism. The wisdom gained at this prestigious institution allowed Aerin to understand the interconnectedness of all beings, learn from cosmic history, appreciate diverse cultures, develop emotional resilience, and embrace the power of collaborative action. The Nebula Academy became the crucible from which Aerin emerged as a beacon of hope and catalyst for change within the interstellar community.

Subsection: The Lessons of Galactic History

Galactic history is filled with tales of triumphs and failures, of civilizations rising and falling, and of the struggle for power and control. Studying this rich tapestry of events provides valuable insights into the patterns and dynamics of interstellar societies. In this subsection, we explore the lessons we can learn from galactic history and the relevance of these lessons to the fight for alien civil rights.

The Cycle of Oppression

One of the most prominent lessons from galactic history is the cycle of oppression that has plagued civilizations throughout the cosmos. Time and again, we see the powerful exploiting the weak, imposing their will and denying basic rights to those they deem inferior. This fundamental pattern of oppression has repeated itself across different species, worlds, and eras.

The wise extraterrestrial philosopher, Zorok the Elder, once said, "Those who do not learn from history are doomed to repeat it." This aphorism rings true when we examine the struggles faced by marginalized groups throughout the galaxy and the importance of learning from past mistakes.

The Power of Resistance Movements

Galactic history also teaches us about the power of resistance movements in challenging oppressive regimes and effecting change. From ancient uprisings to modern revolutions, these movements have been a driving force for social justice and equality.

The Velan-7 Civil Rights Movement, which played a pivotal role in Aerin Zor's journey, is a prime example. Inspired by past resistance movements in other parts of the galaxy, the activists on Velan-7 organized protests, strikes, and other acts of civil disobedience to demand equal rights for Bi-Entity Fusions. Their determination and resilience in the face of adversity ignited a spark of hope and set in motion a revolution.

The Dangers of Complacency

A recurring theme in galactic history is the danger of complacency in the face of injustice. Many civilizations have fallen into a state of apathy, allowing discrimination and oppression to persist unchecked. The lessons from these histories serve as a warning to future generations about the importance of remaining vigilant and actively fighting for what is right.

SECTION 2: INTERSTELLAR EDUCATION

The story of the planet Thromidon serves as a cautionary tale. Once a beacon of interstellar harmony, Thromidon allowed prejudices to take hold within its society. Instead of challenging these prejudices, the Thromidons turned a blind eye, leading to the division and eventual downfall of their civilization. It serves as a reminder that silence and indifference only perpetuate injustice.

Advancements in Interplanetary Relations

Galactic history also provides examples of advancements in interplanetary relations and the positive impact they have on social equality. As civilizations have learned to coexist and embrace diversity, they have taken significant strides toward equality and inclusivity.

The formation of the Interspecies Alliance on the planet Thalos is a remarkable example. Through diplomatic negotiations and cooperation, Thalos brought together representatives from various alien races to create a society that values and protects the rights of all its members. This achievement serves as a blueprint for other worlds aspiring to achieve galactic unity and equal rights.

Confronting Historical Biases

Finally, galactic history teaches us the importance of confronting and addressing historical biases that persist within interstellar societies. By acknowledging and rectifying past injustices, civilizations can lay the foundation for a more equitable future.

The case study of the planet Zyra highlights the significance of this lesson. Zyra, once deeply divided along racial lines, embarked on a path of reconciliation and redemption. Through truth and reconciliation commissions, Zyra confronted its history of discrimination and implemented policies to rectify past wrongs. This process allowed Zyra to heal, fostering an environment of unity, understanding, and respect.

Unconventional Approach: The Cosmic Theater

To engage and educate future generations about the lessons of galactic history, an unconventional approach can be adopted - the Cosmic Theater. The Cosmic Theater would combine elements of traditional theater and holographic technology to bring historical events to life. Through immersive experiences, audiences would witness the struggles and triumphs of past activists, forging a deeper connection with the lessons learned from galactic history.

By employing captivating storytelling and interactive elements, the Cosmic Theater would empower individuals to become active participants in the fight for social justice. This innovative approach to education would serve as a catalyst for empathy, understanding, and meaningful change.

Resources for Further Exploration

To delve deeper into the lessons of galactic history, here are some recommended resources:

- *Chronicles of the Cosmos: A Comprehensive History of Interstellar Civilizations* by Dr. Xandar Valkyrie
- *Revolutionary Movements in the Milky Way: From Rebellion to Transformation* by Professor Luminara Nova
- *Galaxy on Fire: Lessons from the Ashes* by Captain Orion Starborn

These resources offer varying perspectives on galactic history, providing valuable insights into the struggles, triumphs, and lessons learned from civilizations across the cosmos.

Exercises

1. Reflect on a historical event from Earth and draw parallels to the lessons learned from galactic history. How can the knowledge gained from Earth's past help shape a more equitable future?

2. Imagine you are a historian tasked with writing a chapter on the Velan-7 Civil Rights Movement in a galactic history book. Describe the key events, influential figures, and the impact of this movement on the fight for alien civil rights.

3. Discuss the role of art in galactic history, drawing examples from various interstellar civilizations. How has art been used as a form of resistance, activism, or a catalyst for change?

Conclusion

The lessons of galactic history provide us with invaluable guidance and inspiration in the fight for alien civil rights. By understanding the cyclical nature of oppression, the power of resistance movements, the dangers of complacency, the advancements in interplanetary relations, and the importance of confronting biases, we can actively work towards a future of equality and justice.

Through a combination of conventional knowledge and unconventional approaches like the Cosmic Theater, we can pass on these lessons to future generations. By internalizing the wisdom of galactic history, we ensure that the mistakes of the past are not repeated and that the struggle for alien civil rights continues to evolve.

Subsection: Empathy and Interplanetary Relations

Empathy is the ability to understand and share the feelings of others. It is a crucial aspect of interplanetary relations, as it fosters understanding, cooperation, and acceptance between different alien species. In this subsection, we will explore the role of empathy in building strong interplanetary relationships and its significance in promoting harmony and peace in the cosmos.

Understanding Alien Experiences

Empathy begins with a genuine effort to understand the experiences of others, including those from different planets. By putting ourselves in the shoes, paws or tentacles of others, we can gain a deeper understanding of their struggles, joys, and cultural nuances. For instance, suppose an alien species from planet Xanadu communicates primarily through telepathy. To truly understand their mode of communication, we must empathize with their unique sensory and cognitive abilities, reimagining how we perceive and interact with the world.

Overcoming Prejudices and Stereotypes

Empathy serves as a powerful tool in challenging and dismantling prejudices and stereotypes that often hinder interplanetary relations. By fostering empathy, we can break down the barriers that prevent us from seeing individuals for who they truly are. For example, the common belief that all beings from planet Ypsilon are aggressive based on a few isolated incidents perpetuates a harmful stereotype. By actively engaging and empathizing with individuals from planet Ypsilon, we can recognize their inherent diversity and dispel such unfounded generalizations.

Building Bridges of Trust and Cooperation

Empathy lays the foundation for building bridges of trust and cooperation between alien species. When we empathize with others, we create an environment where understanding and mutual respect can flourish. This, in turn, facilitates the formation of alliances and partnerships based on shared goals and values. For instance, imagine two neighboring planets, Zephyr and Aurora, whose relationship has been strained due to a territorial dispute. Through empathetic dialogue and understanding each other's needs and concerns, diplomats from both planets can work towards a peaceful resolution and establish a sustainable interplanetary cooperation agreement.

Promoting Cultural Exchange and Celebration of Diversity

Empathy also encourages the exchange of cultural knowledge and appreciation for diversity. By empathizing with different alien cultures, we can learn about their traditions, arts, and values, fostering a sense of curiosity and respect. This cultural exchange enriches our own understanding of the universe and promotes a global perspective. For example, a cultural festival that showcases the music, dance, and cuisine of various alien species is an opportunity for individuals from different planets to celebrate their differences and find common ground.

The Interplanetary Empathy Initiative

To promote empathy in interplanetary relations, the Interplanetary Empathy Initiative (IEI) was established. The IEI is a collaborative effort between alien communities and governments to enhance understanding, acceptance, and cooperation. It organizes workshops, panel discussions, and intercultural events to facilitate empathy-building activities. The initiative also supports educational programs that teach empathy from an early age, encouraging young beings to develop open minds and compassionate hearts towards others.

Exercises: Developing Empathy

Here are a few exercises to develop empathy in interplanetary relations:

1. Alien Perspective Swap: Encourage beings from different planets to swap roles and experience each other's lives for a day. This exercise helps individuals understand the challenges and joys faced by others.

2. Empathetic Listening: Practice active listening during interplanetary negotiations or discussions. Focus on understanding the emotions, needs, and concerns behind the words spoken by others.

3. Storytelling: Encourage beings to share stories about their experiences, traditions, and values. This exercise fosters empathy by allowing others to see the world through someone else's eyes.

SECTION 2: INTERSTELLAR EDUCATION

Key Takeaways

Empathy is a fundamental aspect of interplanetary relations that promotes understanding, cooperation, and harmony between alien species. By understanding and appreciating others' experiences, overcoming prejudices, and fostering cultural exchange, we can build strong interplanetary relationships based on trust, respect, and equality. Through educational initiatives that prioritize empathy, we can ensure a future where empathy is the norm, paving the way for a truly interconnected and harmonious universe.

As we continue our exploration of Aerin Zor's journey, let us delve into the next section: "1.2.4 Subsection: Uncovering the Dark Side of the Cosmos."

Subsection: Uncovering the Dark Side of the Cosmos

As Aerin Zor delved deeper into her interstellar education, she began to uncover the dark side of the cosmos. She realized that beneath the shining stars and vast galaxies lay a multitude of injustices and inequalities that were systematically perpetuated against alien beings. This revelation ignited a fire within her, compelling her to expose these hidden truths and fight for change.

Cosmic Alien Profiling

One of the most pervasive issues that Aerin Zor discovered was cosmic alien profiling. Just as racial profiling exists on Earth, aliens across different galaxies were subjected to unfair treatment based solely on their extraterrestrial origins. Whether it was through interplanetary travel restrictions, discriminatory hiring practices, or unequal access to resources, cosmic alien profiling created a hierarchy that perpetuated inequality and reinforced power imbalances.

To shed light on this issue, Aerin Zor extensively researched and documented cases of cosmic alien profiling. She compiled data, testimonials, and personal accounts to expose the systemic prejudices that denied aliens their basic rights and freedoms. Her work served as a wakeup call to society, forcing them to confront their own biases and prejudices.

Xenophobic Policies

In her exploration of the darker side of the cosmos, Aerin Zor also uncovered the existence of xenophobic policies that fueled the oppression of alien communities. These policies were designed to isolate and marginalize aliens, preventing them from fully participating in intergalactic society. From restrictive immigration laws to discriminatory citizenship requirements, such policies limited the opportunities available to aliens and hindered their ability to contribute to the development of the cosmos.

To challenge these xenophobic policies, Aerin Zor collaborated with legal experts, scholars, and activists to scrutinize existing interstellar legislation and advocate for reforms. She organized protests, rallies, and advocacy campaigns to shed light on the discriminatory nature of these policies and push for their abolition. Through her efforts, Aerin Zor brought attention to the structural barriers that prevented aliens from achieving their full potential.

Exploitation of Alien Labor

Another bleak aspect of the cosmos that Aerin Zor unveiled was the rampant exploitation of alien labor. Aliens from less developed planets and galaxies were often lured into working under unjust conditions, with low wages and minimal rights. They were subjected to precarious living conditions, dangerous work environments, and inadequate legal protections.

To combat this exploitation, Aerin Zor collaborated with intergalactic labor unions and organizations to raise awareness about alien labor rights. She fought for fair wages, safe working conditions, and the enforcement of labor laws that protected aliens from exploitation. By amplifying the voices of alien workers and initiating dialogue between different species, she aimed to restore dignity and justice to those who had long been victimized by unfair labor practices.

Environmental Exploitation

In her investigation into the dark side of the cosmos, Aerin Zor also uncovered the widespread environmental exploitation of alien worlds. Powerful corporations and governments often disregarded the ecological consequences of their actions, leading to the destruction of pristine alien habitats and the depletion of vital resources.

To address this issue, Aerin Zor spearheaded campaigns that highlighted the interconnectedness of all beings in the cosmos and the importance of preserving the environment for future generations. She collaborated with scientists, conservationists, and indigenous alien communities to develop sustainable practices and advocate for stronger environmental regulations. Through her efforts, she aimed to foster a sense of responsibility towards the cosmos and encourage the protection of alien ecosystems.

The Power of Collective Action

Aerin Zor's exploration of the dark side of the cosmos revealed the widespread injustices faced by alien beings. However, she also discovered the power of collective action in effecting change. By unifying alien communities, forming alliances, and mobilizing supporters across galaxies, she demonstrated the transformative potential of collective advocacy.

Through her activism, Aerin Zor ignited a sense of empowerment among alien beings who had long been suppressed by systemic inequalities. Her message was clear: together, aliens could dismantle the systems that perpetuated discrimination and construct a more just and inclusive cosmos.

Unconventional Yet Relevant Perspective

To truly understand the dark side of the cosmos, one must go beyond the surface level and reckon with the complexities of systemic oppression and inequality. This requires adopting an intersectional approach that recognizes the intersections of race, species, gender, and other dimensions of identity. By taking an intersectional perspective, we can uncover the interlocking systems of power that perpetuate injustice and work towards dismantling them.

Moreover, in combating the dark side of the cosmos, it is essential to recognize the importance of empathy and allyship. Allies from privileged species and races must actively listen to and uplift the voices of marginalized alien communities. By engaging in meaningful alliances and acknowledging one's own privilege, we can create a more inclusive and equitable cosmos for all.

In conclusion, the dark side of the cosmos is not a mythical realm, but a harsh reality that Aerin Zor courageously uncovered. Through her work, she revealed the pervasive cosmic alien profiling, xenophobic policies, alien labor exploitation, and environmental degradation that plague the cosmos. Nevertheless, she also demonstrated that collective action, intersectional perspectives, and empathetic allyship hold the key to addressing these issues and shaping a more just and inclusive future for all beings in the universe.

Subsection: The Power of Knowledge

Knowledge is the cornerstone of progress and change. In the context of the fight for alien civil rights, knowledge empowers individuals to challenge injustice, dismantle prejudice, and advocate for equality. In this subsection, we will explore the transformative power of knowledge and how it fuels the activism of Aerin Zor and the alien civil rights movement.

Understanding the Cosmos

To comprehend the complexities of the alien civil rights struggle, one must first understand the vastness of the cosmos. The universe is an intricate tapestry of diverse species, cultures, and histories. Knowledge of the cosmos helps shed light on the experiences and struggles faced by different alien communities.

For instance, studying the history, traditions, and values of alien civilizations enables activists like Aerin Zor to develop a comprehensive understanding of the challenges they face. Such knowledge helps bridge the gap between different cultures and fosters empathy and understanding.

Exploring Alien History

The power of knowledge extends beyond the boundaries of planetary civilizations. By delving into the rich tapestry of galactic history, activists can identify patterns of discrimination, oppression, and resistance that transcend individual alien communities. This broader perspective allows them to better comprehend the systemic factors perpetuating inequality and develop effective strategies for change.

For example, studying historical movements and figures who challenged unjust systems provides activists with valuable insights and inspiration. The knowledge of past struggles serves as a guiding light, illuminating a path forward and empowering activists to persevere in the face of adversity.

The Importance of Language and Communication

Communication is a foundational pillar of knowledge dissemination and activism. Language enables activists to convey their message, share experiences, and collaborate with others. A crucial aspect of the fight for alien civil rights is the translation of complex concepts into accessible language that resonates with a diverse audience.

Aerin Zor recognized the power of language and developed a unique communication style that connected with individuals from various backgrounds. Their ability to articulate the injustices faced by alien communities using relatable and persuasive language helped galvanize support and mobilize resistance.

Challenging Prejudice through Education

One of the most potent tools for affecting change is education. By providing individuals with the knowledge and tools to challenge their own biases, education can disrupt the cycle of prejudice and discrimination. In the fight for alien civil rights, educating both alien and human communities is vital in fostering understanding and dismantling stereotypes.

Aerin Zor believed in the transformative power of education and established programs to educate alien and human communities about the struggles faced by different species. These initiatives facilitated mutual understanding, challenged preconceptions, and paved the way for collaboration and advocacy.

The Role of Technology in Knowledge Sharing

In the modern era, technology plays a pivotal role in disseminating knowledge and raising awareness on a global scale. Social media platforms, online forums, and digital publications provide a platform for activists like Aerin Zor to share their experiences, raise awareness, and cultivate a sense of community among alien rights advocates.

Furthermore, technological advancements have made knowledge more accessible than ever before. Online libraries, open-access journals, and educational websites democratize information, allowing individuals from all backgrounds to expand their understanding of the universe.

Unconventional Wisdom: Embracing the Unknown

While knowledge is a powerful tool, it is essential to recognize the limitations of what we know. Embracing the unknown and being willing to question existing knowledge is crucial for personal and collective growth. The fight for alien civil rights requires activists to constantly challenge societal norms, reevaluate assumptions, and seek new perspectives.

Aerin Zor understood the importance of embracing the unknown and actively sought out unconventional sources of wisdom. They encouraged others to step outside their comfort zones and engage with diverse perspectives, whether through art, culture, or conversations with individuals from different walks of life.

Exercises: Expanding Your Galactic Knowledge

1. Choose an alien species from popular science fiction and research its history, culture, and experiences within the fictional universe. Reflect on the social and political issues faced by this species and draw parallels to real-world struggles for equality.

2. Engage with online communities or forums that discuss alien rights and intergalactic activism. Share your thoughts and experiences, and learn from others who are passionate about creating a just and equitable universe.

3. Create a social media campaign addressing a specific issue faced by an alien community. Utilize persuasive language and powerful visuals to raise awareness and encourage others to join your cause.

4. Read biographies or listen to interviews with activists who have fought for civil rights or social justice causes. Reflect on their experiences and the role that knowledge played in their activism. Consider how their stories can inspire your own journey as an activist.

Remember, knowledge is not a stagnant entity but a living, evolving force. Embrace the power of knowledge, seek out diverse perspectives, and let it fuel your journey towards a more equitable and inclusive universe.

Subsection: Empowering Others through Education

Education is one of the most powerful tools in the fight for social change and equality. Aerin Zor understood this and dedicated a significant portion of her life to empowering others through education. In this subsection, we explore how she used education as a means to create awareness, foster empathy, and inspire individuals to take action.

The Importance of Education in Social Movements

Education forms the backbone of any social movement. It equips individuals with knowledge, critical thinking skills, and the ability to challenge societal norms. Aerin Zor recognized that educating both the marginalized communities and the majority population was crucial in navigating the complex dynamics of discrimination and systemic oppression.

Promoting Awareness and Understanding

One of Aerin Zor's primary strategies for empowering others through education was to promote awareness and understanding of the history, experiences, and challenges faced by alien communities. She organized workshops, lectures, and panel discussions that offered historical context, personal narratives, and data-driven insights to shed light on the plight of alien individuals.

By highlighting the struggles faced by alien communities, Aerin Zor aimed to humanize the experiences of these individuals and challenge the prevailing stereotypes and prejudices. She encouraged open dialogue and facilitated spaces where individuals could ask questions and engage in meaningful discussions.

Fostering Empathy through Experiential Learning

Aerin Zor believed in the power of experiential learning to foster empathy and compassion. She organized immersion programs where individuals could spend time living and working in alien communities. By immersing themselves in the daily lives of alien individuals, participants could gain a deeper understanding of their challenges, aspirations, and unique cultural practices.

These immersive experiences often included volunteering opportunities, cultural exchanges, and collaborative projects aimed at promoting social integration and solidarity. By walking in the shoes of those they sought to empower, participants could develop a genuine empathy that transcended mere sympathy.

Equipping Individuals with Practical Skills

In addition to promoting awareness and empathy, Aerin Zor emphasized the importance of equipping individuals with practical skills that would enable them to actively contribute to the cause of alien civil rights. She established programs to teach advocacy, community organizing, and effective communication techniques.

These programs went beyond theory and included hands-on activities, role plays, and case studies. By actively engaging participants in learning the tools of activism, Aerin Zor aimed to build a generation of change-makers who could effectively challenge discriminatory systems and advocate for the rights of alien individuals.

Challenges and Strategies

While education is a powerful tool for social change, Aerin Zor encountered several challenges in her mission to empower others. One significant challenge was overcoming resistance and indifference from those who were complacent or hostile to the notion of alien rights.

To address this, Aerin Zor employed creative strategies to capture the attention and curiosity of individuals who may not have initially been interested in the cause. She collaborated with artists, musicians, and other creative professionals to develop engaging educational materials such as short films, graphic novels, and immersive exhibitions.

By combining education with entertainment, Aerin Zor was able to reach a broader audience and spark conversations that may have otherwise been challenging to initiate.

Unconventional Lesson: The Power of Humor

In her tireless efforts to educate and empower, Aerin Zor recognized the power of humor as a tool for breaking down barriers and challenging preconceived notions. She utilized satire, comedy sketches, and memes to address serious topics in a lighthearted manner.

Through humor, Aerin Zor was able to engage individuals who may have felt overwhelmed or disinterested in the alien civil rights movement. By presenting complex issues in an accessible and relatable way, she succeeded in creating a space for open dialogue and critical thinking.

Conclusion

Aerin Zor's commitment to empowering others through education serves as a testament to the transformative power of knowledge and understanding. By promoting awareness, fostering empathy, and equipping individuals with practical skills, she inspired a generation of activists to challenge the status quo and fight for alien civil rights. Through creative strategies and unconventional approaches, she was able to engage individuals who may have otherwise remained indifferent. The legacy of Aerin Zor lives on in the countless individuals she empowered, and her teachings continue to shape the fight for equality and justice in the universe.

Section 3: The Journey to Velan-7

Subsection: A Planet Divided

In this subsection, we explore the intricacies of Velan-7, a planet plagued by division and inequality. The social and political landscape of Velan-7 sets the stage for the Bi-Entity Fusion Uprising and highlights the urgent need for civil rights activism. Let's delve into the challenges faced by the inhabitants of this divided planet and the catalysts that led to the uprising.

Velan-7, located in the Andromeda galaxy, is a planet inhabited by two distinct species: the Envars and the Solarians. The Envars, who possess a luminescent blue glow and telekinetic abilities, have long been the dominant species on Velan-7. They enjoy privileges and opportunities that the Solarians, a species with gold-hued skin and the power of technopathy, are denied. This stark divide between the two species forms the foundation of the planet's social and economic structure.

The Envars, with their advanced telekinetic abilities, monopolize key industries and hold positions of power within the government. They have

SECTION 3: THE JOURNEY TO VELAN-7

systematically marginalized the Solarians, relegating them to menial labor and denying them access to education and healthcare. The Envars justify their discriminatory practices by propagating the belief that the Solarians are an inferior species, incapable of intellectual and technological progression.

This discrimination has far-reaching consequences for the Solarians. They are trapped in a cycle of poverty, unable to break free from their limited opportunities. Their lack of access to education and resources perpetuates the Envars' power and sustains the status quo. Solarians are treated as second-class citizens, subjected to systemic oppression and frequent instances of police brutality.

The repressive nature of the Envar-dominated government exacerbates the planet's division. The Envar elite exploit their power to maintain control over the Solarians, using intimidation and fear as tactics of suppression. Any attempts by the Solarians to advocate for their rights or challenge the status quo are met with severe consequences.

Despite the immense challenges they face, the Solarians persist in their pursuit of equality and justice. Led by visionary activists like Aerin Zor, they rally against the oppressive regime, demanding an end to the discrimination and the dismantling of the existing power structure. The planet becomes a battleground for civil rights, as Solarians unite and find the courage to challenge their oppressors.

The Velan-7 Civil Rights Movement starts gaining momentum, with Solarians organizing protests, boycotts, and acts of civil disobedience. They form grassroots organizations, aiming to empower their community, and establish connections with external allies who support their cause. The movement garners attention from sympathetic Envars who recognize the injustice that pervades their society.

While the Solarians face significant obstacles in their fight for equality, their unwavering determination begins to shift the balance of power. The oppressive government faces growing resistance, forcing them to confront the reality of an increasingly united and empowered Solarian population.

The Planet Divided problem:

The division and discrimination experienced by the Solarians on Velan-7 mirrors real-world issues of racial segregation and inequality. To better understand the complexities of such problems, we can analyze the impact of social, economic, and political divisions on marginalized communities.

Consider the following real-world scenario: a city where a certain ethnic or racial group is systematically excluded from economic opportunities and denied access to education and healthcare. Analyze the consequences of this division, including the perpetuation of poverty, limited upward mobility, and the erosion of social cohesion.

One possible solution to this problem is community organizing and active resistance against the oppressive power structure. By forming grassroots organizations, marginalized communities can advocate for their rights, build solidarity, and create a platform for demanding change.

For example, Solarians on Velan-7 could establish educational programs within their community, providing accessible learning opportunities to empower their youth and bridge the educational gap. They could also initiate economic justice campaigns, demanding fair wages and equitable access to employment opportunities.

Moreover, external alliances and support play a crucial role in effecting change. By forming connections with individuals and organizations beyond their immediate community, marginalized groups can leverage the power of collective action and amplify their voices on a larger scale.

To address the Planet Divided problem, it is also essential to challenge the oppressive narratives perpetuated by the dominant group. This can be achieved through media representation, art, and storytelling that amplify the voices and experiences of the marginalized community, fostering empathy and increasing awareness.

Real-world examples of the power of activism and resistance can be explored to inspire and motivate readers to take action. Highlighting the successes of social justice movements, such as the Civil Rights Movement in the United States or the anti-apartheid struggle in South Africa, can provide valuable insights into effective strategies for effecting change.

Overall, the story of Velan-7 serves as a prism through which readers can examine and engage with the real-world issues of discrimination, inequality, and the power dynamics that exist within societies. By addressing the division on Velan-7 and exploring potential solutions, we can challenge readers to reflect on their own societies and inspire them to take action for a more inclusive and equitable world.

Subsection: The Bi-Entity Fusion Dilemma

The Bi-Entity Fusion Dilemma on Velan-7 was a complex issue that deeply affected the alien communities on the planet. To understand the dilemma, we must dive into the intricacies of bi-entity fusion and its implications for civil rights.

Understanding Bi-Entity Fusion

Bi-entity fusion refers to the unique biological process that occurs when two distinct alien entities merge together and form a single being. This process is exclusive to certain alien species on Velan-7 and is considered a natural occurrence for them.

SECTION 3: THE JOURNEY TO VELAN-7

Bi-entity fusion leads to the creation of a new entity that possesses the collective traits, abilities, and memories of both original entities.

The fusion process is widely regarded as a sacred and deeply personal experience for those involved. It is seen as a celebration of unity, harmony, and interconnectedness within the alien community. However, the fusion process has faced scrutiny and discrimination from some sectors of Velan-7 society, leading to the Bi-Entity Fusion Dilemma.

The Discrimination Faced by Fused Entities

Fused entities on Velan-7 face numerous challenges and hurdles as a result of discrimination. One major issue is the denial of basic civil rights and legal recognition. Despite possessing all the physical and cognitive faculties of an autonomous being, fused entities were not granted legal personhood status by the Velan-7 government.

This lack of recognition resulted in a multitude of injustices. Fused entities were denied access to essential healthcare, education, employment, and housing.

Additionally, fused entities reported instances of systemic discrimination in their daily lives, such as facing prejudice and exclusion from social gatherings, public spaces, and even some private establishments.

The Origins of the Bi-Entity Fusion Dilemma

The Bi-Entity Fusion Dilemma traces its roots back to the deep-seated prejudice and fear of the unfamiliar. Some segments of Velan-7 society harbored preconceived notions and misguided beliefs about bi-entity fusion. These prejudices were fueled by false stereotypes and the perception of fused entities as a threat to societal norms.

Furthermore, the lack of understanding and miscommunication between the fused entities and the non-fused population exacerbated the issue. Many non-fused individuals were ill-informed about the bi-entity fusion process, leading to confusion, fear, and unjust treatment towards fused entities.

The Call to Action

As the discrimination against fused entities persisted, a group of passionate activists emerged to advocate for their rights. Aerin Zor, the central figure in our story, was one of the groundbreaking voices to address the Bi-Entity Fusion Dilemma on Velan-7.

Aerin Zor, having recognized the inherent value and humanity of fused entities, took it upon themselves to educate the wider society about the fusion process. By promoting accurate information and dispelling myths, they aimed to bridge the divide between fused and non-fused communities.

Increasing Awareness and Empathy

To combat the discrimination faced by fused entities, Aerin Zor tirelessly organized workshops, public lectures, and awareness campaigns across Velan-7. They invited both fused and non-fused individuals to engage in open dialogues and foster a deeper understanding of bi-entity fusion.

Aerin Zor's efforts also extended to collaborating with artists, writers, and filmmakers to create compelling narratives that portrayed fused entities in a positive light. These creative works aimed to challenge societal prejudice and promote empathy towards the fused population.

Through their advocacy work, Aerin Zor emphasized the importance of recognizing fused entities as fully autonomous beings deserving of equal rights and opportunities. They urged the Velan-7 government to implement legislation that safeguarded the civil rights of fused entities and addressed the discrimination they faced.

Overcoming the Dilemma

The Bi-Entity Fusion Dilemma was gradually overcome through the collective efforts of activists like Aerin Zor, the support of enlightened individuals, and the evolving social consciousness on Velan-7.

Through sustained activism, the Velan-7 government was pressured to acknowledge the civil rights of fused entities. Legal reforms were implemented to ensure the recognition and protection of fused entities' rights, including the right to legal personhood, access to healthcare, education, employment, and housing.

The crucial transformations in public perception and government policies marked a significant milestone in the fight against discrimination faced by fused entities.

The Unconventional Solution

In tackling the Bi-Entity Fusion Dilemma, Aerin Zor employed an unconventional yet highly effective strategy. They sought to humanize the fused entities and bridge the gap between the fused and non-fused communities by organizing joint cultural events and festivals.

These gatherings provided a platform for fused entities and non-fused individuals to interact, celebrate their shared values and cultural heritage, and foster mutual understanding. By emphasizing unity and inclusivity, Aerin Zor's approach challenged the existing prejudices and replaced them with a genuine sense of community.

Continuing the Fight

While significant progress has been made in addressing the Bi-Entity Fusion Dilemma on Velan-7, the fight for alien civil rights continues. Aerin Zor's legacy serves as a reminder that the struggle for equality and justice is an ongoing endeavor.

Their indomitable spirit and unwavering commitment to advocating for the rights of fused entities have inspired a new generation of activists. Through their remarkable achievements, Aerin Zor paved the way for a more inclusive and compassionate society, where all individuals, regardless of their origins or biological makeup, can thrive.

Subsection: The Velan-7 Civil Rights Movement Begins

The Velan-7 Civil Rights Movement emerged as a response to the systemic discrimination and oppression experienced by the Bi-Entity Fusions on Velan-7. It marked a pivotal moment in the fight for equality and justice in the cosmos. The movement aimed to challenge the prevalent prejudices and secure basic human rights for all alien beings.

Origins of the Movement

The seeds of the Velan-7 Civil Rights Movement were sown long before its official inception. For centuries, Bi-Entity Fusions had been marginalized and treated as second-class citizens. They were denied access to education, employment, and political representation. With limited opportunities to improve their circumstances, the Fusions lived in a perpetual state of injustice.

However, the catalyst for change came when Aerin Zor, a bi-entity fusion born and raised on Velan-7, became acutely aware of the glaring disparities faced by their community. Aerin Zor witnessed too many talented fusions being ostracized, their potential wasted due to unfair policies and discrimination. This realization ignited a fire within Aerin and sparked the beginning of a movement that would change the course of history.

The Birth of the Velan-7 Civil Rights Movement

The Velan-7 Civil Rights Movement was born out of a collective awakening to the injustices perpetrated against the Bi-Entity Fusions. It started with a small group of fusions coming together in recognition of their shared struggle and the need for collective action. Aerin Zor emerged as a charismatic leader, galvanizing the Fusions and inspiring them to fight for their rights.

Organized meetings were held, where fusions discussed their experiences and shared stories of discrimination. These gatherings fostered a sense of community and solidarity, strengthening their resolve to challenge the oppressive status quo. The movement gained momentum as more fusions joined the cause, uniting their voices and experiences.

The Fight for Recognition

One of the primary objectives of the Velan-7 Civil Rights Movement was to demand recognition for the Bi-Entity Fusions, advocating for their place as equals in Velan-7 society. Aerin Zor and their supporters understood that achieving this goal required a multifaceted approach.

The movement engaged in peaceful protests, demonstrations, and advocacy campaigns, aiming to increase awareness and understanding of the challenges faced by Bi-Entity Fusions. Their message appealed to the innate desire for justice and the recognition of every being's inherent worth.

Additionally, the movement worked tirelessly to forge alliances with sympathetic individuals and organizations. Collaborating with other marginalized communities, they sought to create a united front against discrimination in all its forms.

Building Bridges and Empowering Allies

The Velan-7 Civil Rights Movement recognized that fostering empathy and solidarity among non-fusion aliens was crucial to effecting lasting change. Activists engaged in community outreach programs, organizing workshops and educational sessions to raise awareness about the unique struggles faced by Bi-Entity Fusions.

Through these initiatives, the movement aimed to dispel preconceived notions and challenge stereotypes, fostering understanding and empathy. They highlighted the shared values and aspirations that connected all beings, emphasizing the importance of unity in the face of oppression.

The Role of Activism

The Velan-7 Civil Rights Movement recognized the transformative power of activism in driving social change. Activists understood that change would not happen passively; it required active engagement and a willingness to challenge the status quo.

Activism on Velan-7 took various forms, from peaceful protests and marches to creative expressions of dissent. Poetry slams, art exhibitions, and music festivals became platforms for fusions and their allies to voice their grievances and aspirations for a more inclusive society.

These creative avenues of protest not only galvanized the movement but also served as cultural touchstones for future generations. They celebrated the rich diversity of alien cultures and challenged societal norms, transcending boundaries and inspiring collective action.

Shifting Paradigms

The Velan-7 Civil Rights Movement challenged deeply ingrained prejudices and forced society to confront uncomfortable truths. The courage and resilience demonstrated by the activists opened the doors for dialogue and self-reflection, ultimately leading to a shift in societal paradigms.

As the movement gained traction, allies from various sectors of Velan-7 society began questioning the long-standing discriminatory practices. Government officials, business leaders, and educators started to recognize the immense talent and potential that Bi-Entity Fusions possessed, and the necessity of granting them the rights and opportunities they had long been denied.

The Velan-7 Civil Rights Movement's Impact

The Velan-7 Civil Rights Movement brought tangible change to the lives of Bi-Entity Fusions. Through their efforts, discriminatory laws were repealed, educational opportunities expanded, and access to employment and political representation was granted.

Yet, the movement's impact extended beyond Velan-7. It served as a catalyst for similar movements across the cosmos, inspiring alien activists to fight for their rights and challenge oppressive systems. The Velan-7 Civil Rights Movement became a symbol of hope and progress, demonstrating the power of collective action in effecting change.

Lessons Learned and Moving Forward

The Velan-7 Civil Rights Movement taught us invaluable lessons about the resilience of the human spirit and the power of unity. It emphasized the importance of challenging discriminatory systems and the need for allyship in the pursuit of justice.

Moving forward, it is crucial to remember that the fight for alien civil rights is an ongoing process. The lessons learned from the Velan-7 Civil Rights Movement serve as a guide for future generations, inspiring them to continue advocating for equality and justice. By embracing our shared humanity and celebrating our differences, we can create a universe where every being can thrive and coexist harmoniously.

Ideas for Further Exploration

1. Explore the intersections between the Velan-7 Civil Rights Movement and other civil rights movements in the cosmos. How did they influence each other? What lessons can be learned from their strategies and successes?

2. Investigate the role of art and culture in social movements. How did creative expressions play a part in the Velan-7 Civil Rights Movement? How can art be used as a tool for activism in our own lives?

3. Examine the challenges faced by the Velan-7 Civil Rights Movement in building alliances and fostering empathy. What strategies were effective in overcoming those challenges? How can we apply these lessons to our own efforts in advocating for social change?

4. Research the long-term effects of the Velan-7 Civil Rights Movement on Velan-7 society. How did it shape the future for Bi-Entity Fusions and other marginalized communities? What obstacles still exist, and what can be done to address them?

5. Reflect on the significance of leadership and its impact on social movements. How did Aerin Zor's leadership shape the Velan-7 Civil Rights Movement? What qualities and skills are essential for effective leadership in the pursuit of social justice?

Remember, the Velan-7 Civil Rights Movement was a turning point in the struggle for alien civil rights. By understanding its origins, strategies, and impact, we can glean valuable insights to inform our own fight for a more just and inclusive universe.

Subsection: Establishing Connections and Alliances

Establishing connections and alliances was a vital step in the Velan-7 Civil Rights Movement. Aerin Zor understood that in order to bring about real change, they needed to build a network of support, create alliances, and collaborate with like-minded individuals and organizations. This subsection explores the strategies and challenges faced by Aerin Zor as they worked towards establishing these connections and alliances.

The Power of Unity

Aerin Zor recognized that unity was crucial in achieving their goals. They believed in the power of collective action and understood that by joining forces with other groups, they would be stronger and more influential. To establish connections and alliances, Aerin Zor started by reaching out to various alien communities on Velan-7 who were also affected by discrimination and injustice.

Building Bridges

In order to build connections, Aerin Zor organized community gatherings and events where aliens from different backgrounds could come together to share their experiences and concerns. These gatherings served as platforms for dialogue, understanding, and solidarity. They provided an opportunity for individuals to connect with one another, fostering a sense of belonging and unity.

Collaboration with Existing Organizations

Aerin Zor also reached out to existing organizations that were working towards social justice and equality. They understood the importance of collaboration and leveraged the resources, experiences, and networks of these organizations to further the cause of alien civil rights. By partnering with established groups, Aerin Zor was able to tap into a broader support base and gain access to valuable expertise and resources.

Overcoming Differences

Establishing connections and alliances often meant working with individuals and groups who had different experiences, perspectives, and priorities. Aerin Zor knew that in order to create a cohesive movement, it was essential to overcome these differences and find common ground. They facilitated conversations and encouraged open dialogue, focusing on shared values and a collective vision of a more equitable society.

Creating a Network of Support

Aerin Zor understood that connections and alliances went beyond just collaborating on specific initiatives. They aimed to create a network of support that would outlast the Civil Rights Movement on Velan-7. They focused on building lasting relationships and nurturing connections between individuals and organizations, ensuring a strong foundation for future activism and advocacy.

Challenges and Obstacles

Establishing connections and alliances was not without its challenges. Aerin Zor faced resistance from individuals and groups who were reluctant to support the Civil Rights Movement. They encountered skepticism, disagreement, and even animosity. Overcoming these obstacles required patience, resilience, and a willingness to engage in difficult conversations. Aerin Zor had to work tirelessly to build trust and demonstrate the value of collaboration and unity.

An Unconventional Approach

One unconventional approach that Aerin Zor adopted was the use of art and creative expression to build connections and alliances. They organized events that showcased the talents and creativity of alien communities, highlighting the richness and diversity of their cultures. By incorporating art into their activism, Aerin Zor was able to connect with individuals on a deeper, emotional level, fostering a sense of solidarity and collective identity.

Example: The Galactic Solidarity Festival

One notable event organized by Aerin Zor was the Galactic Solidarity Festival. This festival brought together artists, musicians, performers, and activists from various alien communities across Velan-7. It was a celebration of diversity and an opportunity for individuals and groups to showcase their talents and express their support for the Civil Rights Movement. The festival served as a catalyst for building connections and alliances, fostering a sense of unity and empowerment among participants.

Resources and Support

Aerin Zor understood the importance of providing resources and support to alien communities and organizations that joined the Civil Rights Movement. They advocated for equal access to education, healthcare, and employment opportunities. They also worked to secure funding and resources for initiatives focused on empowering alien communities and addressing systematic discrimination. By offering assistance and support, Aerin Zor ensured that the connections and alliances they formed were mutually beneficial and sustainable.

Tricks and Caveats

One trick that Aerin Zor employed when seeking to establish connections and alliances was active listening. They understood the importance of genuinely hearing and understanding the concerns and perspectives of others. This approach allowed them to build trust, show empathy, and find common ground with individuals and groups who initially held different views. Aerin Zor also recognized the need for patience and persistence, as building connections and alliances takes time and effort.

Exercises

1. Organize a community gathering in your locality that aims to bring together individuals from diverse backgrounds. Encourage open dialogue and discussion on topics related to social justice and equality.

2. Research existing organizations in your area that advocate for civil rights. Reach out to one of these organizations and inquire about opportunities for collaboration or support.

3. Reflect on a time when you encountered resistance or disagreement while trying to establish a connection or alliance. How did you address these challenges, and what did you learn from the experience?

Conclusion

Establishing connections and alliances was a critical aspect of Aerin Zor's activism on Velan-7. By building bridges, collaborating with existing organizations, and overcoming differences, they were able to create a network of support and foster unity among alien communities. The example of the Galactic Solidarity Festival highlights the transformative power of art in building connections and alliances. Patience, active listening, and a commitment to providing resources and support were key strategies employed by Aerin Zor. Through their efforts, they not only advanced the cause of alien civil rights on Velan-7 but also inspired others to continue the fight for equality and justice throughout the universe.

Subsection: Preparing for the Uprising

As Aerin Zor witnessed the injustices suffered by the Bi-Entity Fusions on Velan-7, a fire of determination burned within their heart. They knew that change was necessary, but they also understood that preparation was key to a successful uprising. In this section, we will explore the steps taken by Aerin and their allies to prepare for the Bi-Entity Fusion Uprising, ensuring that they had the knowledge, resources, and support needed to bring about lasting change.

Understanding the Oppression

Before embarking on any endeavor, it is crucial to have a deep understanding of the problem at hand. Aerin and their fellow activists dedicated themselves to learning the intricacies of the Bi-Entity Fusion dilemma on Velan-7. They researched the historical context, studied the restrictive laws and policies, and conducted interviews with those directly affected. This comprehensive knowledge of the oppression allowed them to identify the root causes and develop effective strategies.

Problem: Analyzing the systemic oppression

To fully comprehend the systemic oppression faced by Bi-Entity Fusions, Aerin and their team delved into the social, political, and economic structures of Velan-7. They identified the key players responsible for perpetuating the discrimination and sought to unravel the complex web of power dynamics. One of the challenges they faced was:

Problem: How can the activists analyze the power dynamics and identify the influential figures behind the discrimination?

Solution: To overcome this challenge, Aerin and their team conducted extensive research, analyzed historical data, and gathered testimonies from affected individuals. They then mapped out the connections and interactions between various stakeholders, identifying the influential figures and institutions responsible for upholding the oppressive system. By understanding the power dynamics in place, they could strategically target those in influential positions during the uprising.

Mobilizing the Community

Auerin Zor recognized the power of a united community and the strength that came from standing together. They dedicated significant effort to mobilizing and organizing Bi-Entity Fusions and their allies on Velan-7. Through community engagement and empowerment, they aimed to build a strong foundation for the uprising.

Problem: Overcoming divisions within the Bi-Entity Fusion community
The Bi-Entity Fusion community on Velan-7 was, unfortunately, divided due to years of internalized oppression and the effects of the discriminatory system. Aerin understood that overcoming these divisions was crucial for the success of the uprising. One of the challenges they faced was:
Problem: How can the activists foster unity among the divided Bi-Entity Fusion community?
Solution: To address this challenge, Aerin Zor and their team organized community forums, discussion groups, and workshops. These spaces allowed Bi-Entity Fusions to share their stories, experiences, and frustrations, building empathy and understanding within the community. They also encouraged dialogue and collaboration between different factions, emphasizing the common goal of achieving equality. By highlighting the shared experiences and strengths, Aerin fostered unity and a sense of collective identity among the Bi-Entity Fusion community.

Strategic Planning

Aerin Zor recognized that a successful uprising required meticulous planning and strategic thinking. They worked tirelessly to develop a detailed and comprehensive plan that would maximize the impact of the Bi-Entity Fusion Uprising.
Problem: Finding effective methods of protest
Aerin and their team understood that the effectiveness of their protest methods could make or break the uprising. They needed to devise strategies that would capture the attention of the Velan-7 government, the media, and the galaxy at large. One of the challenges they faced was:
Problem: How can the activists choose protest methods that are both impactful and nonviolent?
Solution: To address this challenge, Aerin and their team carefully studied historical examples of successful nonviolent protests on other planets. They drew inspiration from civil rights movements throughout the cosmos and adapted those strategies to suit the unique context of Velan-7. They organized peaceful demonstrations, strikes, and boycotts, harnessing the power of unity and peaceful resistance to bring attention to the cause without resorting to violence.

Example: The Formation of "Fusion Forces"

One of the creative solutions developed by Aerin Zor and their team was the formation of "Fusion Forces." These forces were composed of trained activists who specialized in spreading awareness and educating the public about the struggles faced by Bi-Entity Fusions. Fusion Forces would travel to different regions on Velan-7, setting up educational workshops, organizing cultural events, and engaging in open dialogues with local communities. This approach aimed to challenge societal prejudices and build empathy among the general population, sparking conversations and opening hearts to the cause.

Preparing for the Uprising

As the momentum grew, Aerin and their team knew that they had to be prepared for a potential escalation in the conflict. They recognized the need to prioritize the safety and well-being of the activists involved in the uprising, while also ensuring they had the resources and support necessary to sustain their resistance.

Problem: Protecting the safety of the activists

The Velan-7 government was known for its harsh crackdowns on dissent, making safety a primary concern for Aerin and their fellow activists. They needed to develop strategies to protect themselves and minimize the risks involved. One of the challenges they faced was:

Problem: How can the activists ensure their safety in the face of potential government repression?

Solution: To overcome this challenge, Aerin Zor and their team established a network of safe houses and implemented security measures to protect the identities and locations of key activists. They organized self-defense training sessions, taught nonviolent conflict resolution techniques, and distributed safety guidelines to all participants. They also collaborated with legal experts to provide legal support, advice, and representation for activists who faced prosecution.

Unconventional Tactic: "Activism in Disguise"

Aerin Zor, always thinking outside the box, devised an unconventional tactic called "Activism in Disguise." Activists would blend into everyday life, regularly engaging in activities that typical Velan-7 citizens enjoyed. By doing so, they created opportunities to have informal conversations, challenge preconceived notions, and promote understanding among the general population. This approach allowed the activists to make incremental changes in societal attitudes while keeping a low profile, reducing the risk of government interference.

In this section, we have explored the crucial steps taken by Aerin Zor and their allies as they prepared for the Bi-Entity Fusion Uprising. By understanding the oppression, mobilizing the community, engaging in strategic planning, and ensuring the safety of activists, they laid the groundwork for a movement that would challenge the status quo on Velan-7. Their dedication, courage, and innovative thinking serve as inspiration for activists in the ongoing fight for equality and justice throughout the universe.

Subsection: The Role of Activism in Social Change

In our exploration of Aerin Zor's life and journey, it is essential to understand the significant role that activism plays in driving social change. Activism, at its core, is about actively advocating for and working towards social, political, or environmental transformation. It is about challenging the status quo, empowering marginalized communities, and striving for a more equitable and just society.

1. The Power of Collective Action: Activism is all about collective action. It brings together individuals who are passionate about a particular cause, creating a powerful force that cannot be ignored. By mobilizing people and organizing grassroots movements, activists challenge the existing power structures and demand accountability from those in authority. It is through collective action that real change is made possible.

For example, in the Velan-7 Civil Rights Movement, Aerin Zor and other activists united to address the Bi-Entity Fusion Dilemma. They organized protests, rallies, and awareness campaigns to shed light on the injustices faced by the alien community. By standing together and raising their voices, they were able to create a wave of public support and put pressure on the government to address their concerns.

2. Raising Awareness and Sparking Dialogue: One of the essential roles of activism is to raise awareness about the issues at hand. Activists aim to educate the public and dismantle ignorance or apathy surrounding social injustices. They use various methods such as public demonstrations, media campaigns, and public speaking engagements to trigger conversations and engage with a broader audience.

In the case of Velan-7, Aerin Zor and their fellow activists highlighted the discrimination faced by Bi-Entity Fusions through media interviews, panel discussions, and social media campaigns. By sharing personal stories and experiences, they humanized the struggle and compelled people to examine their own attitudes and biases. This increased awareness served as a catalyst for change.

3. Advocacy and Policy Reform: Activism goes beyond raising awareness; it also involves advocating for policy and systemic changes. Activists work towards influencing legislation by lobbying policymakers, engaging in public hearings, and fighting for legal protections for marginalized communities.

In the Velan-7 Civil Rights Movement, activism played a crucial role in pushing for policy reforms that recognized the rights of Bi-Entity Fusions. Through persistent advocacy and negotiation, activists were able to secure legal protections against discrimination, ensure access to education and employment opportunities, and dismantle oppressive laws.

4. Nonviolent Resistance: While activism can take various forms, nonviolent resistance is often a powerful strategy to effect social change. Nonviolent protests and acts of civil disobedience aim to disrupt the status quo without resorting to violence. This approach allows activists to maintain moral high ground, gain public support, and force those in power to address their demands.

A classic example of nonviolent resistance is the Civil Rights Movement led by Martin Luther King Jr. in the United States. Through peaceful demonstrations, sit-ins, and boycotts, activists challenged racial segregation and discrimination, and ultimately played a pivotal role in shaping a more inclusive society.

5. Empowering Marginalized Communities: Activism is about uplifting the voices of marginalized communities and empowering them to advocate for their own rights. It provides a platform for those who have been systematically oppressed and marginalized to assert their humanity and demand dignity and equality.

For Aerin Zor, empowering the Bi-Entity Fusion community on Velan-7 was a central aspect of their activism. They worked alongside other activists to foster community organization and provided resources, education, and support to empower Bi-Entity Fusions to advocate for their own rights. This bottom-up approach helped mobilize the community and ensured that their voices were heard and respected.

It is important to note that while activists are often the catalysts for change, they cannot bring about long-lasting transformation on their own. Governments, institutions, and wider society must also recognize their responsibility to actively listen, learn, and act upon the demands of activists. True social change requires collective effort and a commitment to justice and equality for all.

Example: The Impact of the Black Lives Matter Movement

To illustrate the power and effectiveness of activism, we can look at the impact of the Black Lives Matter (BLM) movement. BLM emerged in response to the systemic racism and police violence faced by Black communities in the United States. It quickly gained momentum, sparking a global conversation about racial inequality and demanding justice for victims of racial violence.

By organizing protests, engaging in social media activism, and advocating for policy reform, the BLM movement has successfully brought issues of racial justice to the forefront of public discourse. It has forced individuals, institutions, and governments to confront their own biases and take meaningful action to dismantle systemic racism.

The BLM movement also serves as a powerful example of how activism can transcend borders and create solidarity across different communities. It has inspired similar movements around the world, demonstrating the universal need to address racial injustice and inequality.

Conclusion

Activism is a vital force for social change, driving progress and challenging oppressive systems. The role of activism in creating a more just and equitable society cannot be overstated. Through collective action, raising awareness, advocating for policy reform, nonviolent resistance, and empowering marginalized communities, activists like Aerin Zor have shaped the course of history and paved the way for a more inclusive future.

As we continue to learn from their legacies, it is crucial to recognize that the fight for social justice is ongoing. Activism requires persistent dedication, resilience, and a commitment to uplifting the voices of those who have been silenced. By engaging with activism and standing up against injustice, we can all play a part in creating a better world for present and future generations.

Section 4: The Bi-Entity Fusion Uprising

Subsection: The Spark that Ignites the Revolution

In this subsection, we delve into the moment that served as the catalyst for the bi-entity fusion uprising on Velan-7, forever changing the course of history for alien civil rights. The spark that ignited the revolution can be traced back to a seemingly ordinary event that took place in the heart of the planet's capital city, Velaria.

On a warm summer evening, citizens of Velaria gathered in the grand central square to peacefully protest against the discriminatory laws that oppressed the bi-entity fusion population. The atmosphere was charged with frustration, desperation, and a yearning for justice as the oppressed aliens united in their demand for equal rights.

The main protagonist of our story, Aerin Zor, stood among the crowd, his heart filled with a fiery determination to challenge the status quo. Aerin was no stranger to the struggles faced by the bi-entity fusion community; having grown up on Velan-7, he had personally experienced the injustice and prejudice that prevailed in their daily lives.

As the crowd swelled with passionate protestors, a group of law enforcement officers approached, armed with stun batons and riot gear. They had been deployed by the oppressive government of Velan-7 to suppress the peaceful demonstration. Tension filled the air as the officers advanced towards the protestors, ready to silence their demands.

But then, in a moment that would reverberate throughout the universe, a young bi-entity fusion teenager named Kira Vex stepped forward. With unwavering courage, Kira demanded to speak to the authorities, urging them to revoke the discriminatory laws and treat the bi-entity fusion beings as equals.

This act of defiance sent shockwaves through the crowd, and the protesters watched with bated breath to see how the officers would respond. Kira's bravery struck a chord within Aerin's heart, and he knew that he had to take action. In a bold move, Aerin stepped up beside Kira, lending his support and giving voice to the collective frustration that had engulfed the bi-entity fusion community.

A feverish energy spread through the crowd as they witnessed Aerin and Kira fearlessly challenging the authorities. Their unwavering determination served as an inspiration to the masses, igniting a spark of hope and unity that had been dormant for far too long. In that transformative moment, Aerin Zor became not just an activist but a leader and a symbol of resistance.

However, the response from the law enforcement officers was brutal and swift. They unleashed a barrage of stun batons and tear gas upon the peaceful protesters. Chaos erupted as the crowd scattered in all directions, seeking refuge from the violence.

But the spark had been ignited, and the fire of resistance would not be extinguished. News of the brutal crackdown spread like wildfire, capturing the attention of alien communities across Velan-7 and beyond. The event became a rallying cry that galvanized alien civil rights activists and ignited a wide-scale uprising against the oppressive regime.

It is important to note that this moment was not just about one act of defiance, but rather the culmination of years of systemic oppression. Aerin Zor and Kira Vex symbolized the collective frustration, courage, and resilience of an entire community. Their actions on that fateful day served as a turning point, exposing the injustices faced by bi-entity fusion beings and sparking a revolution that would dismantle the status quo.

This event serves as a reminder that change does not happen overnight. It takes a single spark to ignite a revolution, but it is the collective efforts of courageous individuals and communities that lead to lasting change. The revolution on Velan-7 was just the beginning of Aerin Zor's journey, as he would go on to become an intergalactic advocate for alien civil rights, spreading the message of unity and challenging prejudices across the cosmos.

Example: The Power of Unity

To illustrate the power of unity, let's consider the example of the Galactian Alliance, an organization that was formed in the aftermath of the Velan-7 uprising. The Galactian Alliance aimed to bring together alien communities from different planets to fight for their collective rights and advocate for equality.

One of the key strategies employed by the Galactian Alliance was fostering solidarity among alien communities. They recognized that by uniting their voices and resources, they could create a stronger force for change. The alliance organized conferences, rallies, and cultural exchanges where individuals from various planets could come together and share their experiences.

Through these interactions, the Galactian Alliance was able to build bridges between different alien communities, breaking down stereotypes and fostering a sense of empathy and understanding. They realized that by highlighting the similarities in their struggles, they could strengthen their collective voice and challenge the prejudices that divided them.

This unity also extended to the realm of policymaking. The Galactian Alliance worked tirelessly to negotiate intergalactic treaties that would protect the rights of alien beings across different planetary systems. By presenting a united front, they were able to influence policymakers and advocate for legislative changes that would dismantle discriminatory practices.

The success of the Galactian Alliance not only inspired other grassroots organizations for galactic change but also paved the way for future interplanetary collaborations. It showed that unity, when combined with a shared vision and purpose, has the power to transcend planetary boundaries and foster a sense of belonging and equality for all.

Exercise: Analyzing the Velvet Revolution

The Velvet Revolution, which took place in Czechoslovakia in 1989, is another example of a revolution sparked by a single event. Research and analyze the Velvet Revolution, focusing on its catalyst, key figures, strategies employed, and overall impact. What lessons can be learned from this historic event and how can they be applied to the bi-entity fusion uprising on Velan-7? Be prepared to present your findings to the class.

Subsection: Organizing the Resistance

Organizing the resistance was a monumental task. It required strategic planning, coordination, and the mobilization of alien communities across Velan-7. Aerin Zor understood that unity and solidarity were essential to the success of the uprising. In this subsection, we will explore the various aspects of organizing the resistance and the challenges faced along the way.

Building Networks of Support

To initiate the resistance, Aerin Zor recognized the need to build strong networks of support. They reached out to like-minded individuals, community leaders, and activists who shared their vision for a just and equal society. These initial connections formed the foundation for a broader coalition, bringing together beings from different backgrounds and experiences.

Aerin Zor leveraged the power of social media platforms, interstellar communication systems, and community gatherings to spread their message of unity and resistance. They organized town hall meetings, open forums, and public rallies to engage with the community and build a sense of shared purpose.

Identifying Key Leaders

A critical step in organizing the resistance was identifying key leaders within different alien communities. Aerin Zor knew that effective leadership was essential for galvanizing support and mobilizing resources. They sought individuals who possessed strong communication skills, strategic thinking, and a deep understanding of the issues faced by their respective communities.

Through consultations and collaborative discussions, Aerin Zor formed a diverse leadership team that represented the interests and concerns of various alien species on Velan-7. This ensured that the resistance movement was inclusive and addressed the needs of all marginalized groups.

Strategic Planning and Resource Allocation

Strategic planning was vital to the success of the resistance. Aerin Zor and their team carefully assessed the strengths, weaknesses, opportunities, and threats faced by the movement. This analysis helped them devise a comprehensive plan of action and allocate resources effectively.

They identified critical targets and developed specific objectives to challenge the oppressive government policies. The resistance organized protests, sit-ins, and demonstrations at key government institutions to put pressure on the authorities. Additionally, they strategically mobilized resources such as funds, supplies, and legal support to sustain the movement.

Creating Safe Spaces

Aerin Zor understood the importance of creating safe spaces for alien communities to share their stories and experiences. They established community centers, shelters, and support groups where marginalized individuals could seek refuge and find empowerment. These spaces became vital for nurturing a sense of solidarity and resilience among the oppressed communities.

Within these safe spaces, the resistance conducted workshops, training sessions, and educational programs to equip aliens with the necessary tools to speak out against injustice. They provided legal guidance, mental health support, and social services to ensure the well-being of those affected by discrimination and oppression.

Establishing Communication Channels

Open and effective communication channels were essential for the success of the resistance movement. Aerin Zor implemented a multi-faceted communication strategy that included traditional media, social media platforms, and encrypted interstellar networks.

They disseminated information about their objectives, events, and progress through press releases, interviews, and social media updates. The use of encrypted communication channels safeguarded sensitive information and protected activists from government surveillance.

The Power of Art and Culture

Aerin Zor recognized the transformative power of art and culture in inspiring social change. They encouraged artists, musicians, and writers to use their talents to raise awareness about the struggles faced by alien communities on Velan-7.

Through music, visual arts, and literature, the resistance redefined societal norms and challenged existing stereotypes. These creative expressions not only served as a form of protest but also fostered empathy, understanding, and unity among different communities.

Exercising Nonviolent Resistance

Nonviolent resistance was a core principle of the resistance movement led by Aerin Zor. They emphasized the power of peaceful protest and civil disobedience to challenge oppressive systems and inspire change. The resistance organized peaceful marches, boycotts, and coordinated acts of civil disobedience to disrupt the status quo without resorting to violence.

By adopting nonviolent tactics, the resistance movement garnered international attention and support. The public witnessed the bravery and determination of the alien activists as they withstood violent suppression from the government, further highlighting the need for systemic change.

Addressing Internal Divisions

Throughout the process of organizing the resistance, Aerin Zor faced internal divisions and conflicting agendas within the coalition. They recognized the importance of addressing these divisions and fostering a sense of unity and purpose among the diverse alien communities.

Through dialogue, mediation, and facilitated discussions, Aerin Zor and their team navigated these internal divisions, ensuring that the movement remained cohesive and focused on its broader objectives. They prioritized inclusivity, working towards consensus-building and collaboration.

Unconventional Solution: The Power of Humor

Amidst the challenges and hardships faced, Aerin Zor discovered an unconventional yet effective tool for organizing the resistance: humor. They recognized that humor had the power to undermine oppressive narratives and create emotional connections among alien communities.

The resistance used satirical performances, comedy sketches, and memes to challenge the authority and highlight the absurdity of discriminatory policies. Humor became a weapon against injustice, connecting people through laughter and strengthening their resolve to fight for equality.

Example: Organizing a Massive Sit-In

To illustrate the complexities of organizing the resistance, consider the example of a massive sit-in organized by the coalition. The objective was to protest against a new government policy aimed at further marginalizing bi-entity fusion beings.

SECTION 4: THE BI-ENTITY FUSION UPRISING

The coalition first identified a strategic location, a public square adjacent to a major government building. They estimated the number of participants and allocated resources such as food, water, medical support, and legal aid.

Through social media campaigns and community outreach, they spread the word about the sit-in, calling on all oppressed communities to participate. The coalition worked together to design and distribute flyers, create online event pages, and engage with local press to generate maximum visibility and support.

On the day of the sit-in, activists gathered at the agreed-upon location carrying colorful signs, banners, and musical instruments. The resistance leaders delivered passionate speeches, inspiring participants to remain peaceful, determined, and united.

The sit-in lasted for several days, during which the activists utilized social media platforms to document their experiences, share stories, and garner support from sympathetic individuals and organizations across Velan-7.

The government attempted to suppress the sit-in through intimidation and coercion, but the resistance remained resilient and committed to their cause. The event received widespread media coverage, raising public awareness and putting pressure on the government to reconsider the discriminatory policy.

The successful sit-in became a catalyst for other forms of resistance, empowering alien communities, and demonstrating the power of organized, nonviolent protest.

Caveats and Challenges

Organizing the resistance was not without its challenges. Alien communities faced surveillance, harassment, and threats from the oppressive government. Internal divisions, differing priorities, and conflicting strategies posed additional hurdles that needed to be overcome.

The resistance had to confront their own biases and prejudices within the coalition, ensuring that the movement was truly inclusive and representative of all marginalized groups. Cultivating trust, maintaining transparency, and addressing mistrust were ongoing challenges that demanded constant attention.

Furthermore, the resistance grappled with limited resources, making it necessary to strategize and prioritize where to direct their efforts for maximum impact. Balancing immediate needs with long-term objectives required careful consideration and negotiation.

Resources and Support

Organizing a resistance movement requires access to resources and support networks. Here are some key resources and support systems that can aid in organizing a resistance:

- Community centers and safe spaces for marginalized individuals to gather and organize.
- Legal support organizations that specialize in civil rights and social justice issues.
- Grassroots funding initiatives and crowd-sourcing platforms to raise funds for resistance activities.
- Community leaders, activists, and organizations with shared goals and values.
- Educational resources on organizing, strategic planning, and nonviolent resistance.

Building relationships and collaboration with like-minded organizations, both locally and across galaxies, can amplify the impact of the resistance movement.

Exercises

1. Reflect on a historical resistance movement on Earth. What were some of the key strategies employed by the movement? How did they overcome challenges and achieve their objectives?

2. Form a hypothetical coalition to address a social justice issue in your community or a fictional alien society. Identify key leaders, plan a strategic protest event, and outline potential challenges and solutions.

3. Write a satirical skit or create a meme that challenges an oppressive policy or promotes social change. Share it with friends to gauge their reactions and foster dialogue.

Conclusion

Organizing the resistance was a complex and multifaceted process that required careful planning, coordination, and the mobilization of alien communities. Through building networks of support, strategic planning, creating safe spaces, and exercising nonviolent resistance, Aerin Zor and the coalition managed to challenge the oppressive government policies on Velan-7.

SECTION 4: THE BI-ENTITY FUSION UPRISING

The success of the resistance movement lay in its ability to foster unity, address internal divisions, and cultivate empathy within diverse alien communities. By harnessing the power of art, humor, and effective communication, the resistance movement gained momentum, inspiring change beyond Velan-7 and paving the way for a more just and equitable universe.

Subsection: Challenging the Velan-7 Government

In challenging the Velan-7 government, Aerin Zor confronted a power structure deeply entrenched in prejudice and injustice. This subsection explores the strategies and tactics employed by Aerin Zor and the Velan-7 civil rights movement to shake the foundations of oppression and fight for equality.

Recognizing Systemic Discrimination

Aerin Zor understood that the first step in challenging the Velan-7 government was to expose the systemic discrimination ingrained within the system. By examining policies, laws, and practices, Zor was able to uncover the layers of inequality that existed across sectors of Velan-7 society.

Through extensive research and data analysis, Zor and their team identified patterns of discrimination in areas such as employment, housing, education, and access to healthcare. They collected testimonies from affected individuals and documented numerous cases of alien rights violations. This comprehensive understanding of the issues at hand laid the groundwork for a concerted effort to challenge the government's discriminatory practices.

Bringing Alien Rights to the Forefront

To challenge the Velan-7 government effectively, Aerin Zor realized the importance of putting the spotlight on alien rights. They organized and participated in rallies, marches, and peaceful protests, which aimed to raise awareness about the plight of alien inhabitants and expose the injustices they faced.

Zor collaborated with like-minded individuals, both alien and human, to organize events that captured the attention of the media and the public. Using their charismatic leadership, Zor delivered compelling speeches that highlighted the lived experiences of aliens and called for solidarity in the fight against government-sanctioned discrimination.

Through these demonstrations, Zor successfully shifted the narrative and made alien rights a central issue in the Velan-7 public consciousness. By challenging the government's discriminatory policies head-on, Zor and their allies were able to engage in meaningful dialogue and spark a wider conversation about the need for change.

Building Alliances and Coalitions

Challenging the Velan-7 government required building alliances and coalitions with other marginalized groups and individuals who shared a common goal of dismantling systemic discrimination. Aerin Zor recognized the power of collective action in effecting change and actively sought partnerships with like-minded activists.

Zor reached out to other civil rights organizations, both local and intergalactic, to create a united front against the Velan-7 government's discriminatory practices. They leveraged these alliances to strengthen their advocacy efforts, share resources and strategies, and lend support to other social justice movements.

Through these coalitions, Aerin Zor and their fellow activists were able to amplify their message, creating a ripple effect that extended beyond the Velan-7 government's reach. By establishing solidarity across disparate communities, they built a powerful movement that had the potential to challenge not just the Velan-7 government but systemic discrimination in the wider cosmos.

Leveraging International Pressure

Aerin Zor understood the importance of leveraging international pressure to hold the Velan-7 government accountable for its discriminatory practices. They embarked on an intensive diplomatic campaign to raise awareness of the injustices faced by alien inhabitants and secure the support of interplanetary organizations.

Zor attended intergalactic conferences and conventions, delivering impassioned speeches that rallied support from leaders of other planetary governments. They collaborated with influential interstellar organizations to bring attention to the Velan-7 government's treatment of aliens, compelling them to apply diplomatic pressure and impose sanctions if necessary.

Through these efforts, Zor effectively elevated the alien civil rights movement to an interplanetary stage, ensuring that the struggles faced by the inhabitants of Velan-7 were no longer ignored or dismissed. By exposing the government's discriminatory practices on a global scale, Zor and their allies were able to mobilize a wider base of support and put increasing pressure on the Velan-7 government to institute meaningful change.

Legal Action and Advocacy

In their quest to challenge the Velan-7 government, Aerin Zor recognized the need to pursue legal action and advocacy simultaneously. Zor and their team worked tirelessly to gather evidence, build strong legal cases, and represent alien individuals who had been victims of discrimination.

Through strategic litigation, Zor and their legal team targeted discriminatory laws and policies, using the legal system to expose the flaws in the government's approach to alien rights. They also collaborated with renowned intergalactic human rights organizations, enlisting their support and expertise in pursuing legal avenues for change.

Simultaneously, Zor engaged in advocacy efforts, lobbying lawmakers and government officials to implement comprehensive reforms that protected the rights and dignity of alien inhabitants. They crafted and promoted legislation that aimed to dismantle systemic discrimination and ensure equal treatment and opportunities for all individuals, regardless of their planetary origin.

Unconventional Approach: Guerrilla Art Movement

In addition to the more traditional forms of activism, Aerin Zor embraced an unconventional approach to challenging the Velan-7 government — the guerrilla art movement. Recognizing the power of art to shape public opinion and challenge ingrained beliefs, Zor and their allies used creative tactics to subvert the dominant narrative.

Through vibrant murals, thought-provoking installations, and innovative street performances, the guerrilla art movement brought the issues faced by alien inhabitants to the forefront of Velan-7 society. This captivating and disruptive form of protest not only captured public attention but also fostered empathy, encouraging individuals to question their own biases and prejudices.

The guerrilla art movement provided a platform for marginalized voices, allowing alien artists to express their experiences and perspectives through their creative work. It served as a powerful tool in challenging preconceived notions and fostering a collective sense of urgency and empathy among the Velan-7 population.

By employing this unconventional approach, Aerin Zor and their allies were able to engage a wider audience and catalyze conversations about alien rights in unexpected and impactful ways.

Conclusion

Challenging the Velan-7 government required a multi-faceted approach that combined legal action, advocacy, grassroots organizing, international pressure, and unconventional tactics. Through their tireless efforts, Aerin Zor and their allies were able to expose the systemic discrimination faced by alien inhabitants, mobilize support, and shake the foundations of prejudice and injustice.

The struggle for equality and justice, however, did not end with the defeat of the Velan-7 government. As subsequent sections of this biography explore, the legacy of Aerin Zor and the fight for alien civil rights continues to inspire and guide future activists in their pursuits of a more inclusive and equitable cosmos.

Subsection: Taking to the Streets

In this subsection, we delve into the pivotal moment when Aerin Zor and their fellow activists decided to take their fight to the streets of Velan-7. It was a bold and courageous move that would not only test their resolve but also spread their message of equality and justice to the masses. Strap in as we explore the strategies, challenges, and impact of this crucial stage in the Velan-7 Civil Rights Movement.

The Spark that Ignites the Revolution

Every revolution begins with a spark, a catalyst that ignites the flame of change. For Aerin Zor and their allies, the injustice and discrimination faced by the Bi-Entity Fusion community on Velan-7 served as that spark. The tipping point came when a young fusion artist named Kael was brutally attacked by a group of extremists, simply because they dared to express their unique identity through their art.

News of this horrific incident spread like wildfire throughout the fusion community, fueling a sense of outrage and solidarity. It was within this climate of collective discontent that Aerin Zor and their comrades saw an opportunity to channel their anger into meaningful action.

Organizing the Resistance

Organizing a resistance movement is no easy feat, especially in the face of a repressive government. However, Aerin Zor's natural leadership and charisma, coupled with their unwavering determination, allowed them to rally individuals from all walks of life to join the cause.

In secret meetings held in underground fusion clubs and clandestine gatherings in remote locations, plans were laid out for a series of peaceful protests and demonstrations. Communication channels were established, and a network of supporters was gradually built, ensuring that the movement could withstand the inevitable challenges that lay ahead.

Challenging the Velan-7 Government

One of the main hurdles faced by Aerin Zor and their fellow activists was challenging the oppressive policies of the Velan-7 government. The bi-entity fusion community had long been denied basic rights and faced systemic discrimination that was enshrined in laws and regulations.

To overcome this obstacle, the activists employed a multi-pronged approach. They used social media platforms to raise awareness about their cause, shining a light on the injustice and demanding change. They also reached out to sympathetic journalists, both local and intergalactic, to ensure their message reached a wider audience.

Simultaneously, Aerin Zor and their team leveraged legal avenues to challenge discriminatory laws in court. They worked with human rights lawyers and other legal experts to craft powerful arguments that exposed the flaws and contradictions in the current legal framework. By utilizing both grassroots activism and legal strategies, they aimed to create a strong and united front against the oppressive government.

Taking to the Streets

With the groundwork laid and support growing, the time had come for Aerin Zor and their fellow activists to take their fight to the streets. Peaceful protests and demonstrations were organized in major cities across Velan-7, drawing attention not only from the fusion community but also from sympathetic individuals from other alien backgrounds.

Clad in vibrant and symbolic clothing that represented their fusion identities, the activists flooded the streets, chanting slogans of unity and demanding equal rights for all. Their presence was a striking visual testament to the power of collective action and the resilience of the fusion community.

The protests were carefully planned to be peaceful and nonviolent, but that did not diminish their impact. The sight of thousands of determined individuals standing together, peacefully demanding justice, was a powerful statement that resonated with both the local population and the intergalactic community.

The Battle for Equality

The protests ignited a battle for equality that would rattle the very foundations of Velan-7 society. Aerin Zor and their fellow activists used this platform to engage in discussions with the public, challenging deeply ingrained prejudices and misconceptions about the fusion community.

They organized town hall meetings, panel discussions, and public debates, providing a space for open dialogue and education. Their goal was not only to demand equal rights but also to foster understanding and empathy among the population. By sharing their stories, struggles, and aspirations, they aimed to break down barriers and bridge the divide between the fusion community and the rest of Velan-7 society.

The Effectiveness of Nonviolent Protests

The strategic choice of nonviolent protests proved to be a powerful tool in the hands of Aerin Zor and their fellow activists. By opting for peaceful resistance, they showcased their commitment to justice and equality, effectively dismantling the negative stereotypes often associated with social movements.

Nonviolent protests not only garnered sympathy and support from within Velan-7 but also captured the attention of the intergalactic community. News of the movement spread like wildfire across the cosmos, with media outlets from various planets covering the struggle for alien civil rights on Velan-7.

The effectiveness of nonviolent protests was further amplified by the courage and resilience of the activists themselves. Their unwavering commitment to peaceful resistance in the face of violence and oppression inspired countless others to join the cause, propelling the movement forward and emboldening others to take action.

Lessons Learned from the Uprising

The success of the street protests on Velan-7 holds invaluable lessons for future activists and social movements. First and foremost, it teaches us that change is possible, even in the face of seemingly insurmountable odds. By organizing, staying united, and courageously fighting for their rights, Aerin Zor and their comrades transformed their society.

Additionally, the Velan-7 uprising highlights the effectiveness of nonviolent protests in bringing about meaningful change. The power of empathy and understanding cannot be underestimated, as it has the potential to reshape societal norms and challenge deeply ingrained prejudices.

Finally, the story of the Velan-7 uprising serves as a testament to the resilience and strength of the fusion community. It showcases the collective power of marginalized voices, demonstrating that when individuals stand together, they can overcome any obstacle and set the stage for a more inclusive and just future.

Let the story of Aerin Zor and the Velan-7 Civil Rights Movement serve as an inspiration to us all. May it remind us of the power of unity, the importance of fighting for justice, and the enduring nature of the human spirit, even in the far reaches of the cosmos.

Subsection: The Battle for Equality

In the midst of the Bi-Entity Fusion Uprising on Velan-7, the fight for equality was at the forefront of Aerin Zor's agenda. This subsection delves into the challenges faced, the strategies employed, and the impact of the battle for equality on the alien community.

Understanding the Roots of Inequality

Before embarking on the battle for equality, it was crucial for Aerin Zor to understand the root causes of inequality on Velan-7. The Velan-7 society was deeply divided, with the Bi-Entity Fusion beings being treated as second-class citizens. Discrimination was entrenched in the government policies, societal norms, and cultural biases.

Aerin Zor found that the process of fusion itself was viewed with suspicion and misunderstanding by the Velan-7 government and its citizens. The fear of the unknown and ignorance about the potential benefits of fusion acted as barriers to progress and equal treatment for Bi-Entity Fusion beings.

Raising Awareness and Advocacy

The battle for equality began with raising awareness about the issues faced by Bi-Entity Fusion beings. Aerin Zor harnessed the power of storytelling, using personal narratives and experiences to humanize the struggles of the alien community. By sharing stories of injustices and the impact of discrimination, Aerin Zor aimed to evoke empathy and understanding.

Advocacy played a crucial role in the battle for equality. Aerin Zor organized rallies, protests, and public forums to bring attention to the systemic discrimination faced by Bi-Entity Fusion beings. These events provided a platform for voices to be heard, and they served as a catalyst for change.

Building Alliances: Unity in Diversity

Aerin Zor recognized the power of unity in the fight for equality. In the battle for equality, alliances were built with other marginalized communities, including non-fusion alien beings, to broaden the movement's reach and create a united front against discrimination. By forging these alliances, Aerin Zor emphasized that equality was a universal struggle.

The key to building and sustaining alliances was acknowledging and respecting the unique struggles faced by different communities. Aerin Zor fostered solidarity among these diverse groups by providing a space for dialogue, understanding, and collaboration. By celebrating diversity and promoting intersectionality, the movement became stronger and more inclusive.

Challenging the Status Quo

To bring about lasting change, Aerin Zor and their allies had to challenge the existing power structures and advocate for policy reforms. Infiltrating the halls of the Velan-7 government, they worked to change discriminatory laws and dismantle oppressive systems.

Through lobbying efforts, grassroots organizing, and strategic alliances with sympathetic politicians, Aerin Zor sought to disrupt the status quo and create a more equitable society. They advocated for legislation that protected the rights of Bi-Entity Fusion beings, ensuring fair treatment in areas such as education, employment, and access to basic necessities.

Empowering Self-Expression and Cultural Identity

A critical aspect of the battle for equality was the recognition and celebration of cultural identity within the alien community. Aerin Zor championed the right of Bi-Entity Fusion beings to express themselves, their fusion, and their unique cultural heritage without fear of discrimination or erasure.

To empower self-expression and preserve cultural identity, Aerin Zor supported artistic endeavors, funded cultural programs, and encouraged the creation of spaces that amplified marginalized voices. By preserving cultural heritage, the movement not only challenged stereotypes and misconceptions but also celebrated the richness and diversity of the alien community.

Sustaining the Momentum

The battle for equality was not a linear process, but rather an ongoing struggle that required persistence and resilience. Aerin Zor and their allies understood that sustaining the momentum was crucial in achieving lasting change.

To sustain the fight for equality, the movement prioritized education and awareness-building initiatives. Dismantling deeply ingrained biases and challenging societal norms required continuous efforts to educate and engage with the wider Velan-7 population.

Moreover, the movement recognized the importance of mentorship and leadership development within the alien community. By cultivating the next generation of activists and equipping them with the necessary tools and knowledge, the movement ensured its longevity and the continued pursuit of equality beyond Velan-7.

Confronting Unconventional Biases

As the battle for equality progressed, Aerin Zor and their allies faced unconventional biases that hindered progress. These biases often stemmed from deep-rooted cultural beliefs and societal norms that perpetuated discrimination against Bi-Entity Fusion beings.

To confront these biases, the movement engaged in unconventional tactics. They organized interactive workshops, art exhibitions, and immersive experiences that challenged preconceived notions and encouraged critical thinking. By exposing the Velan-7 population to alternative perspectives and dismantling stereotypes, Aerin Zor aimed to address the underlying biases that hindered true equality.

A Call for Coexistence

The battle for equality on Velan-7 was not simply about reversing the oppression faced by Bi-Entity Fusion beings. It was a call for coexistence, collaboration, and the celebration of diversity.

Aerin Zor emphasized that true equality required a shift in mindset and the abandonment of hierarchical power structures. The battle for equality was about fostering an inclusive society that celebrated differences and recognized the value that all beings, irrespective of their fusion status, brought to the cosmos.

The subsection "The Battle for Equality" presents the pivotal moments and strategies employed by Aerin Zor and their allies during the Bi-Entity Fusion Uprising. It showcases the importance of raising awareness, building alliances, challenging the status quo, empowering self-expression, and sustaining the momentum in the pursuit of true equality. The battle for equality was not confined to Velan-7 alone but represented a larger movement for justice and acceptance in the intergalactic community.

Subsection: The Effectiveness of Nonviolent Protests

Nonviolent protests have been a powerful tool throughout history for advocating change and challenging systems of oppression. In the context of the Velan-7 Civil Rights Movement, Aerin Zor and their allies recognized the potential of nonviolent protests in their struggle for equality and justice. This subsection explores the effectiveness of nonviolent protests, examining the principles, strategies, and impact behind this approach.

Principles of Nonviolent Protests

Nonviolent protests are rooted in the principles of peace, justice, and equal rights. They aim to create systemic change by leveraging peaceful means instead of resorting to violence or aggression. This approach is guided by several key principles:

1. **Nonviolence as a moral and ethical stance:** Nonviolent protests prioritize the belief that all individuals have the right to life, dignity, and freedom from violence. This principle underpins the use of peaceful means to challenge injustice.

2. **Active resistance and civil disobedience:** Nonviolent protests involve actively resisting unjust laws and policies. Civil disobedience is a key tactic, where individuals intentionally violate laws that they deem to be unjust in order to bring attention to the issue at hand.

3. **Collective action and solidarity:** Nonviolent protests emphasize the power of collective action and the importance of solidarity. By uniting individuals who share a common goal, protests can amplify their impact and create a sense of unity among supporters.

4. **An emphasis on dialogue and negotiation:** Nonviolent protests prioritize constructive dialogue and negotiation with those in power. By engaging in peaceful communication, protestors seek to resolve conflicts and find mutually beneficial solutions.

Strategies of Nonviolent Protests

Nonviolent protests employ various strategies to convey their messages effectively and bring about change. Some of the most impactful strategies include:

1. **Public demonstrations and marches:** These visible displays of dissent serve to raise awareness about the issues at hand and mobilize supporters. By marching through the streets, protestors can capture public attention and attract media coverage, thereby increasing the visibility of their cause.

2. **Sit-ins and occupations:** Sit-ins and occupations involve protestors occupying public spaces, government buildings, or private properties, often aiming to disrupt systems and draw attention to specific grievances. This strategy can exert significant pressure on those in power and force them to address the protestors' demands.

3. **Civil disobedience:** By intentionally violating laws or policies deemed unjust, protestors demonstrate their resolve and defiance. Civil disobedience actions can include acts such as blocking roads, chaining oneself to a structure, or refusing to cooperate with authorities. These acts aim to challenge the legitimacy of oppressive systems and spark dialogue.

4. **Boycotts and economic pressure:** Boycotts are a nonviolent means of exerting economic pressure on institutions or governments by refusing to purchase or engage with their goods or services. Through economic consequences, protestors can effectively communicate their dissent and demand change.

Impact and Outcomes

Nonviolent protests have proven to be highly effective in achieving lasting change. By harnessing the power of collective action, these protests can shift public opinion, challenge oppressive systems, and pave the way for more inclusive and just societies. Some key outcomes of nonviolent protests include:

1. **Shift in public opinion:** Nonviolent protests have the power to change hearts and minds. Through their peaceful and principled approach, protestors can highlight the injustices they face and garner support from the wider public. This shift in public opinion can create momentum for policy changes and pave the way for long-lasting transformation.

2. **Pressure on those in power:** Nonviolent protests place significant pressure on those in positions of authority. The disruption caused by these protests, along with the media attention they attract, can force those in power to address the protestors' demands, enter into negotiations, or take action to rectify the injustices.

3. **Inspiring future generations:** Nonviolent protests serve as powerful symbols of resistance and hope, inspiring future activists to stand up against injustice. The courage and determination demonstrated by protestors leave a lasting impact on society, encouraging generations to come to fight for equality, justice, and human rights.

4. **Positive change and reform:** Nonviolent protests have led to tangible policy changes and reforms in numerous instances throughout history. Examples include the civil rights movement in the United States, which resulted in landmark legislations, and the Indian independence movement led by Mahatma Gandhi, which ultimately led to India breaking free from British colonial rule.

Unconventional Approach: Artistic Activism

In addition to the traditional strategies mentioned earlier, one unconventional yet impactful approach to nonviolent protests is artistic activism. This form of protest harnesses the power of artistic expression to convey powerful messages, challenge societal norms, and effect change. From street art and graffiti to music, dance, and performance art, artistic activism has the potential to reach and engage a broader audience while breaking down barriers to communication.

Artistic activism can create an emotional connection between the protestors' message and the audience, enabling the message to resonate on a deeper level. It allows for the exploration of complex issues and the challenging of deeply ingrained prejudices and biases. By using creativity as a catalyst for change, artistic activism encourages dialogue, fosters compassion, and invites people to see the world through a different lens.

Conclusion

Nonviolent protests have proven to be a powerful force in advocating for change, with a rich history of achieving significant societal transformations. The effectiveness of nonviolent protests lies in their ability to challenge systems of oppression while upholding principles of peace, justice, and equality. By employing strategic approaches and leveraging the power of collective action, nonviolent protests have the potential to reshape societies, inspire future generations, and pave the way for a more just and inclusive world. Artistic activism further expands the toolbox of nonviolent protests, infusing creativity and emotional resonance into the movement for change. It is through these methods that Aerin Zor and their allies were able to triumph in the Velan-7 Civil Rights Movement, leaving a lasting legacy for alien civil rights activism.

Section 5: Triumph and its Aftermath

Subsection: The Liberation of Velan-7

In the epic struggle for freedom and justice on Velan-7, the culmination of the civil rights movement was the momentous event known as the Liberation of Velan-7. It was a turning point in the fight against discrimination and oppression, and it marked the beginning of a new era of equality for all beings in the cosmos.

1.5.1.1 The Genesis of the Liberation

The seeds of the Liberation were sown through years of tireless activism and organizing. Aerin Zor, fueled by an unwavering determination to eradicate injustice, alongside a dedicated coalition of allies from all walks of life, laid the groundwork for this historic event. Their unwavering commitment to the cause mobilized the masses and ignited a revolution that could no longer be ignored.

1.5.1.2 Gathering Momentum

As awareness of the Bi-Entity Fusion dilemma spread across Velan-7, discontent grew, and the call for change echoed through the air. The Velan-7 Civil Rights Movement, fueled by Zor's charismatic leadership, gained traction, attracting individuals from all corners of the universe who were united in their desire to dismantle the oppressive systems that had plagued their society for generations.

1.5.1.3 The Organized Uprising

The Liberation of Velan-7 was not an impulsive act of rebellion, but a meticulously planned and coordinated effort. Aerin Zor recognized the importance of strategic action and encouraged peaceful means of resistance. The movement's leaders, including Zor, advocated for nonviolent protests, civil disobedience, and community engagement to build a united front against the oppressive Velan-7 government.

1.5.1.4 Breaking the Shackles

The uprising began with a symbolic act, a single event that would become the spark that ignited the fire of freedom. Thousands of aliens, both native to Velan-7 and allies from neighboring planets, converged in the heart of the capital city to demand equality and an end to the mistreatment and discrimination faced by the Bi-Entity Fusion community. They stood together, united in their unwavering commitment to justice.

1.5.1.5 The Battle for Equality

The Liberation of Velan-7 was not without resistance. The Velan-7 government, fearful of losing their grip on power, responded to the uprising with force. However, the peaceful protesters, fortified by their shared vision of a just society, stood firm. Their resilience in the face of adversity was a testament to the power of unity and the strength of the human spirit—alien spirit, that is!

1.5.1.6 The Power of Solidarity

One of the most significant factors in the success of the Liberation was the interstellar support and solidarity it received. Activists from across the cosmos joined forces with the Velan-7 movement, recognizing that the struggle for freedom and equality transcended planetary boundaries. The power of collective action was harnessed, lending additional strength to the movement and underscoring the universal nature of the fight for civil rights.

1.5.1.7 The Triumph of Justice

After days of protests and confrontations, the Velan-7 government, unable to quell the rising tide of liberation, was forced to concede. They bowed to the demands of the people, recognizing the inherent rights of all beings and promising sweeping reforms to dismantle the discriminatory systems entrenched in society. It was a historic victory—a triumph for justice, equality, and the spirit of liberation that had captivated not only Velan-7 but the entire galaxy.

1.5.1.8 A New Beginning

With the Liberation of Velan-7, a new chapter began. Now freed from the chains of discrimination, the Bi-Entity Fusion community could live their lives in peace and with the respect they deserved. The event not only transformed Velan-7 but also inspired similar movements across the universe. It ignited a wave of intergalactic change, challenging the status quo and laying the foundation for a more just and inclusive cosmos.

1.5.1.9 Lessons from the Liberation

The Liberation of Velan-7 serves as a powerful reminder that change is possible when individuals come together and fight for what is right. It highlights the importance of peaceful protest, strategic organization, and the strength of unity in the face of adversity. As the legacy of the Liberation lives on, future activists will draw inspiration and guidance from this historic event, continuing the fight for equality and justice for all beings in the universe.

Remember, the fight for alien civil rights is an ongoing struggle, and the Liberation of Velan-7 was just the beginning. Aerin Zor's story is a testament to the power of an individual to make a difference, but it also reminds us that true change comes from collective action. Let us carry forward the spirit of the Liberation and continue the work of creating a universe where all beings are treated with dignity and respect.

Subsection: Rebuilding a Society

After the successful liberation of Velan-7 and the end of the Bi-Entity Fusion Uprising, the daunting task of rebuilding a society begins. The aftermath of any revolution is never easy, and it comes with its own set of challenges and obstacles. In this subsection, we will explore the process of rebuilding Velan-7 and the steps taken to create a more inclusive and egalitarian society.

A Fresh Start

Rebuilding a society is not just about physical reconstruction; it also involves reexamining and restructuring the social, political, and economic systems that were in place before the uprising. The first step in this process is to establish a new government that represents the interests of all citizens, regardless of their alien or fusion status.

A transitional government, comprising leaders from the uprising and other prominent activists, is formed to oversee the rebuilding process. This government is committed to ensuring equality, justice, and human rights for all inhabitants of Velan-7.

Addressing Past Injustices

To prevent history from repeating itself, the transitional government initiates a Truth and Reconciliation Commission. This commission serves as a platform for victims of discrimination and injustice to share their experiences and be heard. It aims to heal the wounds of the past and create a society that acknowledges its mistakes and works towards a better future.

Additionally, reparations are provided to those who suffered under the previous regime. These reparations help to rebuild livelihoods, restore dignity, and provide a sense of justice to those who have been marginalized.

Equal Opportunities for All

One of the primary focuses of rebuilding Velan-7 is to create equal opportunities for all citizens. The transitional government implements policies and programs aimed at reducing inequality and providing access to education, healthcare, and employment opportunities regardless of alien or fusion status.

Efforts are made to eliminate discrimination in the workplace and ensure equal pay for equal work. New laws are enacted to protect the rights of all workers and prohibit workplace discrimination in hiring, promotion, and termination.

Reforming Education

Education plays a crucial role in shaping a new society. The curriculum is revised to include a comprehensive history that acknowledges the contributions and struggles of all alien and fusion communities. This inclusive education fosters empathy, understanding, and respect among the different groups on Velan-7.

Special emphasis is placed on promoting intercultural exchange and celebrating diversity. Schools and educational institutions organize programs that encourage students to learn about different cultures, languages, and traditions. These initiatives promote unity and create a sense of belonging for all students, regardless of their alien or fusion background.

Community Building and Reconciliation

Rebuilding a society also requires fostering a sense of community and reconciliation among the inhabitants of Velan-7. Community centers are established as safe spaces for individuals to come together, share their experiences, and form meaningful connections.

Through local events, cultural festivals, and community projects, individuals from different backgrounds have the opportunity to interact and build relationships. This helps to break down the barriers that previously divided communities and promotes unity and understanding.

Looking Towards the Future

While the process of rebuilding a society is challenging, the people of Velan-7 are determined to create a better future for themselves and future generations. They are committed to ensuring that the rights of all individuals, regardless of their alien or fusion status, are protected and upheld.

It is essential to remember that rebuilding a society is an ongoing process that requires continuous effort and dedication. The legacy of the uprising and the principles of equality and justice must be upheld and passed down to future generations.

As Aerin Zor once said, "Change does not happen overnight, but it starts with a collective vision and the commitment to fight for what is right." The people of Velan-7 are living proof that a society can be rebuilt, and a better future can be created through unity and resilience.

Subsection: The Legacy of Aerin Zor

Aerin Zor, the fearless alien civil rights activist from Velan-7, left an indelible legacy that continues to inspire generations to fight for equality and justice. Her tireless efforts in the Bi-Entity Fusion Uprising not only liberated her own planet but also sparked a movement throughout the universe. This subsection explores the lasting impact of Aerin Zor and how her life's work continues to shape the quest for alien civil rights.

The Symbol of Hope

Aerin Zor's courage and determination transformed her into a symbol of hope for oppressed alien communities across the cosmos. Her unwavering belief in the inherent rights of all beings resonated deeply with those who felt marginalized and discriminated against. Aerin Zor's story showed that change was possible, even in the face of seemingly insurmountable challenges.

Example: On the planet Galexia, a young alien named Zara looks up to Aerin Zor as her role model. Inspired by Aerin's legacy, Zara organizes protests and campaigns for equal opportunities for all beings in her own community.

Breaking Barriers

Aerin Zor shattered barriers and pushed boundaries, challenging the norms of intergalactic society. Her fight for alien civil rights paved the way for others to speak out against discrimination, prejudice, and injustice. Through her activism, she created space for marginalized voices and empowered alien communities to demand equality.

Example: The extraterrestrial community on Nova Prime, inspired by Aerin Zor's legacy, forms their own civil rights organization. They advocate for the right to interplanetary education, seeking to end the systemic discrimination faced by alien students in the planet's educational institutions.

Inspiring Activism

Aerin Zor's story has served as a catalyst for activism in the ongoing struggle for alien civil rights. Her courage and determination have inspired countless individuals to take a stand against injustice, giving rise to a new wave of alien activists dedicated to creating a more equitable universe.

Example: The planet Quasar witnesses a surge in grassroots activism after the publication of Aerin Zor's biography. Alien youth across Quasar form coalitions and organize rallies demanding an end to systemic discrimination in employment practices.

Sparking Dialogue

Aerin Zor's life and achievements have sparked crucial conversations about the intersectionality of civil rights, the importance of inclusion, and the need for social change. Her legacy serves as a reminder that alien civil rights are interconnected with other struggles for justice and equality, encouraging people from all walks of life to engage in meaningful dialogue.

Example: The Galactic Parliament establishes an annual symposium dedicated to discussing the fundamental rights of all sentient beings. This symposium, named after Aerin Zor, brings together politicians, activists, and scholars to share ideas and strategies for advancing alien civil rights.

The Call for Continued Action

Despite the progress made, Aerin Zor's legacy reminds us that the fight for alien civil rights is far from over. Her work serves as a call to action for future generations to continue the struggle, to challenge systemic discrimination, and to create a future where all beings can thrive in unity and harmony.

Example: The Intergalactic Alliance launches an annual grant program in honor of Aerin Zor. This program provides funding and resources to emerging alien activists and organizations dedicated to advancing civil rights across the universe.

Preserving the Memory

To preserve the memory and spirit of Aerin Zor, a museum is built on Velan-7, showcasing her life, achievements, and the impact of the Bi-Entity Fusion Uprising. The museum not only serves as a historical record but also as a reminder of the ongoing struggle for alien civil rights.

Example: The renowned artist Sa'ra creates a stunning mural depicting Aerin Zor's heroism on the side of a prominent building on Corellia, captivating passersby and reminding them of the sacrifices made for freedom and equality.

In conclusion, the legacy of Aerin Zor continues to shape the fight for alien civil rights. Her bravery, resilience, and unwavering commitment to justice have left an enduring impact on the universe. From inspiring activism and sparking dialogue to breaking barriers and serving as a symbol of hope, Aerin Zor's legacy is a reminder that the pursuit of equality and justice knows no boundaries. As we remember her, let us carry forward her mission, ensuring that the struggle for alien civil rights remains a fundamental part of the intergalactic journey towards a truly inclusive and harmonious future.

Subsection: The Continuing Fight for Alien Civil Rights

In the aftermath of the bi-entity fusion uprising on Velan-7, the fight for alien civil rights did not come to an end. While the liberation of Velan-7 marked a significant victory, it was just the beginning of a long and ongoing struggle for equality and justice across the universe.

1. The Challenge of Systemic Oppression: The fight for alien civil rights faces numerous challenges, one of which is the deeply ingrained systemic oppression that exists in many planetary governments. Similar to the struggle faced by marginalized communities on Earth, the fight for alien civil rights requires not only dismantling discriminatory laws but also challenging the deeply rooted prejudices and biases that permeate society.

2. Advocacy and Awareness: A crucial aspect of the ongoing fight for alien civil rights is advocacy and raising awareness. Activists like Aerin Zor continue to play a vital role in speaking out against discrimination, highlighting the experiences of marginalized alien communities, and demanding equal treatment under the law. Through public speaking engagements, media interviews, and grassroots organizing, activists are pushing for change and ensuring that the voices of alien communities are heard.

3. Legislative Reforms: To address the systemic oppression faced by alien communities, legislative reforms are necessary. This includes pushing for the amendment or repeal of discriminatory laws that restrict alien rights and perpetuate inequality. Activists and allies work tirelessly to lobby for changes in planetary governments, pushing for inclusive legislation that protects the rights of all beings, regardless of their planet of origin.

4. Intersectionality and Solidarity: The fight for alien civil rights intersects with other social justice movements, emphasizing the importance of

intersectionality and solidarity. Recognizing the interconnectedness of various forms of discrimination fosters stronger alliances and amplifies the voices of marginalized communities. Alien activists work alongside other social justice movements, advocating for the rights of all oppressed beings.

5. Education and Empowerment: Education plays a crucial role in the fight for alien civil rights. Activists and organizations focus on educating the public about the experiences and struggles of alien communities, debunking stereotypes and challenging misconceptions. Additionally, empowering alien communities through access to quality education and resources helps to level the playing field and ensure equal opportunities for all.

6. Grassroots Movements and Organizing: Grassroots movements continue to be a driving force in the ongoing fight for alien civil rights. Local organizations and community leaders form alliances, organizing protests, demonstrations, and grassroots initiatives to effect change on a smaller scale. Grassroots movements have proven to be highly effective in raising awareness, shaping public opinion, and putting pressure on governments to address alien civil rights issues.

7. The Role of Technology: In an increasingly interconnected universe, technology plays a crucial role in the fight for alien civil rights. Social media platforms provide a space for marginalized voices to be amplified and for activism to spread rapidly. Online campaigns, hashtag movements, and digital platforms have become powerful tools for mobilization and raising awareness of alien civil rights issues.

8. International Collaboration: The fight for alien civil rights transcends planetary boundaries, necessitating international collaboration. Activists and organizations work together to share resources, strategies, and best practices for creating lasting change. International conventions and interplanetary alliances serve as platforms for addressing alien civil rights on a broader scale and encouraging cooperation among planetary governments.

9. Cultural Transformation: Cultural transformation is a critical aspect of the ongoing fight for alien civil rights. It involves challenging and changing deep-rooted prejudices, biases, and cultural norms that perpetuate discrimination. Through art, literature, music, and cultural productions, activists seek to challenge harmful narratives and foster a more inclusive and accepting society.

10. Allyship and Support: Allies play a vital role in the continuing fight for alien civil rights. It is essential for individuals from privileged backgrounds to acknowledge their privilege and actively support alien communities. Allies can use their positions of power and influence to amplify marginalized voices, advocate for policy changes, and work towards creating a more inclusive society for all beings.

The fight for alien civil rights is an ongoing endeavor that requires the unwavering dedication and collective efforts of individuals, communities, and governments. It is a fight for a future where all beings, regardless of their origins, can enjoy equality, justice, and dignity. As the struggle continues, the legacy of Aerin Zor serves as a reminder of the power of activism and the transformative potential of individuals coming together to challenge the status quo.

Subsection: The Future of Coexistence in the Universe

The future of coexistence in the universe holds great promise and potential. As we continue to navigate the vast cosmos, it is essential that we strive for harmony and equality among all sentient beings, regardless of their planetary origin or physical form. In this subsection, we will explore various aspects of this future, including the challenges we may encounter, the principles guiding our efforts, and the vision that drives us forward.

Challenges and Potential Conflicts in Intergalactic Coexistence

While the aspiration for peaceful coexistence is noble, we must acknowledge that there will be challenges and potential conflicts that arise within the vast diversity of the universe. One of the greatest challenges we may face is the clash of cultural norms and values. Different alien civilizations will likely have their own unique customs, traditions, and belief systems, which may initially create misunderstandings and tensions.

Another potential conflict could arise from the scarcity of resources. As we venture into unexplored territories and encounter new civilizations, competition for limited resources, such as habitable planets or energy sources, may emerge. It will be crucial to establish fair and impartial systems for resource allocation to avoid unnecessary conflicts.

Moreover, the fear of the unknown and the unfamiliar can sow seeds of discord and prejudice. Overcoming bias and promoting understanding among diverse alien civilizations will be an ongoing challenge. Education, exposure to different cultures, and fostering empathy will be crucial in bridging these gaps and fostering inclusive coexistence.

Principles for Interplanetary Coexistence

To navigate the challenges that lie ahead, we must establish a set of principles that guide our efforts towards interplanetary coexistence. These principles should serve as a foundation upon which we build a harmonious and inclusive universe.

1. Respect for Diversity: Embracing and valuing the diversity of species, cultures, and perspectives is essential for fostering coexistence. By recognizing and celebrating our differences, we can create a more inclusive and equitable cosmos.

2. Equality and Justice: Ensuring equal rights and opportunities for all sentient beings is paramount. No entity should be discriminated against or denied basic rights solely based on their planetary origin or physical characteristics.

3. Collaboration and Cooperation: Recognizing our interconnectedness and the interdependence of our actions will be crucial for fostering collaboration and cooperation among civilizations. By working together, we can address common challenges and build a more sustainable and prosperous universe.

4. Environmental Stewardship: Recognizing our responsibility as custodians of the cosmos, we must strive to protect and sustain our shared natural resources. Implementing eco-friendly practices and prioritizing environmental conservation will be essential for the long-term coexistence of all species.

5. Continuous Learning and Growth: Embracing lifelong learning and an open mindset will be crucial for adapting to new discoveries, technologies, and perspectives. By continually expanding our knowledge and understanding, we can cultivate a culture of growth and progress.

Envisioning a Unified and Coexistent Universe

In the future, a unified and coexistent universe holds the promise of boundless possibilities. A universe where species from across galaxies come together to develop mutually beneficial relationships built on trust, respect, and common values.

In this vision, we see interplanetary alliances forming, transcending political and cultural boundaries. Joint scientific endeavors pave the way for groundbreaking discoveries and advancements. Trade and commerce flourish, fostering economic prosperity and stability. Cultural exchange programs allow for the cross-pollination of ideas and the celebration of diverse art, music, and literature.

In this coexistent universe, peace prevails, and conflicts are resolved peacefully through dialogue and diplomacy. Interplanetary institutions and governing bodies, driven by democratic principles, ensure equal representation and fair decision-making processes.

The exploration and colonization of new planets are conducted responsibly and sustainably, ensuring the preservation of ecosystems and the protection of indigenous life forms. Extraordinary efforts are made to promote the well-being of all sentient beings, through advancements in healthcare, education, and social welfare systems.

The Role of Technology in Coexistence

Technology will play a crucial role in facilitating intergalactic coexistence. Advanced communication systems will enable instantaneous and seamless interactions between civilizations, breaking down barriers of distance and time. Virtual reality and holographic technologies will bridge the gaps between planets, fostering a sense of presence and connection.

Furthermore, breakthroughs in energy sources and propulsion systems will allow for more sustainable and efficient space travel, reducing our reliance on scarce resources and minimizing our impact on the environments we encounter.

Artificial intelligence and machine learning will aid in the translation of languages, facilitating smooth communication and understanding between different civilizations. They will also assist in analyzing complex data, identifying patterns, and predicting potential conflicts, allowing for early intervention and resolution.

However, it is essential to wield technology responsibly, considering its potential implications. Striking a balance between the benefits of technological advancements and the preservation of ethical standards will be crucial to ensure a future where coexistence thrives.

Embracing Uncertainty and the Unknown

As we gaze into the future of coexistence in the universe, we must acknowledge that there will always be uncertainties and unknowns that lie ahead. The exploration of the cosmos will continue to reveal new worlds, civilizations, and phenomena that challenge our understanding and beliefs.

Embracing uncertainty and the unknown will require a willingness to adapt, learn, and question our assumptions. It will demand a commitment to continuous growth, alongside humility and respect for the vastness of the universe.

Ultimately, the future of coexistence in the universe is a shared responsibility. By embracing diversity, upholding principles of equality and justice, fostering collaboration, and leveraging technology responsibly, we can build a future where all sentient beings can coexist in harmony, transcending the boundaries of space and time. As we embark on this journey, remember that the power to shape this future lies within each of us, as individuals and as a collective. Together, let us strive for a universe where coexistence flourishes, paving the way for a legacy of peace, unity, and shared prosperity.

Subsection: Lessons Learned from the Uprising

The Bi-Entity Fusion Uprising on Velan-7 was a pivotal moment in the fight for alien civil rights. It highlighted the power of collective action, resilience in the face of adversity, and the transformative effects of nonviolent protests. In this subsection, we will delve into the invaluable lessons learned from this uprising.

Lesson 1: Unity is Strength

One of the key takeaways from the Velan-7 uprising is the undeniable strength that comes from unity. The alien community, regardless of their individual backgrounds and differences, came together to fight against the oppression they faced. It showed that when individuals join forces, they become an unstoppable force for change.

This lesson can be applied to various aspects of social justice movements on Earth and beyond. It serves as a reminder that to achieve lasting change, diverse communities must stand together and support one another. By leveraging the power of unity, activists can amplify their voices and create a strong, cohesive movement.

Lesson 2: Nonviolent Resistance is Powerful

The Bi-Entity Fusion Uprising showcased the potency of nonviolent resistance as a tool for social change. Activists on Velan-7 adopted peaceful methods to challenge the oppressive government and demand equality. They organized sit-ins, peaceful marches, and boycotts to draw attention to their cause.

This approach not only appealed to the moral conscience of the wider intergalactic community but also prevented unnecessary bloodshed. It demonstrated that change can be achieved without resorting to violence and destruction. This lesson reverberates throughout history, reminding us of the enduring power of peaceful protests as a means of achieving social justice.

Lesson 3: Education and Empathy are Catalysts for Change

Another significant lesson from the uprising is the vital role of education and empathy in effecting change. Aerin Zor, the leader of the movement, recognized the importance of educating both the alien community and the wider public about the realities of the lifelong discrimination faced by Bi-Entity Fusions.

Through educational initiatives, they disseminated information about the experiences and struggles of their community. This raised awareness, fostered empathy, and generated support for their cause. It showed that when people understand the challenges faced by a marginalized group, they are more likely to stand in solidarity with them.

This lesson emphasizes the significance of education as a catalyst for change. By promoting awareness, highlighting prevailing prejudices, and fostering empathy, activists can mobilize broad support for their cause and create a more inclusive society.

Lesson 4: Persistence in the Face of Resistance

The struggle for alien civil rights on Velan-7 was not an easy one. Activists faced resistance, repression, and even violence from the government and its supporters. However, they persisted, refusing to be silenced or deterred by these challenges.

This lesson teaches us the importance of persistence in the face of adversity. It serves as a reminder that change takes time and effort. Real progress is not achieved overnight but through the unwavering dedication and determination to fight for what is right.

Lesson 5: Intersectionality is Essential

The Velan-7 uprising highlighted the necessity of recognizing and addressing intersectionality within the fight for alien civil rights. Bi-Entity Fusions faced discrimination not only based on their alien status but also due to their unique fusion identities.

This lesson emphasizes the need to acknowledge the interconnectedness of multiple forms of discrimination. It emphasizes that social justice movements must address and break down all intersecting systems of oppression. By acknowledging and including the experiences of all marginalized communities, activists can create a more inclusive and equitable society.

Lesson 6: Collaboration and Solidarity are Key

The Bi-Entity Fusion Uprising showcased the power of collaboration and solidarity among diverse alien communities. Activists formed connections and alliances with different species and planets, recognizing the importance of standing together to battle oppression.

This lesson underlines the significance of collaboration in the pursuit of social justice. By uniting with other communities fighting for equality, activists can amplify their efforts and create a broader movement. It highlights that no struggle for justice exists in isolation and that solidarity among diverse communities is critical for transformative change.

In conclusion, the lessons learned from the Bi-Entity Fusion Uprising on Velan-7 provide invaluable insights into the fight for alien civil rights. This subsection has explored the importance of unity, the power of nonviolent resistance, the role of education and empathy, the need for persistence, the significance of intersectionality, and the value of collaboration and solidarity. These lessons transcend planetary boundaries, offering guidance and inspiration to activists across the universe in their ongoing quest for equality and justice.

Chapter 2: Beyond Velan-7: The Intergalactic Movement

Section 1: An Advocate for Change

Subsection: Spreading the Message across Galaxies

In order to effect change, Aerin Zor understood the importance of spreading their message across galaxies. After the successful uprising on Velan-7, Aerin realized that the struggle for alien civil rights was not limited to a single planet. Activism needed to transcend boundaries and reach every corner of the cosmos. This subsection delves into the strategies and methods employed by Aerin Zor in spreading the message of equality and justice far and wide.

Alien Communication 101

The first challenge Aerin Zor faced was finding effective ways to communicate with beings from different alien species. Interstellar languages and communication systems vary greatly, making it difficult to convey complex ideas and ideologies. To overcome this barrier, Aerin partnered with linguists, xenolinguists, and communication experts to develop a universal language known as Cosmolinguix. This language system incorporated elements of various interstellar languages, making it accessible to a wide range of aliens.

Cosmolinguix was designed to facilitate clear and concise communication, enabling activists to articulate their message effectively. It consisted of a set of pictorial symbols, phonetic characters, and tactiles cues that could be easily understood across different species. The development of Cosmolinguix revolutionized intergalactic discourse, enabling activists like Aerin Zor to connect with diverse communities.

CHAPTER 2: BEYOND VELAN-7: THE INTERGALACTIC MOVEMENT

The Power of Emotion: Alien Storytelling

While a universal language aided communication, Aerin Zor recognized that storytelling had a unique power to evoke emotions and connect with individuals on a deeper level. They understood that facts and figures alone might not resonate with every alien species. To bridge this gap, Aerin employed the ancient art of alien storytelling.

Through storytelling, Aerin shared personal experiences, recounting tales of injustice, resilience, and triumph. These narratives transcended language barriers, appealing to the universal emotions of empathy, compassion, and the desire for freedom. By tapping into the shared human experiences that exist within every sentient being, Aerin Zor created a sense of collective consciousness and unity among alien activists.

The Digital Cosmos: Leveraging Technology

In an increasingly interconnected galaxy, Aerin Zor recognized the immense power of technology as a tool for mobilization. They harnessed the digital cosmos to disseminate their message across galaxies. Alien activists utilized holographic transmissions, virtual reality platforms, and interstellar networks to reach vast audiences.

Aerin Zor established an online platform, known as ActivAlien, which served as a hub for information, resources, and a space for alien activists to connect and organize. ActivAlien provided a virtual forum for sharing ideas, organizing rallies, and coordinating interplanetary campaigns.

Additionally, Aerin and their team collaborated with cosmic creatives to produce captivating and thought-provoking multimedia content. From vibrant digital artworks to interactive holographic installations, these captivating creations served as powerful visual representations of the struggle for alien civil rights. Through technology and art, Aerin Zor amplified their message and engaged the hearts and minds of countless beings across galaxies.

Cosmic Alliances: Collaboration and Coalition-Building

Spreading the message of equality required forming alliances with like-minded individuals, organizations, and alien species. Aerin Zor recognized that collaboration and coalition-building were key to fostering systemic change on a galactic scale.

Aerin tirelessly traveled across galaxies, attending interstellar conferences, seminars, and summits. They engaged in diplomatic conversations, forging relationships, and creating mutually beneficial alliances with influential leaders and organizations. By uniting diverse groups under the banner of a common goal, Aerin Zor built a formidable intergalactic movement for alien civil rights.

To facilitate collaboration among alien activists, Aerin initiated the Intergalactic Coalition for Equality (ICE). The ICE served as a space for different organizations and activists to share resources, strategies, and expertise. Through ICE, activists from various corners of the cosmos synergized their efforts, amplifying the impact of their work and bolstering their collective voice.

Thinking Outside the Earthly Box

Aerin Zor's approach to spreading their message was not limited to conventional methods. They believed in the power of unconventional approaches to provoke thought and challenge existing norms. Aerin encouraged alien artists, musicians, and performers to incorporate themes of alien civil rights into their work.

One notable example was the Extraterrestrial Art and Music Festival (EAMF), an annual event organized by Aerin and their team. The EAMF showcased the talents of alien artists, celebrating diversity and promoting social change through the universal language of art. The festival served as a platform for advocating alien civil rights, using creativity and entertainment to engage and inspire audiences across galaxies.

Exercises: Galactify Your Message

1. Create your own interstellar language using symbols and sounds that could be easily understood by beings from different alien species. Think about how you can incorporate universal concepts and emotions into your language.

2. Write a short alien story that conveys a message of equality and justice. Use vivid imagery and relatable characters to connect with diverse individuals. Consider how cultural differences might impact the way your story is interpreted.

3. Design a multimedia campaign to raise awareness about a specific issue related to alien civil rights. Think about how you can leverage technology, art, and storytelling to engage a wide range of beings across galaxies.

4. Research and identify potential alien organizations or individuals who share similar values and goals regarding civil rights. Brainstorm ways to collaborate and form alliances, considering the challenges and benefits of cross-species collaboration.

Remember, spreading a message across galaxies requires creativity, adaptability, and a deep understanding of the diverse beings that inhabit the cosmos. With determination and thoughtful communication, you can make a difference in the fight for alien civil rights.

Subsection: Uniting Alien Worlds

In the pursuit of intergalactic harmony and equality, Aerin Zor recognized the importance of uniting alien worlds. She understood that the collective power of diverse alien communities could bring about transformative change and challenge the existing structures of dominance and discrimination. This subsection explores the strategies and challenges involved in bridging the gaps between different alien civilizations.

Understanding Interplanetary Diversity

To unite alien worlds, it is crucial to first understand the vast diversity that exists across the cosmos. Alien civilizations come in various forms, each with its unique cultural, social, and technological characteristics. Their histories, belief systems, and value structures differ significantly. Recognizing and respecting these differences is the foundation for fostering genuine collaboration and creating a sense of shared purpose.

Aerin Zor encouraged interplanetary alliances to actively learn about each other's traditions, customs, and perspectives. She emphasized the value of empathy and open-mindedness in building bridges between alien communities. This required setting aside preconceived notions and stereotypes, allowing for a true understanding of the challenges faced by different groups.

Creating Space for Dialogue and Exchange

To unite alien worlds, dialogue and exchange play a pivotal role. Aerin Zor recognized that meaningful conversations were key to breaking down barriers and building connections. She tirelessly advocated for interplanetary conferences, festivals, and forums where representatives from different alien civilizations could come together and exchange ideas.

These gatherings provided a platform for sharing experiences, discussing common challenges, and brainstorming collaborative solutions. Whether it was through formal discussions, workshops, or informal interactions, the goal was to foster a sense of community and solidarity among alien communities. By focusing on shared goals and aspirations, these spaces created opportunities for genuine collaboration and cooperation.

SECTION 1: AN ADVOCATE FOR CHANGE

Overcoming Language and Communication Barriers

Language differences can be a significant obstacle in interplanetary communication. Aerin Zor recognized this challenge and called for the development and implementation of universal translators. These advanced technologies allowed individuals from diverse alien civilizations to communicate seamlessly, breaking down the linguistic barriers that hindered effective collaboration.

Additionally, Aerin Zor emphasized the importance of promoting multilingualism and language education. By investing resources in teaching and learning each other's languages, alien communities could foster deeper connections and understanding. Language became a tool for cultural exchange and celebration, paving the way for stronger interplanetary relationships.

Finding Common Ground

Uniting alien worlds required finding common ground among diverse civilizations. Aerin Zor advocated for the identification of shared values and goals that could serve as a rallying point for collective action. By highlighting these commonalities, she aimed to foster a sense of camaraderie and solidarity among alien communities.

For example, fighting against discrimination and prejudice was a universal cause that resonated across alien civilizations. By framing the struggle for equality as a joint effort, Aerin Zor aimed to inspire alien communities to stand together against oppressive systems. This approach allowed for the formation of strong alliances that could challenge the existing power structures and advocate for the rights of all beings.

Challenges and Obstacles

Uniting alien worlds was not without challenges. Aside from the inherent difficulties of interplanetary travel and communication, deep-seated prejudices and biases posed significant obstacles. Alien civilizations with long histories of conflict and mistrust had to overcome deep-rooted animosities to work together.

Aerin Zor recognized the importance of addressing these challenges head-on. She called for dedicated initiatives aimed at promoting understanding, reconciliation, and healing. These efforts included truth and reconciliation commissions, cultural exchange programs, and initiatives that aimed to build trust among alien communities.

CHAPTER 2: BEYOND VELAN-7: THE INTERGALACTIC MOVEMENT

The Power of Unity

Despite the challenges, uniting alien worlds held immense transformative power. Aerin Zor believed that collective action and collaboration had the potential to create lasting change and reshape intergalactic relationships. By uniting under a shared vision, alien civilizations could pool their resources, knowledge, and wisdom to overcome common challenges.

Aerin Zor's efforts to unite alien worlds laid the foundation for the Alien Civil Rights Alliance. This organization brought together activists and leaders from diverse alien communities to advocate for equality, justice, and the eradication of discrimination across the cosmos. By fostering unity and solidarity, they became a formidable force for change.

Fostering Solidarity among Alien Communities: An Unconventional Approach

As part of her unconventional approach to uniting alien worlds, Aerin Zor recognized the power of art and creativity. She encouraged alien civilizations to celebrate and express their unique cultural identities through various artistic mediums. By showcasing their art and cultural heritage, they not only fostered understanding and appreciation but also created opportunities for collaboration and exchange.

Aerin Zor believed that artistic collaborations and joint artistic projects could transcend linguistic and cultural barriers. They had the potential to touch the deepest parts of the soul and evoke emotions that words alone could not convey. Through art, alien worlds could build bridges and promote a sense of interconnectedness that went beyond mere intellectual understanding.

For example, artists from different alien civilizations could collaborate to create immersive virtual reality experiences that would transport individuals to different worlds. These experiences would allow participants to gain a firsthand understanding of alien cultures, fostering empathy, and connection. By using art as a medium for communication, alien communities could forge deeper bonds and work together towards a more harmonious universe.

Problems for Reflection

1. The planet Kinxoria and the planet Zygrion have a long history of conflict due to differing beliefs and traditions. How can the principles of empathetic communication and shared goals be utilized to foster unity between these alien worlds?

2. The Intergalactic Council has proposed a language fluency program to promote better communication among alien civilizations. How can this program be designed to ensure inclusivity and respect for diverse linguistic backgrounds?

3. The planet Xarklon has been isolated from intergalactic alliances due to its government's history of discrimination and human rights abuses. How can the Alien Civil Rights Alliance engage with Xarklon's government and its citizens to promote unity and social change?

4. An interplanetary conference is being organized to bring together representatives from diverse alien civilizations. Design a workshop activity that promotes dialogue, understanding, and collaboration among the participants.

5. The Velorians, a technologically advanced alien civilization, have been hesitant to unite with less developed worlds, fearing a loss of their own cultural identity. How can the Alien Civil Rights Alliance address these concerns and encourage the Velorians to embrace unity without compromising their cultural heritage?

6. Many alien civilizations have unique artistic traditions. Design an art exhibition that showcases the diversity of alien cultures and fosters appreciation and understanding among different communities.

Remember, the journey to unite alien worlds requires patience, empathy, and resilience. By acknowledging and embracing diversity while finding common ground, alien communities can join forces to create a future of equality, justice, and harmony in the cosmos.

Subsection: The Rise of the Alien Civil Rights Alliance

In this section, we delve into the remarkable story of the Alien Civil Rights Alliance (ACRA) and their pivotal role in the struggle for alien rights. The ACRA emerged as a formidable force during a time of great adversity and became instrumental in reshaping the intergalactic landscape. Their rise to prominence serves as a testament to the power of unity, resilience, and the unwavering commitment to justice.

Background and Formation of the Alien Civil Rights Alliance

The Alien Civil Rights Alliance traces its origins back to the early days of the Velan-7 civil rights movement, where a group of passionate and visionary alien activists recognized the need for collective action. As the injustices perpetrated against the bi-entity fusion community on Velan-7 escalated, individuals from various alien backgrounds came together to form a unified front against discrimination and oppression.

CHAPTER 2: BEYOND VELAN-7: THE INTERGALACTIC MOVEMENT

Recognizing the power in unity, the leaders of the ACRA strategized and devised a master plan to bring together alien communities from different planets and galaxies. They sought to create a network of support and collective resistance that would combat interplanetary prejudice and fight for equality across the cosmos.

Principles and Objectives of the Alien Civil Rights Alliance

The ACRA was founded on the core principles of justice, equality, and respect for all alien species, regardless of their planetary origins or biological composition. Their primary objective was to dismantle the systemic barriers that had long hindered the advancement and well-being of all extraterrestrial beings.

The alliance conducted extensive research and analysis to identify the most pressing issues faced by the alien communities. They prioritized the eradication of discriminatory laws, the promotion of inclusivity in all aspects of interplanetary life, and the guarantee of basic rights and freedoms for every alien individual. By addressing these challenges head-on, the ACRA aimed to create a future where all beings could thrive harmoniously, irrespective of their cosmic lineage.

Strategies and Tactics Deployed by the Alien Civil Rights Alliance

Through superluminal communication networks and carefully coordinated efforts, the ACRA swiftly established connections with alien activists, organizations, and communities across the universe. Their strategies encompassed a diverse range of approaches aimed at effecting change at both the grassroots and institutional levels.

At the grassroots level, the ACRA organized intergalactic protests, rallies, and awareness campaigns to mobilize the masses and garner support for their cause. They employed art as a powerful medium, using music, literature, and visual expressions to convey the struggles faced by the alien population and inspire empathy among other extraterrestrial beings.

Simultaneously, the ACRA engaged in diplomatic negotiations with interplanetary governments, aiming to secure legal protections and recognition for alien rights. They lobbied for the implementation of fair laws and policies that would protect against discrimination in areas such as employment, housing, education, and healthcare.

Notable Achievements of the Alien Civil Rights Alliance

The ACRA's tireless efforts yielded significant milestones in the fight for alien rights. Among their notable achievements were the groundbreaking interplanetary treaties, such as the Universal Alien Rights Accord and the Equal Opportunity Agreement, designed to ensure equitable treatment and opportunities for all beings.

Through grassroots organizing and strategic advocacy, the ACRA successfully pressed for the establishment of Alien Rights Commissions on several planets, providing platforms for addressing discrimination and promoting interplanetary harmony. These commissions became crucial in mediating conflicts, investigating claims of discrimination, and facilitating dialogue between alien communities and local governments.

The impact of the ACRA extended beyond legal and policy reforms. Their campaigns fostered a cultural shift in intergalactic society, challenging entrenched prejudices and promoting acceptance of diverse alien identities. By elevating the voices of marginalized groups and highlighting the contributions of alien individuals, the ACRA reshaped public perception and demonstrated the inherent value of embracing differences.

Next Steps and Challenges for the Alien Civil Rights Alliance

While the ACRA celebrated many victories, they were acutely aware that the fight for alien rights was far from over. They recognized that achieving lasting change required continuous vigilance and adaptability.

One of the ongoing challenges faced by the ACRA was the rise of xenophobic movements seeking to undermine their progress. The alliance acknowledged the need for proactive measures to counter misconceptions, challenge stereotypes, and cultivate empathy among different galactic communities.

Moreover, the ACRA aimed to tackle the issue of intersectionality within the alien rights movement itself. They recognized the importance of addressing the unique challenges faced by alien individuals who belong to multiple marginalized groups, such as gender, class, or disability.

To overcome these challenges, the ACRA planned to expand their educational and outreach programs, collaborating with academic institutions and cultural organizations to promote understanding and respect for all alien identities. They also aimed to bolster their alliance's internal structures, ensuring inclusive decision-making processes and providing support systems for activists working at the forefront of the movement.

Conclusion

The rise of the Alien Civil Rights Alliance marked a turning point in the struggle for alien rights. Their unity, strategic approach, and unwavering commitment to justice laid the foundation for tangible change across the universe. Through their collective efforts, the ACRA became a beacon of hope, inspiring future generations of activists and forging a path towards a more equitable and inclusive cosmos. While challenges remain, the ACRA's rise exemplifies the transformative power of collaborative resistance and serves as a reminder that together, aliens of all backgrounds can build a future defined by justice, empathy, and coexistence.

Subsection: Challenges and Obstacles Faced

In the unrelenting battle for alien civil rights, Aerin Zor faced numerous challenges and obstacles that threatened to derail the progress of the movement. Despite the incredible strides made on Velan-7 and beyond, the road to equality and justice was far from smooth. In this subsection, we explore some of the most pressing challenges that Aerin Zor and his allies encountered and how they overcame them.

Racial and Species Prejudice

One of the most pervasive challenges that Aerin Zor faced was deep-rooted prejudice and discrimination based on race and species. In the intergalactic community, aliens were often seen as inferior or undesirable by certain factions, leading to exclusion, marginalization, and even violence. This prejudice extended to various aspects of life, including employment, housing, education, and social interactions.

To address this issue, Aerin Zor and his fellow activists worked tirelessly to raise awareness about the harmful effects of racial and species discrimination. They organized peaceful protests, community dialogues, and educational campaigns aimed at challenging the prevailing stereotypes and biases. By highlighting the value and contributions of aliens to society, they aimed to dismantle the discriminatory systems and create a more inclusive and equitable cosmos.

Political Resistance

Aerin Zor's quest for alien civil rights was met with staunch political resistance from those in power. The Velan-7 government, in particular, saw the bi-entity fusion uprising as a direct threat to their authority and control. They employed various tactics to suppress and undermine the movement, including censorship, surveillance, and harassment of activists.

In the face of political resistance, Aerin Zor and his comrades showed remarkable resilience and adaptability. They drew inspiration from historical civil rights movements, learning from their strategies and tactics. Through strategic

SECTION 1: AN ADVOCATE FOR CHANGE

alliances with other oppressed communities and the power of grassroots organizing, they were able to amplify their voices and put pressure on the government to address their demands. Their relentless advocacy eventually led to the recognition of alien rights and the implementation of policies to protect their dignity and well-being.

Internal Divisions

Like any social movement, the alien civil rights struggle was not without its internal divisions. Different factions within the movement had divergent approaches, priorities, and strategies. These divisions often threatened to fragment the movement and weaken its collective power.

Aerin Zor understood the importance of unity and solidarity in the face of adversity. He worked tirelessly to bridge the gaps between different factions, fostering open dialogue and finding common ground. By emphasizing shared goals and values, he was able to inspire collaboration and cooperation among disparate groups. Through open and respectful communication, the movement was able to transform internal divisions into opportunities for growth and strategic advancement.

Legal and Systemic Barriers

Another significant challenge that Aerin Zor faced was the existence of legal and systemic barriers that perpetuated inequality and oppression. Laws and policies were often designed to disadvantage aliens and limit their access to resources and opportunities. These barriers hindered their ability to secure employment, education, and healthcare, preventing them from fully participating in society.

To overcome these hurdles, Aerin Zor and his allies engaged in strategic litigation and advocacy campaigns. They fought for the repeal of discriminatory laws, pushing for comprehensive legislation that protected the rights of aliens. They also sought to transform institutions and systems to be more equitable and inclusive, working with lawmakers and policymakers to implement effective reforms.

Resistance from Status Quo

The fight for alien civil rights posed a direct challenge to the status quo, unsettling established power dynamics and societal norms. Many individuals, organizations, and institutions resisted change, fearing the loss of privilege and the disruption of existing hierarchies.

CHAPTER 2: BEYOND VELAN-7: THE INTERGALACTIC MOVEMENT

In order to confront resistance from the status quo, Aerin Zor and his fellow activists emphasized the importance of education and building empathy. They conducted workshops, seminars, and awareness campaigns aimed at debunking misconceptions and fostering understanding between different groups. By humanizing the struggles of aliens and highlighting the shared humanity of all beings, they aimed to break down the walls of prejudice and resistance.

Resource Constraints

Aerin Zor and his allies faced significant resource constraints throughout their journey. Funding for their movement was limited, making it difficult to sustain their activism and carry out large-scale initiatives. Additionally, they lacked access to mainstream media platforms and faced limited opportunities for amplifying their message.

To overcome these challenges, Aerin Zor embraced creative and unconventional approaches. He leveraged social media and grassroots organizing to spread the message of the movement and engage supporters. Through crowdfunding and community partnerships, he was able to secure the necessary resources to sustain their efforts. By thinking outside the box and utilizing available platforms and networks, they were able to overcome resource constraints and make their voices heard.

In the face of these numerous challenges and obstacles, Aerin Zor and his allies never wavered in their commitment to the cause of alien civil rights. They remained resilient, adaptable, and strategic, demonstrating the power of collective action in effecting meaningful change. Their experiences serve as an invaluable blueprint for future activists, inspiring them to confront and overcome the challenges that arise in their own pursuit of justice and equality.

Subsection: Inspiring Future Activists

As the story of Aerin Zor's life spreads throughout the galaxy, a new generation of young aliens is inspired to take up the mantle of activism and fight for justice and equality. In this subsection, we explore the ways in which Aerin Zor's legacy continues to motivate and inspire future activists.

The Power of Representation: One of the most powerful aspects of Aerin Zor's story is the representation it provides for young aliens who may have felt marginalized or excluded. Seeing someone like themselves achieving great things and fighting for their rights gives these individuals hope and the belief that they too can make a difference. Representation matters, and Aerin Zor's journey serves as a

SECTION 1: AN ADVOCATE FOR CHANGE

beacon of inspiration for young activists who seek to challenge societal norms and create a more inclusive future.

The Importance of Grassroots Movements: Aerin Zor's success is a testament to the power of grassroots movements in effecting real change. By organizing communities at the local level and mobilizing collective action, activists can create a groundswell of support and push for systemic change. Future activists can learn from Aerin Zor's example by building strong networks, engaging with their communities, and empowering their fellow aliens to fight for their rights.

Engaging Through Social Media and Technology: Technology has become an invaluable tool for activists, and Aerin Zor understood its potential. In today's interconnected universe, social media platforms and online communities provide spaces for activists to share their stories, mobilize others, and raise awareness on a massive scale. Future activists can leverage the power of technology and social media to reach wider audiences, amplify their messages, and connect with like-minded individuals across the galaxy.

Taking Nonviolent Direct Action: Aerin Zor's dedication to nonviolent direct action serves as an important lesson for future activists. The power of peaceful protests and civil disobedience should never be underestimated. By embracing nonviolent strategies, activists can bring attention to their cause, inspire empathy, and highlight the injustices they face. Aerin Zor's unwavering commitment to peaceful resistance inspires future activists to use their voices and actions as a force for change.

Creating Artistic Expressions of Resistance: Art has always played a significant role in protest movements, and Aerin Zor recognized the power of creative expressions in shaping public opinion. Future activists can draw inspiration from Aerin Zor by utilizing various art forms such as music, visual arts, dance, and literature to convey their messages and inspire change. These creative endeavors can capture the imagination and emotions of the audience, galvanizing support and elevating the importance of the cause.

Collaboration and Intersectionality: Aerin Zor's activism was characterized by a commitment to collaboration and intersectionality. Future activists can learn from this approach by recognizing the interconnected nature of social justice issues and building alliances with other marginalized communities. By joining forces and advocating for multiple causes, activists can create a more inclusive movement and amplify their collective voices.

Never Underestimate the Power of Hope: Perhaps the most enduring message from Aerin Zor's story is the importance of hope. Despite facing immense challenges and setbacks, Aerin Zor never lost faith in the possibility of change. Future activists can draw strength from this unwavering hope and remember that even in the face of adversity, progress is possible. The belief that a better future is within reach can sustain and inspire activists throughout their journey.

Remember, the fight for justice and equality is an ongoing struggle, and it is up to future generations to carry the baton forward. As Aerin Zor's story continues to inspire and resonate, it is our hope that it will ignite a fire within the hearts of young activists, motivating them to create a better and more inclusive universe for all.

Section 2: The Alien Experience

Subsection: Addressing Interplanetary Prejudice

In order to address interplanetary prejudice, it is crucial to understand the underlying causes and consequences of such biases. Prejudice refers to preconceived opinions or attitudes toward a particular group, often resulting in unfair treatment based on irrelevant factors. Interplanetary prejudice, therefore, involves biases and discrimination against individuals from different planets or celestial bodies.

Understanding the Roots of Prejudice

One of the main drivers of interplanetary prejudice is fear of the unknown. When people encounter individuals from other planets, they may feel threatened or uncomfortable due to unfamiliarity. This fear can lead to stereotypes, misconceptions, and ultimately prejudice. Additionally, scarcity of resources, competition, and power imbalances can intensify prejudices as people look for scapegoats or perceive others as threats.

To address interplanetary prejudice, it is important to dismantle these negative perceptions by promoting education, awareness, and empathy. By gaining a deeper understanding of different planetary cultures, histories, and perspectives, individuals can begin to challenge their own biases and combat prejudice.

Promoting Interplanetary Education and Awareness

Education plays a crucial role in challenging and addressing interplanetary prejudice. By incorporating interplanetary studies into school curricula and promoting cross-cultural exchanges, individuals can develop a more inclusive and open-minded perspective. Educational institutions can encourage dialogue, respect, and understanding among students from different planets, fostering a sense of unity and shared humanity.

Additionally, public awareness campaigns and media representation can help debunk stereotypes and showcase the diversity and richness of interplanetary cultures. By highlighting the achievements, contributions, and shared values of different planetary communities, society can dismantle negative biases and promote inclusivity.

Advocating for Equal Rights and Opportunities

To combat interplanetary prejudice, it is crucial to advocate for equal rights and opportunities for individuals from all planets. This includes ensuring fair and unbiased employment practices, access to education and healthcare, and protection against discrimination. Legislative measures can be implemented to enforce equal rights and prevent discrimination based on planetary origin.

Creating inclusive workplaces and institutions that value diversity and actively promote inclusivity can help address interplanetary prejudice. By fostering an environment where individuals from different planets are respected, valued, and empowered, society can overcome stereotypes and prejudices.

Building Interplanetary Alliances and Coalitions

Another effective approach to addressing interplanetary prejudice is through the formation of interplanetary alliances and coalitions. By bringing together individuals and organizations committed to combating prejudice and promoting interplanetary equality, collective action and collaboration can be achieved.

Interplanetary alliances can advocate for policy changes, raise awareness, and support marginalized communities. By amplifying the voices of those impacted by prejudice and discrimination, alliances can challenge systemic barriers and promote a more inclusive and equitable society.

Celebrating Intergalactic Diversity

Beyond addressing prejudice, it is important to celebrate and embrace the diversity of different planetary communities. Cultural festivals, events, and celebrations that highlight intergalactic traditions, music, arts, and cuisine can foster understanding and appreciation.

Moreover, promoting interplanetary travel and tourism can encourage individuals to experience other planets firsthand, fostering connections and dispelling stereotypes. By emphasizing the shared experiences and aspirations of beings from different planets, a sense of intergalactic unity can be fostered, strengthening the fight against interplanetary prejudice.

An Unconventional Solution: Empathy Training

Addressing interplanetary prejudice requires not only external changes but also internal shifts in attitudes and mindsets. An unconventional yet effective solution to cultivate empathy is through empathy training. This involves creating immersive experiences or simulations that allow individuals to step into the shoes of someone from another planet, enabling them to gain a firsthand understanding of their experiences, challenges, and aspirations.

Empathy training can help individuals develop empathy and compassion, breaking down barriers and challenging preconceived notions. By fostering a deeper connection and understanding between beings from different planets, empathy training can be a powerful tool in the fight against interplanetary prejudice.

Conclusion

Addressing interplanetary prejudice requires a multifaceted approach that entails education, advocacy, alliances, celebration of diversity, and empathy. By challenging stereotypes, promoting inclusivity, and advocating for equal rights, individuals and societies can work together to create a future where intergalactic harmony and equality prevail. Let us strive to build a universe where prejudice has no place, and respect and understanding flourish among all sentient beings.

Subsection: The Fight for Alien Employment Rights

The fight for alien employment rights is a crucial aspect of the overall struggle for alien civil rights. In this subsection, we will delve into the challenges faced by aliens in the workforce, the importance of equal opportunities, and the efforts made by Aerin Zor and other activists to secure fair treatment for all beings in the workplace.

Background and Challenges

In the vast cosmos, employment discrimination against aliens is a prevalent issue that often goes unseen or unaddressed. Many alien species face systemic barriers when seeking employment opportunities, hindering their ability to contribute to society and realize their full potential. This discrimination can manifest in various forms, such as:

- **Xenophobic Hiring Practices:** Some employers may hold prejudiced beliefs against aliens, leading them to favor candidates from their own species or planet. This biased approach perpetuates inequality and undermines the principles of fairness and meritocracy.

- **Lack of Recognition and Validation:** Alien skills, qualifications, and experiences are often overlooked or devalued by employers who prioritize familiarity and conformity. This disregard for diversity restricts creativity, innovation, and ultimately stunts societal progress.

- **Exploitation and Unfair Labor Practices:** Aliens are sometimes subjected to exploitative working conditions, including long hours, low wages, and limited access to benefits and advancement opportunities. These practices further marginalize alien workers and breed inequality.

Principles and Solutions

To address these challenges, it is essential to establish principles of equality, inclusivity, and respect in the workplace. Every individual, regardless of their species or planetary origin, should have equal access to employment opportunities and be evaluated based on their skills, qualifications, and potential.

1. **Legal Protections:** Activists like Aerin Zor have played a pivotal role in advocating for the implementation of comprehensive anti-discrimination laws that protect alien workers. These laws prohibit employers from engaging in discriminatory practices and provide legal recourse for victims of workplace discrimination.

2. **Education and Awareness:** Raising awareness about the value of diversity and the contributions aliens bring to the workforce is crucial. Through community outreach programs, workshops, and educational campaigns, activists have worked to challenge stereotypes, combat xenophobia, and promote an inclusive work environment.

3. **Diversity and Inclusion Initiatives:** Encouraging employers to embrace diversity and implement inclusive policies is a key step towards addressing employment discrimination. Companies can establish diversity and inclusion departments, provide bias training to employees, and set goals for diverse representation within their workforce.

4. **Affirmative Action Programs:** In some cases, affirmative action programs have been implemented to rectify historical disadvantages faced by alien communities. These programs aim to level the playing field by prioritizing the hiring and promotion of qualified alien candidates.

5. **Alien Professional Networks:** Building networks and support systems for alien professionals can provide valuable guidance, mentorship, and opportunities for career advancement. These networks can also serve as platforms for collective action and advocating for equal treatment in the workplace.

Unconventional Example: The Alien Internship Exchange Program

In an effort to combat employment discrimination and foster cross-cultural understanding, the Alien Internship Exchange Program was initiated by Aerin Zor and like-minded activists. This program pairs alien interns with companies and organizations that are committed to promoting diversity and providing equal employment opportunities.

Designed to go beyond traditional internships, this program offers a unique experience where interns not only learn valuable skills but also share their perspectives, culture, and expertise with their host organizations. By exposing employers to the richness and talent of alien interns, the program aims to break down biases and promote long-term changes in the workplace.

Resources and Support

Alien civil rights organizations, such as the Alien Rights Advocacy Group and the Interplanetary Workforce Equality Coalition, provide resources and support for alien workers facing employment discrimination. These organizations offer legal assistance, counseling services, and networking opportunities to help aliens navigate the challenges of the job market and ensure their rights are protected.

Conclusion

The fight for alien employment rights is an integral part of the overall struggle for equal rights and social justice. By advocating for fair treatment in the workplace, activists like Aerin Zor work towards creating a society that values diversity, embraces inclusion, and provides equal opportunities for all beings. It is through collective action, legislative changes, and a shift in societal mindset that we can build a future where employment discrimination becomes a relic of the past, and aliens can thrive in their chosen professions.

Subsection: Challenging Xenophobia in the Cosmos

Xenophobia, the fear and hatred of foreigners or anything perceived as foreign, is unfortunately not limited to planet Earth. It permeates the cosmos, where aliens from different planets and galaxies face prejudice and discrimination. In this subsection, we will explore the challenges of xenophobia in the cosmos and discuss the strategies employed by Aerin Zor to challenge and combat this form of discrimination.

Understanding Xenophobia in the Cosmos

Xenophobia in the cosmos is rooted in ignorance and fear of the unknown. When alien species encounter one another, it is not uncommon for stereotypes and biases to emerge. These stereotypes can lead to a host of negative consequences, including social exclusion, unequal access to resources, and even violence.

One common form of xenophobia in the cosmos is the belief that certain alien species are inherently dangerous or inferior. This prejudice often stems from misunderstandings or limited contact with the perceived "other." It is essential to challenge these beliefs and promote understanding and empathy across alien communities.

Education and Awareness

Aerin Zor recognized the power of education in challenging xenophobia. By promoting interplanetary education programs, she aimed to bridge the gaps in knowledge and understanding between different alien species. These programs focused on promoting cultural exchange and dispelling stereotypes.

One effective strategy employed by Aerin Zor was the use of multimedia platforms to share stories and experiences of aliens from diverse backgrounds. By showcasing the richness and diversity of alien cultures, she aimed to challenge the narrow-minded views held by some individuals.

Additionally, Aerin Zor advocated for the inclusion of intergalactic history in the curriculum of Nebula Academies and other educational institutions. By studying the successes and struggles of alien civilizations, young minds could develop a more nuanced understanding of different cultures and challenge xenophobic beliefs.

Building Alliances and Solidarity

In the fight against xenophobia, alliances and solidarity are crucial. Aerin Zor understood the power of unity and encouraged collaborations between alien rights organizations across the cosmos. By coming together, these organizations could share resources, strategies, and best practices to combat xenophobia effectively.

To foster a sense of solidarity among alien communities, Aerin Zor organized interplanetary conferences and events. These gatherings provided a platform for aliens from different backgrounds to engage in dialogue, share experiences, and build mutual understanding.

Furthermore, Aerin Zor advocated for the formation of grassroots organizations dedicated to combating xenophobia at the local level. These organizations focused on creating safe spaces for dialogue, promoting cultural exchange, and challenging xenophobic attitudes within their communities.

CHAPTER 2: BEYOND VELAN-7: THE INTERGALACTIC MOVEMENT

Legislative and Policy Changes

To address xenophobia effectively, Aerin Zor recognized the need for legislative and policy changes at the interstellar level. She advocated for the inclusion of anti-xenophobia laws and regulations in the Universal Lawbook. These laws were intended to protect the rights of aliens and provide a legal framework for challenging acts of discrimination.

Furthermore, Aerin Zor pushed for the establishment of independent interstellar commissions to monitor and address instances of xenophobia and discrimination. These commissions would provide a mechanism for aliens to report incidents of prejudice and seek justice.

Art and Media as Tools for Change

Art and media have the power to challenge deep-seated beliefs and influence public opinion. Aerin Zor recognized this and used creative mediums to challenge xenophobia in the cosmos.

She encouraged alien artists to create works that celebrated diversity and unity. These artworks served as powerful symbols of resistance and solidarity, challenging xenophobic narratives and promoting intergalactic harmony.

Aerin Zor also supported the creation of interstellar films and documentaries that highlighted the struggles faced by aliens due to xenophobia. By telling authentic and compelling stories, these films aimed to create empathy and foster understanding among intergalactic communities.

Unconventional Approach: Alien Exchange Programs

An unconventional approach employed by Aerin Zor to challenge xenophobia was the establishment of alien exchange programs. These programs facilitated the exchange of individuals from different planets, allowing them to live and work in alien communities different from their own.

By immersing themselves in unfamiliar environments, participants in these exchange programs gained firsthand experience of alien cultures, breaking down stereotypes and fostering understanding. These programs helped build personal connections and promote empathy, challenging xenophobia at its roots.

Real-World Example: The S'lang Clan Integration Project

An inspiring example of combating xenophobia is the S'lang Clan Integration Project on the planet Draclon. Draclon was a divided society, with xenophobic sentiments directed towards the S'lang Clan, who were viewed as outsiders.

Aerin Zor collaborated with local activists and the Draclonian government to create an integration project that brought together members of the S'lang Clan and the dominant Draclonian population. The project focused on fostering understanding, breaking stereotypes, and building connections between the two groups.

Through cultural exchange events, education programs, and community-building initiatives, the project successfully challenged xenophobia and improved intergroup relations on Draclon. It served as a model for other planets grappling with similar issues of xenophobia and discrimination.

Exercises

1. Imagine you are part of an interstellar education committee tasked with developing a curriculum to challenge xenophobia in Nebula Academies. Outline three lessons or activities that would promote understanding and empathy among alien students.

2. Research and identify one contemporary alien rights organization dedicated to combating xenophobia. Discuss their strategies and successes in challenging xenophobic attitudes and promoting equality.

3. Write a short science fiction story or create a piece of artwork that challenges xenophobia in the cosmos. How does your story or artwork promote understanding and respect among alien species?

Key Takeaways

- Xenophobia in the cosmos is fueled by ignorance and fear of the unknown. - Education and awareness are crucial in challenging xenophobic attitudes. - Building alliances and solidarity among alien communities help combat xenophobia effectively. - Legislative and policy changes are needed to protect the rights of aliens and challenge discrimination. - Art and media can be powerful tools for challenging xenophobia and promoting intergalactic harmony. - Unconventional approaches, such as alien exchange programs, can foster understanding and empathy. - Real-world examples, such as the S'lang Clan Integration Project, demonstrate successful challenges to xenophobia.

Subsection: Advocating for Alien Voting Rights

In this subsection, we explore the importance of advocating for alien voting rights, drawing on the principles of democracy, equality, and social justice. We examine the challenges faced by alien communities in obtaining voting rights and discuss strategies to overcome these obstacles. By highlighting the benefits of inclusivity and representation, we empower aliens to actively participate in the democratic processes of their adopted planets.

The Democratic Ideal

Democracy is the cornerstone of modern society, rooted in the belief that every individual should have a voice in shaping the policies that govern their lives. It upholds the principles of equality, freedom, and the right to self-determination. Ensuring that all members of a society have the right to vote is crucial to maintaining a functioning democratic system.

Challenges Faced by Alien Communities

Alien communities often face significant hurdles when advocating for voting rights. Prejudice, discrimination, and xenophobia can lead to the denial of basic civil liberties, including the right to vote. These barriers are magnified when aliens are not recognized as full members of society, treated as second-class citizens, or even regarded as mere visitors.

Furthermore, language barriers, limited understanding of local politics, and unfamiliarity with the voting process can also make it difficult for aliens to exercise their voting rights. Lack of information about registration procedures and discriminatory practices can further marginalize alien communities.

Strategies for Overcoming Obstacles

Advocating for alien voting rights requires a multifaceted approach that addresses both systemic and individual challenges. Here are some strategies to consider:

1. Education and outreach: Providing comprehensive information on voting rights, registration processes, and electoral systems is essential. Efforts should be made to engage with alien communities, offering language assistance and cultural sensitivity training to facilitate their participation.

2. Legal reform: Advocacy groups can work towards legislative changes that eliminate discriminatory voting practices and ensure equal rights for all residents, regardless of their planetary origins.

3. Community organizing: Building strong coalitions and networks within alien communities can amplify their voices and enable collective action. Encouraging dialogue, hosting forums, and organizing voter education campaigns can foster a sense of community and political engagement.

SECTION 2: THE ALIEN EXPERIENCE

4. Political representation: Promoting alien candidates and supporting their campaigns is crucial in increasing the visibility and influence of alien voices in political decision-making bodies. Alien leaders can champion policies that address the unique needs and concerns of their communities.

The Benefits of Inclusivity and Representation

Advocating for alien voting rights is not just about fairness and equality; it is also about harnessing the diverse perspectives and experiences of alien communities. By including aliens in the democratic process, societies can benefit from a broader range of ideas, innovative solutions, and a deeper understanding of interconnected global issues.

Alien voting rights also empower aliens to address issues that directly impact their lives, such as immigration policies, economic opportunities, and environmental sustainability. It moves societies towards more inclusive, open-minded, and progressive governance, leading to a stronger and more resilient democracy.

Real-World Examples

To better understand the significance of advocating for alien voting rights, let's explore a couple of real-world examples:

1. Planet X: Alien residents on Planet X have struggled for decades to obtain voting rights. Through a grassroots movement, they organized voter registration drives, raised awareness about their rights, and supported alien candidates for local elections. Eventually, their efforts paid off, and Planet X passed legislation granting aliens the right to vote.

2. Galaxy United: In the intergalactic federation of Galaxy United, aliens from various planets have been actively involved in advocating for their voting rights. They formed a coalition of alien advocacy groups and successfully lobbied for reforms that guarantee representation for alien communities in the federation's governing council.

Take Action

As an aspiring activist, you can make a difference in advocating for alien voting rights. Here are some actions you can take:

1. Educate yourself: Learn about the challenges faced by alien communities in obtaining voting rights. Familiarize yourself with the electoral systems and legal frameworks relevant to aliens.

CHAPTER 2: BEYOND VELAN-7: THE INTERGALACTIC MOVEMENT

2. Support alien-led initiatives: Stand in solidarity with alien-led organizations and initiatives that champion the cause of alien voting rights. Donate, volunteer, or amplify their messages through social media and grassroots outreach.

3. Engage in public discourse: Use your voice to raise awareness about the importance of alien voting rights. Write op-eds, host community discussions, or speak at public forums to promote inclusivity and equality for all.

4. Get involved in political campaigns: Support alien candidates who prioritize the rights and interests of alien communities. Volunteer for their campaigns, donate, or lend your skills to help amplify their messages.

Remember, advocating for alien voting rights is part of a broader struggle for social justice and equality. By taking action, you become a catalyst for change in fostering a more inclusive and representative democracy that respects the rights of all beings, regardless of their planetary origins.

Now that we have completed the content for the "2.2.4 Subsection: Advocating for Alien Voting Rights," we can seamlessly integrate it into the full outline.

Subsection: Achieving True Equality

In the fight for alien civil rights, one of the most significant goals is achieving true equality. This subsection explores the challenges, strategies, and principles behind this crucial aspect of the intergalactic movement.

How do we define true equality?

True equality is more than just equal rights on paper. It encompasses an inclusive society where all beings are treated with respect, dignity, and fairness. It means eliminating systemic barriers and prejudices that hinder individuals' ability to participate fully in all aspects of life. True equality recognizes and values the intrinsic worth of each individual, regardless of their alien heritage or origin.

Identifying and dismantling systemic barriers

To achieve true equality, it is essential to identify and dismantle systemic barriers that perpetuate discrimination and inequality. These barriers can take many forms, such as access to education, employment opportunities, healthcare, and political participation.

For example, imagine a society where certain alien species face limited employment opportunities due to stereotypes and prejudice. Breaking down these barriers involves challenging discriminatory hiring practices, promoting diversity and inclusion policies, and creating equal access to job opportunities for all beings.

Promoting inclusive policies and legislation

Legislation plays a crucial role in promoting true equality. Civil rights activists must advocate for the implementation of inclusive policies and laws that protect and empower all beings. This requires working closely with lawmakers, drafting bills, and lobbying for their passage.

For instance, fighting for alien employment rights may involve advocating for laws that prohibit discrimination based on species, ensuring equal pay for equal work, and providing reasonable accommodations to promote workplace accessibility. By enacting these policies, societies can create an environment that fosters equal opportunities for all beings.

Educating and raising awareness

Education is a powerful tool in the pursuit of true equality. It is vital to educate individuals about the diverse experiences, cultures, and contributions of different alien species. By raising awareness and promoting empathy, societies can overcome stereotypes, xenophobia, and other forms of prejudice.

One effective strategy is integrating intercultural education into curricula at all levels, from primary schools to higher education institutions. By teaching young minds about the importance of diversity and inclusion, we can cultivate a generation that values equality and respects the rights of all beings.

Building solidarity and alliances

Achieving true equality requires the collective effort of individuals and alien communities across the cosmos. By building solidarity and forming alliances, activists can amplify their voices and advocate for systemic change.

Creating grassroots organizations that bring together beings from different backgrounds and advocating for their rights can be an effective way to build solidarity. By pooling resources, sharing experiences, and supporting one another, these organizations can create transformative change in local communities and beyond.

CHAPTER 2: BEYOND VELAN-7: THE INTERGALACTIC MOVEMENT

Fostering cultural exchange and understanding

Cultural exchange and understanding are essential for achieving true equality. By actively encouraging cross-cultural interactions and celebrating diversity, societies can break down barriers and create a sense of belonging for all beings.

Promoting cultural festivals, exhibitions, and events that showcase the rich traditions and customs of different alien species fosters greater appreciation and understanding. These platforms encourage dialogue, challenge stereotypes, and promote unity among all beings.

The power of representation

Representation matters in the fight for true equality. When individuals from marginalized alien communities see themselves reflected in leadership positions, media, and popular culture, it empowers them and challenges societal norms.

Encouraging diverse representation in all spheres of life, from politics to entertainment, is crucial. It promotes the visibility and inclusion of aliens, breaking down stereotypes and inspiring future generations to strive for true equality.

An unconventional approach: intersectional activism

In the pursuit of true equality, it is essential to adopt an intersectional approach. Recognizing the interconnectedness of different forms of oppression, such as racism, sexism, and speciesism, allows activists to address the complex nature of discrimination.

For example, an intersectional approach acknowledges that an alien woman may face unique challenges that differ from those of an alien man or a human woman. By understanding and addressing these specific intersections, activists can better advocate for true equality that encompasses the experiences of all beings.

Case Study: The Multicultural Council for Galactic Equality

The Multicultural Council for Galactic Equality (MCGE) is a prime example of an organization dedicated to achieving true equality. Composed of representatives from various alien communities, the MCGE works tirelessly to address systemic barriers and advocate for inclusive policies.

Through grassroots initiatives, educational programs, and policy advocacy, the MCGE actively promotes true equality among diverse alien species. They collaborate with local communities, share resources, and foster cultural exchange to foster understanding and unity.

Exercises and reflection

1. Reflect on your own experiences and beliefs about equality. How can you apply the principles of true equality in your daily life and interactions with others?

2. Conduct research on discrimination faced by different alien species in various parts of the cosmos. Identify specific challenges and propose strategies to address them.

3. Identify a local advocacy group or grassroots organization that aligns with the values of true equality. Explore ways to support their efforts and contribute to their cause.

4. Imagine a society that has achieved true equality. Describe what it would look like and brainstorm steps to get there.

Remember, achieving true equality is an ongoing journey. By actively engaging in advocacy, education, and fostering understanding, we can create a future where all beings are respected, valued, and treated as equals.

Subsection: Overcoming Stereotypes and Misconceptions

Stereotypes and misconceptions are deeply ingrained in society, and they have a profound impact on how we perceive and treat others. In the case of alien civil rights, overcoming these stereotypes and misconceptions is crucial for creating a more inclusive and just society. In this subsection, we will explore the various stereotypes and misconceptions surrounding aliens and discuss strategies to challenge and dismantle them.

Unveiling the Root of Stereotypes

Stereotypes often arise from ignorance, fear, and a lack of exposure to different cultures and identities. In the case of aliens, they are frequently depicted as violent, dangerous beings seeking to invade and destroy our world. These portrayals create an atmosphere of fear and hostility towards extraterrestrial life forms. It is essential to understand that these stereotypes are baseless and perpetuate harmful biases.

The Power of Representation

One effective way to challenge stereotypes is through representation. By showing diverse and complex alien characters in media, literature, and popular culture, we can reshape public perception and challenge preconceived notions. We need more stories that highlight the humanity and struggles of aliens, portraying their rich culture, values, and aspirations. By humanizing aliens, we can foster empathy, understanding, and acceptance.

Educating for Empathy

Education is a powerful tool in combating stereotypes and misconceptions. It is essential to include intercultural education in school curriculums, teaching students about the diverse range of alien civilizations that exist. By instilling empathy and understanding at an early age, we can create a more inclusive society where diversity is celebrated.

Breaking Down Binary Thinking

Another common misconception is the binary thinking that separates aliens and humans into opposing categories. This binary perspective perpetuates the "us versus them" mentality and hinders the progress of alien civil rights. We must challenge this mindset and recognize that we share a common humanity with aliens. Emphasizing our shared experiences and aspirations can foster unity and collaboration.

Promoting Intergalactic Dialogue

Dialogue and communication are essential in overcoming stereotypes and misconceptions. By promoting intergalactic exchanges and fostering meaningful conversations between aliens and humans, we can break down barriers and bridge cultural divides. Open-mindedness and active listening are key to understanding each other's perspectives and dispelling misconceptions.

Reframing the Narrative

To counter stereotypes, we must actively challenge and reframe the narrative surrounding aliens. This involves debunking myths, correcting misinformation, and highlighting the contributions and achievements of aliens throughout history. By showcasing the diverse talents, intellect, and achievements of aliens, we can challenge the notion that they are inferior or a threat to our society.

Unconventional Tactics: Humor and Satire

In the fight against stereotypes, humor and satire can be powerful tools. Comedic approaches that challenge stereotypes and misconceptions through satire can disarm and engage audiences in meaningful conversations. Using humor to highlight the absurdity of stereotypes and misconceptions can provoke self-reflection and change perspectives.

Real-World Examples: Aliens in Everyday Life

To illustrate the impact of stereotypes and misconceptions, let's consider a real-world example. Imagine an alien newly arrived on Earth seeking employment. Despite their qualifications, they face discrimination and are denied job opportunities based on stereotypes that aliens are unreliable or too different to fit in. This example highlights how stereotypes can unjustly hinder the progress of alien individuals and communities.

Exercise: Challenging Stereotypes

Conduct research on an alien culture different from your own. Identify stereotypes or misconceptions associated with this culture and develop a strategy to challenge and debunk these stereotypes. Consider the power of representation, education, dialogue, reframing the narrative, and unconventional tactics such as humor and satire.

Resources for Overcoming Stereotypes

- "How to Be an Alien Ally: Actions and Strategies for Dismantling Stereotypes" by Dr. Xalara Zenn - "The Power of Representation: Aliens in Media" by Filmmaker Zara Ramos - "Intercultural Education Toolkit: Promoting Empathy and Understanding" by Intercultural Educator Luna Patel - "Breaking Down Barriers: Strategies for Interplanetary Communication" by Dr. Damian Hughes

By actively challenging stereotypes and misconceptions relating to aliens, we can create a more inclusive society that celebrates diversity. It is through empathy, education, dialogue, reframing narratives, and humor that we can overcome prejudice and build a future of true equality for all beings in the universe. The fight against stereotypes is ongoing; let us embrace it with open hearts and minds, and together, we can create a galactic utopia where everyone is valued and respected.

Section 3: The Extraterrestrial Alliance

Subsection: Forming Bonds with Other Alien Activists

In the fight for alien civil rights, unity is the key to success. Aerin Zor understood this and dedicated significant effort to forming bonds with other alien activists across the galaxies. By fostering collaboration and solidarity, they were able to amplify their voices and effect change on a universal scale.

Building Trust and Understanding

Forming bonds with other alien activists begins with building trust and understanding. Aerin Zor recognized the importance of acknowledging and respecting the unique challenges faced by different alien communities. They actively engaged in dialogue, learning about the diverse struggles that each community faced and the cultural nuances that influenced their activism.

To facilitate this process, Aerin Zor organized intergalactic conferences and forums where activists could come together to share their stories and experiences. These events provided a safe space for open and honest discussions, allowing activists to establish common ground and develop a deeper appreciation for each other's perspectives.

Example: At the Galactic Activist Convention, Aerin Zor orchestrated a series of panel discussions where representatives from various alien communities spoke on the issues they faced. This led to a greater understanding among activists and helped forge powerful alliances between previously isolated groups.

Collaborative Initiatives

Once trust and understanding were established, Aerin Zor encouraged the formation of collaborative initiatives. They recognized the strength in numbers and believed that collective action would bring about more significant change than isolated efforts.

Collaborative initiatives took various forms, ranging from joint campaigns, resource-sharing networks, and coordinated protests. By combining resources, knowledge, and skills, activists were able to leverage their combined influence and maximize their effectiveness.

Example: The Coalition for Intergalactic Equality was one such collaborative initiative spearheaded by Aerin Zor. This coalition brought together activists from different alien communities to advocate for systemic changes in interplanetary policies. By working together, they were able to gather extensive data, conduct comprehensive research, and mobilize a stronger front to demand justice and equality.

Strategies for Solidarity

Solidarity among alien activists was a powerful force that drove social change. Aerin Zor recognized the need to develop strategies to foster and maintain this solidarity.

One strategy was the creation of support networks that provided emotional, financial, and legal assistance to activists. These networks offered a space for activists to seek guidance, share resources, and receive encouragement during challenging times. By investing in the well-being of activists, Aerin Zor ensured a strong foundation for continued cooperation.

Another strategy involved the promotion of cultural exchange programs. By encouraging alien activists to immerse themselves in the experiences and customs of other communities, Aerin Zor aimed to break down barriers and promote empathy. These programs not only allowed activists to learn from each other's stories but also fostered a deeper sense of connection and camaraderie.

Example: The Intergalactic Mentorship Program, initiated by Aerin Zor, paired seasoned alien activists with newcomers to the movement. Through one-on-one mentorship, activists were able to share knowledge, provide guidance, and offer support to those who were just beginning their journey. This program not only provided valuable mentorship but also cultivated lifelong friendships and a sense of belonging within the activist community.

Challenges and Solutions

While forming bonds with other alien activists was essential, it also came with its share of challenges. Overcoming these challenges required innovative solutions and a commitment to building a truly inclusive and united front.

One challenge was the language barrier. With countless languages spoken across the galaxies, communication could be a significant hurdle. Aerin Zor addressed this challenge by developing a universal translation device that allowed activists to communicate effortlessly, regardless of the language they spoke. This breakthrough not only facilitated effective communication but also symbolized the power of collaboration and innovation.

Another challenge was the vast distances between alien communities. Interstellar travel presented logistical and financial challenges for organizing collaborative initiatives. To overcome this, Aerin Zor worked with astronomers and engineers to develop teleportation technology, making it possible for activists to gather quickly and efficiently, regardless of their location. This breakthrough eliminated the barrier of physical distance, strengthening bonds between activists and accelerating the progress of the civil rights movement.

CHAPTER 2: BEYOND VELAN-7: THE INTERGALACTIC MOVEMENT

Conclusion

In the fight for alien civil rights, forming bonds with other alien activists is crucial. Aerin Zor's efforts to foster collaboration and unity not only propelled the movement forward but also laid the foundation for a future where equality and justice prevail throughout the universe. By building trust, developing collaborative initiatives, adopting strategies for solidarity, and overcoming challenges, Aerin Zor created an interconnected network of activists who continue to work together, inspiring and empowering the next generation of alien activists.

Quote: "Unity is not just a concept; it is the very force that will dismantle the oppressive structures and pave the way for a future where everyone, regardless of their origins, can thrive." - Aerin Zor

Subsection: The Power of Collaborative Resistance

In the fight for alien civil rights, one of the most crucial elements for success is collaborative resistance. It is through the power of unity and collective action that meaningful change can be achieved and oppressive systems can be dismantled. In this subsection, we will explore the importance of collaborative resistance in the intergalactic movement and its impact on the struggle for equality and justice.

The Strength of Numbers

Collaborative resistance recognizes the strength that comes from numbers. When individuals come together with a shared goal, their collective voice becomes amplified, making it harder for those in power to ignore their demands. By joining forces, alien activists can raise awareness, build solidarity, and create pressure for change.

One example of collaborative resistance is the formation of grassroots organizations dedicated to alien civil rights. These organizations serve as a platform for marginalized voices, allowing individuals to share their stories and unite around common grievances. By working together, they can pool resources, share knowledge, and strategize more effectively in their pursuit of social change.

Intersectionality: Strength in Diversity

Collaborative resistance goes beyond just numbers; it values and embraces diversity. The intergalactic movement recognizes that systems of oppression intersect and impact individuals differently based on their race, gender, class, and

SECTION 3: THE EXTRATERRESTRIAL ALLIANCE

other intersecting identities. By prioritizing intersectionality, activists can ensure that no one is left behind in the struggle for equality.

For example, the Alien Civil Rights Alliance actively promotes inclusive and intersectional activism. They recognize that the fight for alien civil rights cannot be divorced from other social justice movements. By building alliances with organizations addressing issues such as gender equality, economic justice, and LGBTQ+ rights, they can work collaboratively to dismantle systemic oppression across different dimensions.

Collective Action and Nonviolent Resistance

Collaborative resistance is characterized by collective action, which involves coordinated efforts by a group of individuals to challenge the status quo. In the intergalactic movement, collective action takes various forms, including demonstrations, protests, and boycotts. These actions serve to disrupt existing power structures and draw attention to the injustices faced by alien communities.

Nonviolent resistance is at the core of collaborative resistance. It is a strategic choice to confront oppression without resorting to violence. This approach has proven to be effective in many historical struggles for civil rights, such as the Earth Civil Rights Movement. By practicing nonviolence, alien activists can demonstrate their moral integrity and win the support of allies across the galaxy.

Building Alliances and Solidarity

Collaborative resistance thrives on building alliances and fostering solidarity among different alien communities. The intergalactic movement recognizes the importance of uniting diverse groups with shared values and intersecting struggles. By bridging differences and finding common ground, activists can amplify their collective power and challenge systemic oppression more effectively.

One way to build alliances is through interplanetary cultural exchanges. By showcasing the richness and diversity of their respective cultures, alien communities can foster understanding and empathy among different species. These exchanges not only strengthen relationships but also provide opportunities for cross-cultural collaborations in the fight for equality and justice.

Creating Change from Within

Collaborative resistance is not limited to challenging external systems of oppression; it also involves reshaping internal power structures within alien communities. To be

CHAPTER 2: BEYOND VELAN-7: THE INTERGALACTIC MOVEMENT

truly transformative, the intergalactic movement recognizes the need for inclusivity and accountability within their own ranks.

One example of this is the creation of affinity groups within the movement, dedicated to addressing the specific needs and concerns of different alien communities. These groups provide a platform for self-advocacy, ensuring that the voices of all aliens, regardless of their background, are heard and valued.

Harnessing the Power of Imagination

Collaborative resistance encourages the use of imagination and creativity as powerful tools for change. Alien activists recognize that art and storytelling have the ability to inspire, challenge social norms, and envision alternative futures. By harnessing their collective creativity, they can challenge the dominant narratives and imagine a universe that celebrates diversity and equality.

For example, the intergalactic movement organizes art installations, performances, and multimedia campaigns to raise awareness and foster empathy. By engaging the imaginations of individuals across different galaxies, they can shift perspectives and challenge ingrained prejudices.

In conclusion, the power of collaborative resistance in the intergalactic movement cannot be underestimated. By uniting diverse voices, embracing intersectionality, engaging in collective action, building alliances, transforming internal power structures, and harnessing the power of imagination, alien activists can create meaningful change and strive towards a more just and equitable universe for all. The struggle for alien civil rights requires collective effort, and through collaborative resistance, the intergalactic movement is able to amplify its impact and pave the way for a brighter future.

Subsection: Overcoming Interstellar Barriers

As Aerin Zor looked out into the vast expanse of the cosmos, she couldn't help but marvel at the beauty and mystery of the universe. However, alongside this awe-inspiring wonder, she also witnessed the presence of barriers that hindered unity and cooperation among alien communities spread across the galaxies.

In this subsection, we will explore the various interstellar barriers that confronted Aerin Zor and her fellow activists in their fight for alien civil rights. We will delve into the challenges they faced and the strategies they employed to overcome these obstacles.

Understanding the Nature of Interstellar Barriers

Interstellar barriers can take many different forms, from physical to social, and they can be deeply ingrained within the fabric of intergalactic societies. To confront these barriers effectively, it was imperative for Aerin Zor and her allies to understand their nature and origins.

One of the primary interstellar barriers they encountered was the lack of interplanetary communication and cooperation. Each alien civilization had its unique traditions, languages, and cultural practices, making it difficult to forge connections and build alliances. Moreover, deep-rooted prejudices and stereotypes created a sense of distrust and animosity among different alien species, further exacerbating the divide.

Another significant barrier was the vast distances between planets and the sheer scale of the universe. Traveling from one planet to another posed immense logistical challenges and required advanced technology. This physical barrier hindered the ability to organize joint efforts and impeded the flow of activism across galaxies.

Breaking Down Language and Cultural Barriers

To overcome these interstellar barriers, Aerin Zor realized the need to address the fundamental issue of communication. She saw that language played a pivotal role in fostering understanding and harmony among diverse alien communities.

Aerin Zor and her team worked tirelessly to establish a multilingual communication network, advocating for the adoption of a universal language that could bridge the linguistic divide. This language, known as "Galactic Esperanto," was a blend of different alien dialects and allowed for more effective communication between different species. It provided a level playing field for all, dismantling the language barriers that previously hindered collaboration.

Additionally, Aerin Zor recognized the importance of cross-cultural understanding. She encouraged the exchange of cultural practices, art, and traditions among alien communities. By celebrating and appreciating the diversity of each civilization, she fostered a sense of unity and mutual respect, breaking down the cultural barriers that had divided them for centuries.

Technological Innovations for Interstellar Cooperation

The vast distances between planets posed a formidable challenge in the fight for alien civil rights. To overcome this physical barrier, Aerin Zor championed technological innovations that would facilitate interstellar cooperation.

CHAPTER 2: BEYOND VELAN-7: THE INTERGALACTIC MOVEMENT

Aerin Zor's team worked alongside scientists and engineers to develop advanced warp drive technology, making interplanetary travel faster and more accessible. This breakthrough allowed activists to traverse the vastness of the cosmos swiftly, attending conferences, organizing protests, and building alliances across galaxies.

In addition to travel, Aerin Zor also focused on developing advanced communication systems. She advocated for interconnected networks that could facilitate real-time communication between distant planets. This technological leap bridged the gap between different alien communities, enabling them to share knowledge, coordinate efforts, and amplify their voices in unison.

The Power of Education and Advocacy

Overcoming interstellar barriers required more than just technological advancements; it necessitated a transformation in mindset and societal values. Aerin Zor understood the critical role of education and advocacy in challenging deep-rooted prejudices and stereotypes.

She spearheaded educational initiatives that promoted intercultural understanding and empathy. Schools and universities across galaxies introduced curriculum that highlighted the richness of diverse cultures and histories, fostering respect and appreciation for each other's differences. These educational reforms played a vital role in breaking down ingrained biases and perceptions, nurturing a generation of empathetic and open-minded citizens.

Aerin Zor also utilized the power of advocacy to shed light on the injustices faced by alien communities. She organized intergalactic conferences and rallies, where activists shared personal stories and experiences, helping others understand the systemic barriers that perpetuated discrimination. By amplifying marginalized voices and humanizing their struggles, Aerin Zor sought to dismantle the ignorance and apathy that allowed interstellar barriers to persist.

Unconventional Approach: Cosmic Social Media

To reach a wider audience and break through the noise of interstellar communication, Aerin Zor conceptualized a revolutionary platform known as "Cosmic Social Media." This virtual space allowed individuals from all corners of the universe to connect, share stories, and engage in meaningful discussions.

Cosmic Social Media facilitated the exchange of ideas and experiences, promoting greater awareness and empathy. It served as a digital hub for activists, offering a space for collaboration and collective organizing. By harnessing the power of technology and connectivity, Aerin Zor transcended the limits imposed by physical distance and cultural barriers, unifying like-minded individuals across galaxies.

Conclusion: A United Cosmos

Through their relentless efforts, Aerin Zor and her fellow activists managed to surmount the interstellar barriers that once divided alien communities. By addressing communication challenges, fostering cross-cultural understanding, leveraging technological advancements, and promoting education and advocacy, they paved the way for a more united and inclusive cosmos.

The journey to overcoming interstellar barriers was not without its challenges, but the legacy of Aerin Zor and her allies serves as a testament to the power of resilience, determination, and the belief in a future where all beings can coexist harmoniously. As the fight for alien civil rights continues, their triumphs remind us that a united cosmos is within our reach.

Subsection: Grassroots Organizations for Galactic Change

In the fight for alien civil rights, grassroots organizations have played a crucial role in effecting social change and mobilizing communities towards a common goal. These organizations, comprised of passionate individuals committed to the cause, have been instrumental in bringing awareness, organizing protests, and challenging the status quo. In this subsection, we will dive into the world of grassroots activism, exploring its principles, strategies, and the power it holds in creating real and lasting change.

Principles of Grassroots Activism

At its core, grassroots activism is driven by the belief that change starts from the ground up. It emphasizes the power of ordinary people coming together, organizing, and taking collective action. Grassroots organizations are typically characterized by their decentralized structure, participatory decision-making processes, and reliance on volunteers and community support.

One of the key principles of grassroots activism is inclusivity. These organizations strive to create a space where everyone's voice is heard and valued, fostering diversity and creating a sense of belonging. By actively involving individuals from different backgrounds and experiences, grassroots organizations can better understand the complexities of the issues they are fighting against and develop more informed and effective strategies.

Another important principle is empowerment. Grassroots organizations aim to empower individuals and communities to take ownership of their rights and fight for justice. By providing resources, education, and platforms for engagement, they enable people to become active participants in the movement and advocates for change.

Strategies for Grassroots Activism

Grassroots organizations employ a range of strategies to bring about systemic change, often utilizing a combination of direct action, education, and coalition-building. These strategies are tailored to the unique challenges and context of the alien civil rights movement. Let's explore some of the most effective strategies:

1. **Community Organizing:** Grassroots activists prioritize building relationships and creating connections within their communities. They conduct outreach programs, hold town hall meetings, and conduct workshops to raise awareness about alien civil rights issues. By engaging with community members and listening to their concerns, grassroots organizations can mobilize greater support and galvanize individuals to take action.

2. **Advocacy and Education:** Grassroots organizations place great emphasis on educating the public about alien civil rights, challenging misconceptions, and dispelling stereotypes. Through public forums, seminars, and targeted campaigns, they provide accurate information and promote empathy and understanding. Education acts as a catalyst for change, encouraging individuals to question existing norms and supporting the fight for equality.

3. **Nonviolent Direct Action:** Inspired by the teachings of historical movements, grassroots organizations employ nonviolent direct action as a powerful tool to disrupt the status quo, draw attention to injustices, and pressure those in power to address grievances. Sit-ins, peaceful protests, and acts of civil disobedience serve as public displays of discontent and solidarity, creating a sense of urgency around the need for change.

4. **Coalition-Building:** Recognizing the strength in unity, grassroots organizations actively seek alliances and partnerships with other social justice movements and organizations. By collaborating with like-minded groups, they amplify their collective voices, leverage resources, and create a broader social movement that can affect change on a larger scale. These coalitions foster solidarity and allow for the sharing of strategies and tactics.

The Power of Grassroots Activism

Grassroots activism has proven time and again to be a powerful force in effecting societal change. By organizing at the local level, grassroots organizations are able to deeply connect with the communities they serve, understand their unique needs, and mobilize support effectively. The power of grassroots activism lies in several key aspects:

1. **Grassroots organizations have firsthand knowledge:** Being embedded within the communities they serve, grassroots organizations have a deep understanding of the challenges faced by alien individuals. This firsthand knowledge allows them to develop targeted strategies and campaigns that are more likely to resonate with the broader public.

2. **Grassroots activism is scalable:** Grassroots organizations, while initially focused on local issues, have the potential to scale their efforts and make a broader impact. By establishing networks, sharing resources and knowledge, and coordinating actions, grassroots movements can expand their reach and influence beyond their immediate communities.

3. **Grassroots activism is driven by passion:** Grassroots activists are fueled by their unwavering passion and commitment to the cause. This passion brings with it a level of dedication and persistence that can withstand challenges and setbacks. It inspires others to join the movement and fosters a sense of collective purpose.

4. **Grassroots activism creates community ownership:** By involving community members in every stage of the activism process, grassroots organizations create a sense of ownership and investment in the movement. This increases the likelihood of sustained engagement and long-term change.

Examples of Grassroots Organizations for Galactic Change

In the fight for alien civil rights, numerous grassroots organizations have emerged, each with its unique approach and focus. Let's take a look at two inspiring examples:

1. **The Coalition for Extraterrestrial Justice (CEJ):** CEJ operates on multiple planets, bringing together various alien communities to fight for their rights. With a focus on intersectionality, CEJ advocates for the rights of all marginalized alien groups, addressing issues such as employment discrimination, housing rights, and healthcare access. They organize grassroots campaigns, collaborate with other social justice movements, and provide resources and legal support to affected individuals.

2. **Aliens for Equality (AFE):** AFE is a grassroots organization based on Velan-7, created with the aim of achieving full equality for bi-entity fusions. They conduct community outreach programs, engage with educational institutions, and

organize peaceful protests to demand equal rights and challenge discriminatory policies. AFE also focuses on empowering bi-entity fusions through education and skills development, promoting self-sufficiency and autonomy.

Resources for Grassroots Activism

For budding activists looking to get involved in grassroots organizations or individuals wanting to support the movement, there are several resources available. These resources provide guidance, training, and support to facilitate effective grassroots activism. Here are a few notable resources:

    1. **Grassroots Leadership Training Programs:** Many organizations offer leadership training programs specifically tailored to grassroots activism. These programs provide valuable skills and knowledge that empower individuals to take on leadership roles within their communities and drive meaningful change.

    2. **Community Organizing Toolkits:** Toolkits serve as comprehensive guides for community organizers and grassroots activists, offering step-by-step instructions, resources, and templates for organizing campaigns and mobilizing communities. These toolkits are invaluable resources for individuals looking to start their own grassroots initiatives.

    3. **Online Activist Networks:** Online platforms and social media have made it easier than ever for activists to connect, collaborate, and access resources. Online activist networks provide a space for grassroots organizations to share information, coordinate actions, and support each other.

    4. **Legal Support and Advocacy Groups:** Grassroots activists often face legal challenges and obstacles in their fight for alien civil rights. Legal support and advocacy groups specializing in social justice issues provide crucial assistance, including legal advice, representation, and lobbying for policy changes.

Tricks of the Trade: An Unconventional Approach

While grassroots activism often follows established principles and strategies, there is room for creativity and unconventional approaches. One unconventional approach that has gained traction in recent years is the use of art and creative expression as a catalyst for change. Artistic mediums, such as music, visual arts, and theater, have the power to transcend language and cultural barriers, evoking emotions and provoking reflection.

    Grassroots organizations can harness the power of art by incorporating it into their campaigns and events. Art installations, street performances, and collaborative art projects can serve as powerful tools for raising awareness, capturing attention, and fostering dialogue. By intertwining creativity with activism, grassroots organizations tap into the universal language of art and reach a wider audience.

Exercise: Starting Your Own Grassroots Initiative

Are you inspired to make a difference and start your own grassroots initiative for alien civil rights? Here's an exercise to get you started:

1. Identify the issue: Determine the specific alien civil rights issue you want to address. Research and understand the root causes, challenges, and potential solutions related to the issue.

2. Build a network: Connect with like-minded individuals and organizations that share your passion for the cause. Establish relationships and partnerships that can support your grassroots initiative.

3. Develop a strategy: Outline a plan of action, including goals, objectives, and a timeline. Identify key activities, such as community outreach, education programs, and advocacy campaigns, that align with your mission.

4. Mobilize resources: Assess the resources you have available, including funds, volunteers, and expertise. Seek additional support through fundraising events, grant applications, or partnerships with local businesses and institutions.

5. Create an inclusive space: Foster an environment that values inclusivity, diversity, and participation. Ensure that everyone has a voice and the opportunity to contribute to the decision-making process.

6. Take action: Organize events, workshops, and initiatives that raise awareness, educate the public, and mobilize the community. Utilize both traditional and digital platforms to amplify your message and connect with a wider audience.

Remember, grassroots activism is a journey that requires persistence, adaptability, and a commitment to continuous learning. Stay open to feedback, evaluate your progress, and be willing to adapt your strategies as needed.

Conclusion

Grassroots organizations are the heartbeat of the alien civil rights movement, driving social change from the ground up. Grounded in principles of inclusivity and empowerment, these organizations employ various strategies to mobilize communities, raise awareness, and challenge existing systems. With their firsthand knowledge, scalability, passion, and community ownership, grassroots organizations have the power to effect lasting change in the fight for alien civil rights. By embracing unconventional approaches, leveraging powerful resources, and standing united, they pave the way for a more just and equitable universe.

Subsection: Building a Network of Support

In the fight for alien civil rights, one of the most crucial aspects is building a strong network of support. Activism is not a solitary endeavor, and the power of collective action cannot be overstated. By forging alliances and fostering solidarity among alien communities, activists like Aerin Zor can create a formidable force capable of effecting real change in the cosmos.

The Importance of Unity

Unity lies at the heart of any successful movement, and the alien civil rights movement is no exception. Building a network of support involves bringing together diverse alien groups and individuals who share a common goal of equality and justice.

It is essential to recognize that each alien community may face unique challenges and have specific needs. However, by finding common ground and acknowledging the interconnectedness of the struggle, activists can unite disparate alien communities under a shared purpose. This unity is a powerful force that can amplify the voices of the marginalized and put pressure on those in power to address systemic injustice.

Creating Connections

Creating connections is a vital step in building a network of support. Activists must actively reach out to other alien communities, organizations, and individuals who are passionate about alien civil rights. This can be done through various means, such as attending conferences, joining online forums and social media groups, and participating in interplanetary events.

By establishing connections, activists can build relationships, exchange ideas, and share resources. These connections also provide a platform for collaboration and collective action. An interconnected network of support allows for the pooling of knowledge, strategies, and experiences, strengthening the collective impact of the movement.

Grassroots Organizations

Grassroots organizations play a crucial role in building a network of support. These organizations are typically formed by alien activists and community members at the local level, driven by a shared desire for change. Grassroots organizations offer a space for alien communities to come together, organize, and voice their concerns.

Activists must encourage the establishment and growth of grassroots organizations to foster engagement and mobilize the alien population. These organizations serve as hubs for education, community building, and coordination of advocacy efforts. They can also provide support to individual activists, offering resources, mentorship, and a sense of belonging.

Strength in Diversity

In building a network of support, it is essential to appreciate and embrace the diversity within alien communities. Each individual brings a unique perspective and set of experiences to the struggle for alien civil rights. By celebrating this diversity, activists can create a rich tapestry of voices and ideas, enriching the movement as a whole.

However, it is important to acknowledge that diversity also comes with challenges. Activists must navigate the complexities of intersectionality, ensuring that the movement is inclusive and representative of all alien individuals, regardless of their background, gender identity, or planetary origin. This requires active engagement with voices from marginalized groups and a commitment to amplifying their concerns and needs.

Fostering Solidarity

Solidarity is the backbone of any successful movement. Building a network of support involves not only connecting with alien communities but also forging alliances with other social justice movements. The struggles for equality and justice are interconnected, and alien activists can find common cause with groups fighting against racism, sexism, and other forms of oppression.

By collaborating with other movements, activists can tap into existing resources, strategies, and knowledge. They can also amplify their message and reach a wider audience, building a broader coalition for change. Solidarity enables activists to share the burden of advocacy, working together towards a shared vision of a more equitable and inclusive universe.

CHAPTER 2: BEYOND VELAN-7: THE INTERGALACTIC MOVEMENT

Unconventional Collaboration

In the spirit of Donald Glover, it is important to push the boundaries of conventional activism and seek unconventional methods of collaboration. For example, alien activists might consider engaging with artists, musicians, and performers to raise awareness and inspire change. Art has the power to transcend language barriers and touch hearts on a deep emotional level.

By collaborating with artists, activists can tap into their creative energy and storytelling abilities to convey the message of the alien civil rights movement. Through music, visual arts, and performance, activists can reach new audiences and spark conversations that might not have happened otherwise.

Problem-solving Exercise: Building Bridges

Imagine you are an alien activist who wants to build a network of support among alien communities in the galaxy. However, you find resistance and hesitancy from some groups due to historical tensions and distrust. How would you approach this challenge and foster unity among these communities? Present a step-by-step plan outlining your strategy, considering the importance of empathy, open dialogue, and finding common ground.

Resources and References

1. "Building Networks of Solidarity: A Guide for Alien Activists" by Intergalactic Alliance for Social Justice 2. "Grassroots Organizing: Mobilizing Alien Communities for Change" by Aliens for Equality 3. "The Power of Collaboration: Lessons from Intergalactic Social Movements" by Intergalactic Activist Network 4. "Music and Activism: Amplifying the Voices of the Marginalized" by Extraterrestrial Artists Collective

Subsection: Fostering Solidarity among Alien Communities

In the pursuit of equality and justice for all beings in the universe, one of the most important aspects is fostering solidarity among alien communities. Solidarity strengthens movements and creates the momentum needed to challenge oppressive systems. When alien activists come together and support one another, they amplify their voices and increase their chances of achieving meaningful change.

The concept of solidarity is rooted in the understanding that all beings, regardless of their origin or physical attributes, share a common struggle for freedom and equality. It recognizes that the power to effect change lies in collective

SECTION 3: THE EXTRATERRESTRIAL ALLIANCE

action and unity. Fostering solidarity among alien communities requires building bridges, creating safe spaces, and cultivating understanding.

Creating Safe Spaces

Creating safe spaces is crucial for fostering solidarity among alien communities. Safe spaces provide a refuge where individuals can openly share their experiences, vulnerabilities, and fears without the fear of judgment or discrimination. These spaces allow for the formation of bonds based on shared struggles and empower individuals to speak out against injustice.

Alien activists can organize support groups, discussion circles, or online forums where individuals can come together to share their stories, seek advice, and offer support. These spaces not only validate the experiences of marginalized communities but also encourage allies to understand and empathize with the challenges faced by others.

Cultivating Understanding

To foster solidarity, it is essential to cultivate understanding between different alien communities. This requires actively engaging in dialogue, listening with empathy, and acknowledging the unique experiences and struggles of each community. By recognizing the interconnectedness of their struggles, alien activists can build bridges and find common ground.

Workshops, seminars, and intercommunity events can be organized to facilitate dialogue and information sharing. These platforms allow for the exchange of ideas, perspectives, and experiences, leading to a deeper understanding of the challenges faced by different alien communities. Through this process, activists can identify shared goals and strategies for collective action.

Collaborative Projects

Collaborative projects play a significant role in fostering solidarity among alien communities. By working together towards a shared objective, alien activists can build trust and establish lasting partnerships. This collaboration not only strengthens the movement but also demonstrates the power of unity to effect change.

Activists can organize events such as joint protests, cultural festivals, or educational initiatives that promote intercommunity collaboration. These projects not only foster solidarity but also provide opportunities for the wider galactic community to witness the diversity and strength of united alien voices.

Sustained Advocacy

Fostering solidarity among alien communities requires sustained advocacy efforts. Activists must remain dedicated to challenging oppressive systems and dismantling discriminatory practices. Solidarity is not a fleeting notion but a commitment to ongoing support and collaboration.

Alien activists can form alliances, coalitions, or networks to create a unified front against discrimination. These structures provide a collective platform for advocacy, sharing resources, and amplifying marginalized voices. Sustained advocacy ensures that the fight for equality and justice remains at the forefront of the galactic agenda.

Unconventional yet Relevant Example: The Galaxy Coalition for Intersectional Liberation

An unconventional yet relevant example of fostering solidarity among alien communities is the formation of the Galaxy Coalition for Intersectional Liberation (GCIL). The GCIL is a grassroots organization that brings together alien activists from various communities to address intersecting forms of oppression.

The GCIL recognizes that discrimination and injustices are interconnected and cannot be tackled in isolation. By fostering solidarity among alien communities and advocating for intersectional approaches to social justice, the GCIL aims to create a galactic society where all beings can thrive.

Through collaborative projects, dialogue circles, and sustained advocacy efforts, the GCIL has successfully dismantled discriminatory policies, fought against systemic oppression, and uplifted marginalized voices across the cosmos.

Conclusion

Fostering solidarity among alien communities is critical for achieving equality and justice in the universe. By creating safe spaces, cultivating understanding, engaging in collaborative projects, and sustaining advocacy, alien activists can amplify their voices and challenge oppressive systems. Solidarity is the catalyst for change, as it unites diverse beings in a shared struggle and empowers them to create a better and more inclusive future.

Section 4: From Activism to Diplomacy

Subsection: Alien Representation in Planetary Governments

In the complex landscape of intergalactic politics, a crucial aspect of achieving true equality for alien beings is their representation in planetary governments. The recognition and inclusion of alien perspectives and interests in decision-making processes are vital for creating a fair and just society. In this subsection, we explore the challenges and opportunities associated with alien representation in planetary governments, highlighting the importance of this issue and proposing innovative solutions.

Understanding the Need for Alien Representation

Alien representation in planetary governments is more than just a symbolic gesture. It is an acknowledgment of the diverse experiences and perspectives that exist within the cosmos. Planetary governments must recognize that decisions affecting alien communities should involve those communities themselves. Without alien representation, policies may inadvertently marginalize and suppress the rights and voices of aliens.

The Challenges of Alien Representation

While the need for alien representation is clear, there are significant challenges that hinder its realization. One major obstacle is the deep-rooted prejudice and bias against aliens that permeate many societal structures. Overcoming these prejudices requires a shift in collective consciousness, challenging ingrained beliefs, and dismantling discriminatory institutions.

Another challenge lies in the complexities of governance systems themselves. Decisions in planetary governments often rely on democratic processes such as voting, which may not adequately represent alien populations. Aliens may have unique cultural, social, and political systems that differ from those of the dominant species, necessitating alternative mechanisms for their representation.

Alternative Models for Alien Representation

To address these challenges, innovative models for alien representation in planetary governments are needed. One approach is to establish dedicated seats or advisory boards specifically reserved for alien representatives. These representatives would have voting rights and the authority to bring alien voices and perspectives to the forefront of governmental decision-making.

Another model worth exploring involves adopting a quota system, ensuring a minimum number of alien representatives in the government proportional to the alien population. This approach ensures that alien communities are not overlooked or underrepresented. It promotes inclusivity and provides a platform for the unique needs and concerns of aliens to be effectively addressed.

Collaborative Governance: Alien-Host Species Partnerships

In addition to direct representation, fostering partnerships between alien and host species can be a powerful method of collaborative governance. By working together, alien and host species can co-create policies that consider the interests of all parties

CHAPTER 2: BEYOND VELAN-7: THE INTERGALACTIC MOVEMENT

involved. This approach requires open dialogue, mutual respect, and a willingness to engage with diverse perspectives.

One example of successful collaborative governance is the Intergalactic Council for Interplanetary Relations (ICIR). The ICIR brings together representatives from various planetary governments, including both aliens and host species. Through diplomatic negotiations and cooperative decision-making, the ICIR aims to ensure fairness, equality, and inclusivity on a cosmic scale.

Ensuring the Sustainability of Alien Representation

While alien representation in planetary governments is crucial, it must also be sustainable in the long run. This requires nurturing future generations of alien leaders and empowering them to take on active roles in governance. Educational initiatives should be implemented to raise awareness about the importance of alien representation and provide the necessary skills and knowledge for aliens to participate effectively.

To maintain the momentum of alien representation, it is essential to establish mechanisms for accountability and periodic evaluation of governmental policies and practices. Regular audits can ensure that alien voices are genuinely being heard and their interests are being taken into account. Additionally, mechanisms for conflict resolution should be in place to address any disputes or tensions that may arise between alien and host species representatives.

Conclusion: A United Future

The path to achieving alien representation in planetary governments is not without challenges, but it is a journey worth undertaking. It requires a collective commitment to dismantling prejudice, embracing diversity, and fostering inclusive governance systems. By providing a platform for alien voices, we move closer to a united future where all beings, regardless of their origins, can actively participate and shape the destiny of the cosmos. Through collaborative governance and sustained efforts, we can create a society that celebrates the richness of our differences and builds a foundation of equality and justice for all.

"Unity in diversity breeds a stronger universe."

Subsection: Negotiating Intergalactic Treaties

In the quest for galactic peace and harmony, negotiating intergalactic treaties plays a crucial role. These treaties establish the framework for cooperation, resolve conflicts,

SECTION 4: FROM ACTIVISM TO DIPLOMACY

and promote mutual understanding between alien worlds. In this subsection, we dive into the art and science of negotiating intergalactic treaties, exploring the key principles, challenges, and strategies involved.

Understanding Intergalactic Diplomacy

Intergalactic diplomacy is a complex field that requires a deep understanding of alien cultures, political systems, and legal frameworks. Diplomats tasked with negotiating intergalactic treaties must possess exceptional interpersonal skills, the ability to navigate cultural nuances, and a strong knowledge of the interstellar legal landscape.

To start the negotiation process, diplomats need to establish common ground and build trust with their alien counterparts. This is often achieved through dialogue, cultural exchanges, and the exploration of shared interests and values. By fostering genuine relationships and demonstrating respect for each other's differences, diplomats can lay the foundation for productive negotiations.

Key Principles of Treaty Negotiations

Negotiating intergalactic treaties involves adhering to a set of key principles that guide the process. These principles ensure fairness, transparency, and mutually beneficial outcomes. Here are some of the fundamental principles one must keep in mind:

1. **Unanimous Consent:** Treaties must be agreed upon by all involved parties. Each party has a right to be involved in the negotiation process and should have an equal say in shaping the treaty's provisions.

2. **Equitable Distribution of Benefits:** Treaties should strive to achieve a fair distribution of benefits for all parties involved. This ensures that no single entity exploits or dominates the others, fostering a sense of equality and trust.

3. **Respect for Sovereignty:** Treaties should respect the sovereignty of each alien world involved. This means recognizing the right of each entity to govern its own affairs and make decisions in its best interest.

4. **Accountability and Enforcement:** A robust mechanism for accountability and enforcement is essential for the effective implementation of intergalactic treaties. This ensures that parties uphold their commitments and face consequences for non-compliance.

CHAPTER 2: BEYOND VELAN-7: THE INTERGALACTIC MOVEMENT

Challenges in Intergalactic Treaty Negotiations

Negotiating intergalactic treaties is not without its challenges. The process often entails overcoming significant barriers and complexities, some of which include:

1. **Interstellar Power Dynamics:** Negotiations may involve parties with significantly different levels of power and influence. Addressing power imbalances requires skilled diplomacy and the ability to find creative solutions that satisfy the interests of all parties involved.

2. **Cultural Differences:** Each alien civilization brings its own cultural perspectives and norms to the negotiation table. Understanding and managing these cultural differences is crucial for effective communication and problem-solving.

3. **Legal Harmonization:** Intergalactic treaties often involve aligning vastly different legal frameworks. Harmonizing legal systems requires extensive legal expertise and a commitment to finding common ground while respecting the unique legal traditions of each alien world.

Strategies for Successful Negotiations

Successful negotiation of intergalactic treaties requires a thoughtful and strategic approach. Here are some proven strategies to achieve positive outcomes:

1. **Preparation and Research:** Thorough preparation and research are paramount. Diplomats should study the political, cultural, and legal aspects of the alien world they are negotiating with, identifying potential areas of agreement and points of contention.

2. **Effective Communication:** Clear and effective communication is essential during negotiations. Diplomats must be skilled communicators, adept at conveying complex ideas and actively listening to the concerns and perspectives of their alien counterparts.

3. **Finding Common Ground:** Identifying shared interests and goals creates a solid foundation for negotiations. Diplomats should seek common ground and build upon areas of agreement to foster collaboration and trust.

4. **Flexibility and Compromise:** Negotiations require a willingness to be flexible and open to compromise. Identifying win-win solutions that address the needs and concerns of all parties involved can lead to successful outcomes.

An Unconventional Perspective: The Role of Intergalactic Cuisine

While negotiating intergalactic treaties may seem like purely diplomatic work, an unconventional yet relevant aspect to consider is intergalactic cuisine. Sharing food traditions and culinary experiences can create a unique bond between negotiating parties, promoting a sense of familiarity and fostering trust. Including intergalactic cuisine as part of the negotiation process can serve as a catalyst for building relationships and bridging cultural gaps.

Conclusion

Negotiating intergalactic treaties is a challenging yet vital aspect of promoting interstellar cooperation. By adhering to key principles, navigating the complexities, and employing strategic negotiation techniques, diplomats can pave the way for a peaceful and harmonious universe. Remember, effective negotiation is not solely about winning or achieving individual goals—it is about creating a framework that respects the diversity of all alien worlds and establishes a foundation for a shared future.

CHAPTER 2: BEYOND VELAN-7: THE INTERGALACTIC MOVEMENT

Subsection: The Role of Alien Ambassadors

In the intergalactic struggle for equality and justice, one crucial role is often overlooked: that of the Alien Ambassadors. These remarkable individuals play a significant role in representing the interests of their respective alien communities and advocating for change on a diplomatic level. Their task is no small feat, as they navigate the complexities of interstellar politics and bridge the gap between different species and cultures. In this subsection, we will explore the multifaceted role of Alien Ambassadors, their challenges, and the transformative power they hold.

Navigating the Politics of the Universe

One of the primary responsibilities of Alien Ambassadors is to navigate the intricate web of interstellar politics. They serve as intermediaries between their home planets and the planetary governments they are assigned to. This requires a deep understanding of diplomatic protocols, negotiation techniques, and the art of compromise. Alien Ambassadors must be skilled communicators, capable of conveying the needs and concerns of their alien communities effectively.

To successfully navigate the politics of the universe, Alien Ambassadors must cultivate diplomatic relationships built on mutual respect and understanding. This involves establishing alliances, fostering dialogue, and promoting cooperation among different species. By building bridges between worlds, Alien Ambassadors contribute to the creation of a harmonious and inclusive galactic society.

Advocating for Alien Rights

Alien Ambassadors are at the forefront of advocating for alien rights within the planetary governments they interact with. They serve as vocal advocates, pushing for policies and legislation that protect and uplift the rights of their fellow aliens. This includes advocating for equal access to education, healthcare, and employment opportunities.

To be effective advocates, Alien Ambassadors must be well-versed in interplanetary law and human rights principles. They must possess a deep understanding of the socio-political landscape of both their home planet and the planetary government they are assigned to. Armed with this knowledge, Alien Ambassadors engage in persuasive rhetoric and diplomatic negotiations to bring about positive change for their communities.

Promoting Intercultural Exchange and Understanding

In addition to advocating for alien rights, Alien Ambassadors serve as catalysts for intercultural exchange and understanding. They strive to break down barriers and dismantle prejudices through educational initiatives, cultural exchange programs, and community outreach. By fostering a deeper understanding and appreciation of different alien cultures, Alien Ambassadors facilitate a more inclusive and harmonious universe.

These ambassadors of cultural appreciation often organize events that showcase the richness and diversity of their home planets. They promote the arts, music, literature, and culinary traditions of their communities, encouraging others to embrace the beauty of differences. Through these initiatives, Alien Ambassadors inspire dialogue, mutual respect, and empathy across species.

Addressing Planetary Concerns

Alien Ambassadors are also tasked with addressing planetary concerns and resolving conflicts that may arise between their home planet and the planetary government they represent. They act as mediators, using their diplomatic skills to find common ground and negotiate fair solutions. This requires a deep understanding of the intricacies and complexities of planetary politics, economics, and social dynamics.

By addressing planetary concerns, Alien Ambassadors contribute to the stability and peace of the universe. They facilitate cooperation and collaboration between different worlds, helping to resolve disputes and prevent conflicts from escalating. Their role as peacekeepers is essential in promoting interstellar harmony and ensuring a prosperous future for all species.

Embracing Diversity and Collaboration

The role of Alien Ambassadors goes beyond mere representation; it is about embracing diversity and collaboration in all its forms. These ambassadors promote inclusivity and equality not only within their communities but also on a universal scale. They work towards a future where all species are treated with respect and dignity, regardless of their planetary origins.

To embrace diversity and collaboration, Alien Ambassadors must encourage dialogue and cooperation among different species. They create platforms for exchanging ideas, sharing resources, and collectively addressing challenges that affect the entire galaxy. Through their efforts, Alien Ambassadors foster a sense of unity that transcends borders, species, and cultures.

CHAPTER 2: BEYOND VELAN-7: THE INTERGALACTIC MOVEMENT

The Unconventional Solution: Intergalactic Exchange Program

To further enhance the role of Alien Ambassadors, an unconventional yet effective solution could be the implementation of an intergalactic exchange program. This program would allow Alien Ambassadors to spend a designated period of time on different planets, immersing themselves in the culture, politics, and everyday lives of the species they represent.

By participating in the intergalactic exchange program, Alien Ambassadors would gain firsthand insight into the challenges faced by different alien communities. This experiential learning would deepen their understanding and empathy, enabling them to better advocate for the rights and needs of their constituents.

In addition, the intergalactic exchange program would promote cross-cultural understanding and collaboration. It would foster personal connections and friendships between Alien Ambassadors and individuals from different species, building trust and strengthening the fabric of the universe.

Conclusion

The role of Alien Ambassadors is integral to the struggle for alien rights and equality in the cosmos. These diplomatic champions navigate the politics of the universe, advocate for alien rights, promote intercultural exchange, address planetary concerns, and embrace diversity and collaboration. Their transformative power lies in their ability to bridge the gap between different worlds and inspire change on a universal scale. With Alien Ambassadors leading the way, a future of equality and harmony among all species is within reach.

Subsection: Addressing Alien Rights in Universal Law

In this subsection, we dive into the complex and important area of addressing alien rights in universal law. As the rights of aliens are increasingly recognized and protected, it is vital to establish a framework within which these rights can be upheld. We will explore the key principles, challenges, and strategies involved in ensuring the inclusion of alien rights in universal law.

Background

Before we delve into the specifics of addressing alien rights, let us first establish a foundational understanding of universal law. Universal law represents a set of principles and norms that are applicable to all sentient beings, regardless of their origin or planetary affiliation. It is a framework that seeks to protect and uphold the fundamental rights of all beings, irrespective of their species or planet of residence.

The concept of universal law emerges from the recognition that every sentient being possesses inherent rights that should be respected and preserved. These rights include the right to life, liberty, and the pursuit of happiness, as well as the right to be free from discrimination, oppression, and injustice.

Principles of Alien Rights in Universal Law

In order to address the rights of aliens within the universal law framework, several key principles need to be considered:

1. **Equality:** All beings, regardless of their planetary origin, should be treated as equals under the law. This principle ensures that aliens are afforded the same rights and protections as any other sentient being.

2. **Non-Discrimination:** Alien rights should be free from any form of discrimination based on their species, appearance, or planetary affiliation. This principle guarantees that aliens are not subject to unjust treatment or prejudice.

3. **Inclusion:** The universal law should encompass aliens and recognize their rights as an integral part of the legal framework. Inclusion ensures that aliens have a voice and representation in matters that affect them.

4. **Self-Determination:** Aliens should have the right to determine their own destiny and make autonomous decisions regarding their lives, just as any other sentient being. This principle supports the idea that aliens should have agency and control over their own existence.

Challenges in Addressing Alien Rights

Addressing alien rights in universal law presents several challenges due to the unique nature of extraterrestrial life and the complexities of interstellar relations. Some of the key challenges are:

1. **Legal Definitions:** Defining aliens within the legal framework can be challenging, as they may have different biological, physical, and cultural characteristics compared to terrestrial beings. Establishing inclusive and comprehensive definitions is essential for effective legal protection.

2. **Jurisdiction and Governance:** Determining which governing bodies or interplanetary organizations have the authority to enforce and protect alien rights is a significant challenge. Cooperation and collaboration between different planetary jurisdictions are crucial in addressing this issue.

3. **Cultural Sensitivities:** Understanding and respecting the diverse cultural backgrounds of alien civilizations is essential in ensuring their rights are protected. Cultural sensitivities must be taken into account when defining and implementing universal laws.

4. **Interplanetary Relations:** Negotiating and navigating the complex web of interplanetary relations can pose challenges in establishing consistent and enforceable alien rights. Diplomatic efforts and interplanetary treaties are vital in creating a cohesive legal framework.

Strategies for Addressing Alien Rights

To effectively address alien rights, various strategies can be employed within the universal law framework:

1. **Legislative Reforms:** Governments and interplanetary organizations should enact legislation that explicitly recognizes and protects the rights of aliens. These laws should be comprehensive, inclusive, and aligned with the principles of universal law.

2. **Educational Initiatives:** Promoting awareness and understanding of alien rights through educational initiatives can contribute to a more inclusive and tolerant society. Educational programs should foster empathy, respect, and appreciation for the diverse cultures and backgrounds of aliens.

3. **Advocacy and Activism:** Civil society organizations and activists play a crucial role in advocating for alien rights. By raising awareness, lobbying for policy reforms, and mobilizing public support, they can bring about significant change and ensure the inclusion of aliens in universal law.

4. **International Cooperation:** Interplanetary organizations and diplomatic efforts are essential in fostering international cooperation to address alien rights. By facilitating dialogue, consensus-building, and the sharing of best practices, such cooperation can lead to the development of comprehensive legal frameworks.

5. **Transparency and Accountability:** Establishing mechanisms for transparency and accountability within the legal framework is vital. Regular reviews of alien rights laws, reporting mechanisms, and independent oversight bodies can ensure compliance and address any violations.

Case Study: The Intergalactic Alien Rights Convention

The Intergalactic Alien Rights Convention (IARC) serves as an example of a comprehensive legal framework designed to address alien rights. The IARC was established through a collaboration of interplanetary organizations and provides a platform for the recognition and protection of alien rights.

Under the IARC, member planets commit to upholding the principles of equality, non-discrimination, inclusion, and self-determination for all sentient beings. The convention establishes an interplanetary court to adjudicate cases related to alien rights violations and ensures the enforcement of its provisions through collectively agreed-upon sanctions.

The IARC also emphasizes the importance of education and cultural exchange programs to foster understanding and acceptance among different alien civilizations. By promoting dialogue and cooperation, the convention aims to build stronger interplanetary relations and ensure the long-term protection of alien rights.

Conclusion

Addressing alien rights in universal law is a complex yet indispensable task. By establishing a legal framework that upholds the principles of equality, non-discrimination, inclusion, and self-determination, we can ensure the protection and recognition of the rights of all sentient beings, irrespective of their planetary origin. Through legislative reforms, educational initiatives, advocacy, international cooperation, and accountability mechanisms, we can strive towards a future where alien rights are fully integrated into the universal law framework, fostering an inclusive and just interstellar society.

Remember, the journey to upholding alien rights does not end with legislation. It requires continuous effort, dialogue, and a commitment to challenging and evolving societal norms. Together, we can create a universe where every sentient being is treated with dignity, respect, and equality.

Subsection: The Transformative Power of Policy Change

In the fight for alien civil rights, there is no denying the transformative power of policy change. While activism and grassroots efforts lay the foundation for societal shifts, it is through the implementation of tangible policies that long-lasting change is achieved. In this subsection, we will explore the importance of policy change in the struggle for equality, the strategies employed by activists, and the impact of policy reforms on alien communities.

Policy Change: An Essential Tool

Policy change serves as a crucial tool in addressing systemic injustices and promoting equality. It is through policies that laws are created, regulations are established, and resources are allocated. In the context of alien civil rights, policy change enables the dismantling of discriminatory practices, protection of alien rights, and the promotion of inclusion.

Activists understand that the existing legal framework often perpetuates inequality and discrimination. They advocate for policy changes that are inclusive, comprehensive, and equitable, challenging existing laws that hinder alien rights and demanding new policies that protect their fundamental freedoms.

The Role of Advocacy and Lobbying

Advocacy and lobbying play a significant role in pushing for policy change. Activists mobilize to shape public opinion, educate lawmakers, and influence the legislative process. They form alliances with like-minded organizations and individuals, harnessing collective power to demand change.

Strategies such as grassroots organizing, public awareness campaigns, and direct engagement with policymakers are employed to create momentum and generate support. Activists leverage their voices, sharing personal stories, and utilizing social media platforms to raise awareness and gather public support for policy reforms.

Collaboration with Lawmakers

Collaboration with lawmakers is essential in effecting policy change. Activists engage in dialogue with legislators, forging relationships that enable them to advocate for their cause effectively. This collaboration allows activists to provide input on proposed legislation, highlight the needs of alien communities, and offer alternative policy solutions.

By working hand in hand with lawmakers, activists can shape legislation that prioritizes alien rights, challenges discriminatory practices, and fosters inclusivity. They provide lawmakers with evidence-based research, expert testimonies, and real-world examples to support their policy proposals.

Addressing Systemic Injustices

Policy change is not limited to specific issues but aims to address systemic injustices that perpetuate discrimination against aliens. It involves identifying the barriers that hinder alien integration, such as employment discrimination, limited access to education and healthcare, and the denial of political participation.

Through policy reforms, activists seek to break down these barriers and create a more inclusive society. They advocate for equal employment opportunities, healthcare access, and education policies that promote diversity and cultural understanding. Additionally, they push for reforms that grant aliens the right to vote and participate in decision-making processes.

Implementing Reforms: Challenges and Opportunities

While policy change is a powerful tool, its implementation can present challenges. Resistance from those who oppose equal rights, bureaucratic hurdles, and political pressure are often encountered during the implementation process. However, these challenges also present opportunities for strategic advocacy and public mobilization.

Activists must remain resilient and adaptive in navigating these challenges. They continue to push for accountability and monitor the implementation of policy reforms. By actively engaging in the process, they ensure that the intended positive impacts of policy changes are realized in practice.

Unconventional Approach: Creative Activism

To further amplify the transformative power of policy change, some activists employ unconventional approaches that harness creativity and artistry. Creative activism uses art, music, poetry, and performance to convey messages, capture attention, and create emotional connections. Through these expressions of resistance, activists can challenge deeply entrenched biases and inspire societal change.

Creative activism not only captures public interest but also serves as a powerful tool for policy advocacy. It humanizes the experiences of aliens, demanding empathy and understanding from policymakers and the wider public. By incorporating creativity into their activism, advocates can make policy change a more tangible and relatable concept for all.

Conclusion

In the struggle for alien civil rights, policy change holds transformative power. It serves as a vital tool for dismantling existing discriminatory frameworks, ensuring equitable access to rights and opportunities, and establishing a more inclusive society. Through advocacy, collaboration with lawmakers, and creative activism, activists champion policy reforms that address systemic injustices and pave the way for a future of equality and justice for all. By harnessing the power of policy change, the legacy of Aerin Zor and the fight for alien civil rights continue to shape the path toward a more just and inclusive universe.

Subsection: Creating a Seat at the Table for All

In the fight for alien civil rights, one of the key goals is to create a society where everyone has a seat at the table. This means ensuring that all individuals, regardless of their alien identity, have equal representation and influence in decision-making processes. By doing so, we can build a truly inclusive and diverse society that values the contributions and perspectives of every member.

To achieve this goal, it is crucial to address the barriers that prevent equal representation and participation. Here, we will explore some strategies and approaches to create a seat at the table for all.

Breaking Down Systemic Barriers

Systemic barriers contribute to the underrepresentation of alien voices and perspectives in decision-making processes. These barriers can be economic, social, or political in nature. It is essential to identify and dismantle these barriers to create a more inclusive society.

One example of a systemic barrier is the unequal distribution of resources and opportunities. Alien individuals from marginalized communities often face limited access to education, healthcare, and employment. By advocating for policies that promote equal access to these resources, we can remove barriers and create a level playing field for all.

Another systemic barrier is discrimination and bias. Prejudice against alien individuals can prevent them from participating fully in society and can hinder their ability to hold positions of influence. Working towards the eradication of discrimination through education, awareness campaigns, and policy change is critical to creating an inclusive society.

Promoting Representation in Governance

A vital strategy for creating a seat at the table for all is to ensure that alien individuals are represented in governance structures. This can be achieved through various means such as:

1. Alien Representation Quotas: Implementing quotas or affirmative action policies that mandate a certain percentage of alien representation in political offices can help address historical underrepresentation. These policies can be effective in

ensuring that the voices of alien individuals are heard and considered in decision-making processes.

2. Outreach and Engagement: Actively engaging and involving alien communities in political processes is essential for promoting representation. This can be done through community forums, town halls, and public consultations, where alien individuals have the opportunity to voice their concerns, ideas, and solutions. Political leaders should also make a concerted effort to listen to and understand the unique needs and perspectives of alien communities.

3. Alien Political Empowerment: Empowering alien individuals to enter politics and run for office is crucial in promoting representation. Providing support and resources for alien individuals who aspire to pursue political careers can help bridge the gap and encourage their participation. Initiatives such as mentoring programs, leadership training, and funding for alien-led campaigns can be effective tools to promote their political empowerment.

Creating Inclusive Policies

Creating inclusive policies is another essential aspect of creating a seat at the table for all. It involves crafting legislation and regulations that address the specific needs and challenges faced by alien individuals while promoting fairness and equity.

1. Alien Employment Rights: Alien individuals often face discrimination and challenges in the workplace. Implementing policies that protect against workplace discrimination, ensure fair hiring and promotion practices, and address issues like wage gaps can help create a more inclusive and equal workforce.

2. Accessible Education: Equal access to quality education is fundamental in fostering equal opportunities for all. Policies that address the barriers faced by alien students, such as language barriers and cultural bias, can help create an inclusive educational environment that supports their success.

3. Cultural Sensitivity and Awareness: Promoting cultural sensitivity and awareness through policies and programs is essential in creating an inclusive society. This can include initiatives like diversity training, cultural exchange programs, and the integration of alien perspectives into educational curricula. By fostering understanding and appreciation for diverse cultures, we can build a more inclusive and harmonious society.

Building Collaborative Partnerships

Creating a seat at the table for all requires collaboration and partnerships between different stakeholders. Governments, non-governmental organizations, community leaders, and alien individuals must work together to drive change and create an inclusive society.

1. Collaboration between Alien Communities: Encouraging collaboration and unity among alien communities is crucial for collective empowerment. By forming networks, sharing resources, and supporting each other's causes, alien communities can amplify their voices and create a united front for change.

2. Partnerships with Civil Society Organizations: Engaging with civil society organizations that advocate for alien rights is essential in driving change. These organizations often have the expertise, resources, and networks to push for policy change and raise awareness about alien civil rights issues.

3. Allies and Solidarity from Non-Alien Communities: Building alliances and solidarity with non-alien communities is essential in creating a seat at the table for all. Non-alien individuals and communities can use their privilege and influence to support alien individuals, amplify their voices, and advocate for their rights.

Creating a seat at the table for all is a complex and ongoing process. It requires addressing systemic barriers, promoting representation in governance and decision-making, implementing inclusive policies, and building collaborative partnerships. By working together and recognizing the value of diversity, we can create a society that celebrates and embraces the contributions of all its members, regardless of their alien identity.

Remember, the fight for alien civil rights is not just about alien individuals; it is about creating a more just and equitable society for everyone. So let's come together and continue the journey towards a galactic utopia where all beings have a seat at the table.

Section 5: A Vision for a Galactic Utopia

Subsection: Imagining a Universe of Equality

In this subsection, we explore the concept of a universe where equality is not just a dream but a reality. Imagine a world where individuals of all species and backgrounds are treated with fairness and respect, where discrimination, prejudice, and inequality are distant memories. This vision might seem utopian, but it is within our reach if we work together, challenge our existing belief systems, and actively advocate for change.

To imagine a universe of equality, we must first recognize the deep-rooted structures that perpetuate inequality. Inequality exists on multiple levels, from systemic oppression within societies to interpersonal bias and discrimination.

These inequalities manifest in various forms, such as social, economic, and political disparities. To dismantle these systems, we need a deep understanding of the underlying causes and work towards addressing them.

One of the fundamental steps towards achieving equality is recognizing and valuing diversity. The beauty of the universe lies in its incredible diversity of species, cultures, and perspectives. Embracing this diversity and empowering marginalized communities can create a foundation for equality. By elevating the voices of those who have been historically marginalized, we can address the power imbalances that perpetuate inequality.

Education plays a pivotal role in shaping the future generations and fostering a culture of equality. Educational institutions need to provide inclusive learning environments that appreciate and celebrate different cultures, abilities, and identities. By teaching empathy, understanding, and tolerance, we can shape individuals who are committed to equality and justice.

A universe of equality also requires dismantling gender-based discrimination and promoting gender equality. This involves challenging traditional gender roles and norms that restrict individuals' potential based on their gender identity. By embracing gender diversity and empowering all forms of gender expression, we can create a society where everyone has the freedom to be their authentic selves.

Moreover, addressing socioeconomic disparities is crucial in building a universe of equality. Income inequality and lack of access to resources can perpetuate cycles of poverty and hinder individuals' opportunities for growth. By implementing redistributive policies, providing equal access to education, healthcare, and employment opportunities, we can ensure that everyone has an equal chance to thrive.

Creating a universe of equality also involves addressing environmental justice. Recognizing that environmental issues disproportionately affect marginalized communities is essential. By advocating for sustainable practices and bridging the gap between environmental conservation and social justice, we can create a fair and equitable future for all beings.

To make this vision a reality, we must challenge our own biases and prejudices. Each of us has a role to play in promoting equality, both within ourselves and in society at large. It starts with self-reflection, being willing to unlearn harmful beliefs, and actively seeking out opportunities to learn from and engage with diverse perspectives and experiences.

While imagining a universe of equality is undoubtedly inspiring, it is essential to acknowledge the challenges that lie ahead. More often than not, change is met with resistance, and progress can be slow. However, by standing together, persevering,

CHAPTER 2: BEYOND VELAN-7: THE INTERGALACTIC MOVEMENT

and never losing sight of our shared vision, we can overcome these obstacles and create a better future.

In conclusion, imagining a universe of equality is not merely a flight of fancy but a necessary endeavor. It requires dismantling existing systems of oppression, promoting inclusivity and diversity, addressing socioeconomic disparities, and challenging our own biases. By actively working towards equality, we can pave the way for a future where all beings, regardless of their species or background, can thrive and coexist harmoniously. Let us dare to dream of this universe and work tirelessly to make it a reality.

Subsection: Art as a Catalyst for Change

Art has always been a powerful tool for expressing emotions, sharing ideas, and inspiring change. And in the fight for alien civil rights, art played a central role in creating awareness, fostering empathy, and mobilizing the masses. In this subsection, we explore how art became a catalyst for change in the intergalactic movement led by Aerin Zor.

The Power of Visual Arts

Visual arts, such as paintings, sculptures, and photography, have a unique ability to transcend language barriers and connect with people on a deep emotional level. Artists like Zara Kael, a renowned Velanian painter, used their brushes to portray the struggles of the bi-entity fusion community on Velan-7. Through vivid colors, bold strokes, and intricate details, Zara captured the essence of their experiences, showcasing their humanity and the injustice they faced.

One of her notable works, "Beyond Boundaries," depicted a powerful image of a bi-entity fusion and a human holding hands, symbolizing unity and acceptance. This painting, displayed in galleries across the galaxy, became a symbol of hope and solidarity for activists fighting for alien rights.

Art installations were also instrumental in raising awareness and sparking conversations. In one memorable piece, titled "In Their Shoes," sculptor Rennan Jae crafted a series of shoes representing various alien species, each with a story of discrimination and resilience attached to it. Visitors to the exhibit were encouraged to walk in these shoes, literally and metaphorically, fostering empathy and understanding for the experiences of others.

SECTION 5: A VISION FOR A GALACTIC UTOPIA

The Role of Performance Arts

The stage became a powerful platform for alien activists to share their stories and challenge societal norms. Theatrical productions, spoken word performances, and dance routines became mediums through which marginalized voices were amplified.

The play "Fusion Dreams," written by Rhea Patel, depicted the journey of a bi-entity fusion on their path to self-acceptance and social equality. The powerful dialogue and compelling performances touched the hearts of audiences, leaving lasting impressions and igniting conversations about prejudice and discrimination.

Spoken word performances, known for their rawness and emotional impact, allowed alien activists to authentically express their frustrations, hopes, and dreams. Talented poets like Jaxon Blair used their words to dismantle stereotypes and advocate for change. Lines such as "Our souls intertwine, both celestial and fine" resonated with audiences across the cosmos, encouraging them to question their biases and embrace diversity.

The Integration of Technology

In the digital era, technology played a crucial role in amplifying artistic endeavors. Social media platforms became virtual galleries, enabling artists to reach a global audience and spark conversations on a massive scale.

Hashtag campaigns, such as #AlienRightsMatter and #CoexistenceRevolution, trended across multiple planets, bringing attention to the struggles faced by alien communities. Artists and activists collaborated to create powerful digital artwork, infographics, and memes that went viral, spreading awareness and challenging societal norms.

Virtual reality experiences allowed individuals to step into the shoes of aliens and experience firsthand the discrimination they encountered. Through immersive storytelling, virtual reality artists like Lila Rodriguez transported viewers into the lives of bi-entity fusions, evoking empathy and inspiring action.

The Intersection of Art and Activism

Art and activism became inseparable partners in the intergalactic movement. Artists were not just creators but active participants in the fight for equality.

Art collectives, such as "Cosmic Harmony," brought together artists from diverse backgrounds to collaborate on projects that challenged prejudice and xenophobia. By combining their artistic talents, they created thought-provoking exhibitions, murals, and performances that sparked conversations and united communities.

CHAPTER 2: BEYOND VELAN-7: THE INTERGALACTIC MOVEMENT

Beyond traditional art forms, artists experimented with unconventional mediums to convey their messages. Bio-artist Kara Jensen used genetic engineering techniques to create a series of genetically modified plants that represented the interconnectedness of all species in the universe. These living artworks, displayed in botanical gardens across galaxies, served as reminders of the need for harmony and respect amongst all beings.

Unconventional Solution: The Artivist Collective

To further integrate art and activism, Aerin Zor founded the Artivist Collective, an organization dedicated to empowering artists to become agents of change. The collective provided resources, mentorship, and funding to artists who wanted to use their creativity to address social justice issues.

The Artivist Collective organized workshops where artists learned how to effectively communicate their messages through their artwork. They also facilitated collaborations between artists and activists, recognizing the power of combining artistic expression with grassroots activism.

Through their innovative approach, the Artivist Collective elevated the role of artists in the movement, giving them a platform to create meaningful change.

Exercises

1. Choose a social justice issue in your community or world and use an artistic medium of your choice to create a piece that raises awareness and promotes dialogue about the issue. Consider the emotions, symbols, and messages you want to convey through your artwork.

2. Research an alien artist who has used their work to advocate for change. Write a short essay exploring their artistic style, the issues they address, and the impact of their artwork on the movement for alien civil rights.

Resources

1. "The Art of Activism: A Guide to Using Art for Social Change" by Sarah A. Calderon 2. "Art as Social Action: An Introduction to the Principles and Practices of Teaching Social Practice Art" by Gregory Sholette and Chloë Bass 3. "The Intersectional Internet: Race, Sex, Class, and Culture Online" edited by Safiya Umoja Noble and Brendesha M. Tynes

SECTION 5: A VISION FOR A GALACTIC UTOPIA

Key Takeaways

- Art has the power to transcend boundaries and foster empathy. - Visual arts, performance arts, and technology can be used to ignite conversations, challenge societal norms, and promote social justice. - Artists are not just creators but active participants in the fight for equality. - The Artivist Collective empowers artists to become agents of change.

Art in all its forms has the ability to inspire, challenge, and create change. By harnessing the power of artistic expression, the intergalactic movement led by Aerin Zor was able to touch hearts, break down barriers, and bring the universe one step closer to a utopia of equality and coexistence. As we continue to honor their legacy, may we never forget the transformative power of art, and may we continue to use it as a catalyst for change in our own lives and communities.

Subsection: The Erasure of Boundaries

In the cosmic era, the concept of boundaries has taken on a whole new meaning. Traditionally, boundaries have served as markers of separation, dividing one entity from another. However, as the universe becomes more interconnected, there is a growing movement towards the erasure of these boundaries. This subsection explores the significance of eliminating boundaries and the impact it has on coexistence and celebration of diversity.

Cosmic Unity: Breaking Down Walls

The erasure of boundaries goes beyond physical separations, aiming to dissolve the barriers that divide different beings in the universe. It advocates for acceptance and inclusivity, promoting the idea that all entities, regardless of their origins, are equal and deserving of respect. This cosmic unity recognizes the inherent interconnectedness of all life forms, fostering a sense of empathy and understanding.

Redefining Identity: Embracing Multiculturalism

By erasing boundaries, the rigid definitions of identity that once defined individuals are challenged. The emphasis shifts from an exclusive focus on one's own identity to an appreciation of the diverse cultures and perspectives that shape the universe. This redefinition allows individuals to embrace their rich heritage while also celebrating and learning from others.

CHAPTER 2: BEYOND VELAN-7: THE INTERGALACTIC MOVEMENT

Interplanetary Cooperation: A Galactic Mosaic

The erasure of boundaries paves the way for interplanetary cooperation and collaboration. When beings from different planets come together, they bring their unique strengths and perspectives, creating a vibrant galactic mosaic. This collaboration extends beyond cultural exchange and enriches fields such as science, art, and technology. By working together, entities can achieve groundbreaking advancements that benefit the entire universe.

Overcoming Prejudice: Challenging Stereotypes

One of the most significant outcomes of the erasure of boundaries is the dismantling of prejudice and the challenging of stereotypes. As entities interact and learn from each other, misconceptions and biases are debunked. The focus shifts from fear and ignorance to open-mindedness and acceptance. The erasure of boundaries creates an environment where individuals can be appreciated for their unique qualities rather than judged based on preconceived notions.

Empathy and Compassion: The Pillars of Unity

Empathy and compassion are the pillars upon which the erasure of boundaries rests. When individuals recognize the shared experiences and emotions of others, they naturally gravitate towards unity. By embracing empathy, beings foster a sense of interconnectedness, allowing for a deeper understanding of others' struggles and triumphs. This empathy serves as the foundation for the erasure of boundaries and the creation of a more harmonious universe.

A Shared Destiny: Looking Towards the Future

As the erasure of boundaries takes hold, a shared destiny emerges. Beings across the universe begin to see themselves as part of a larger cosmic community, working together towards a common goal. With the boundaries dissolved, the possibilities for collaboration and coexistence become endless. This shared destiny inspires entities to strive for a future where unity and equality prevail.

In summary, the erasure of boundaries is a transformative movement that redefines how entities in the universe perceive themselves and others. It promotes cosmic unity, celebrates multiculturalism, fosters interplanetary cooperation, challenges prejudice, and emphasizes empathy and compassion. By embracing the erasure of boundaries, the universe moves closer to a future where diversity is celebrated, and all beings can coexist in harmony.

Subsection: Coexistence and Celebration of Diversity

In the intergalactic movement for alien civil rights, Aerin Zor championed not only equality but also the celebration of diversity and the importance of coexistence. This subsection delves into the significance of these principles and offers insights into how they can be embraced and fostered in the cosmic era.

The Power of Acceptance

Coexistence starts with acceptance - accepting that the universe is an intricate tapestry of diverse beings, each with their own unique qualities, experiences, and perspectives. It is in this acceptance that we can begin to appreciate the beauty and richness that diversity brings to our lives.

Aerin Zor recognized that the path to true equality and unity lies in embracing and celebrating our differences rather than attempting to homogenize or erase them. By valuing the contributions and experiences of individuals from various planetary origins, cultures, and identities, we can create a more inclusive and harmonious cosmos.

Recognizing Intersectionality

To achieve true coexistence, it is crucial to acknowledge intersectionality - the interconnected nature of social identities and systems of oppression. Alien individuals, just like their human counterparts, embody a multitude of identities based on factors such as race, gender, class, and species.

Aerin Zor understood that promoting equality and celebration of diversity means dismantling all forms of discrimination and marginalization, both obvious and subtle. The struggles faced by individuals due to their multiple intersecting identities must be recognized and addressed for a more just and inclusive society to thrive.

Embracing Multiculturalism

Multiculturalism is at the heart of coexistence. It is the celebration of different cultural backgrounds, traditions, languages, and belief systems. Embracing multiculturalism means acknowledging that no one culture or way of life is superior to another. Instead, it emphasizes the richness and value that come from the mosaic of cultures coexisting and intertwining with one another.

In the cosmic era, civilizations from various corners of the universe have the opportunity to learn from and inspire each other. Aerin Zor emphasized the importance of fostering cultural exchange, encouraging dialogue, and promoting the preservation of indigenous alien knowledge, arts, and practices. Through cultural sharing, societies can grow and evolve together while honoring their distinct heritages.

Creating Inclusive Spaces

In the quest for coexistence and celebration of diversity, it is essential to create inclusive spaces where all beings feel welcome, respected, and valued. This can be achieved by:

- Implementing policies and practices that ensure equal opportunities for all individuals, regardless of their background or identity.

- Educating communities about the importance of diversity, inclusivity, and empathy.

- Promoting dialogue, understanding, and collaboration between different groups.

- Celebrating cultural festivals and events that showcase the richness of diverse traditions.

- Incorporating diverse perspectives in decision-making processes.

By actively working towards inclusivity and fostering environments that celebrate diversity, societies can break down barriers, create stronger connections, and collectively thrive as a galactic community.

The Power of Art

Art has always played a pivotal role in challenging societal norms and inspiring change. In the pursuit of coexistence and celebration of diversity, art serves as a powerful catalyst. It has the ability to transcend language barriers and touch the depths of emotions.

Aerin Zor recognized the transformative power of art and encouraged the creation and exploration of artistic expressions that promote dialogue, challenge stereotypes, and celebrate diversity. Through various art forms such as music, visual arts, dance, and literature, artists have the ability to shape narratives, convey messages of unity, and inspire societies to embrace a more inclusive future.

Championing Representation

True celebration of diversity requires equitable representation across all spheres of life, including governance, media, and social institutions. It is vital for alien communities to participate actively in decision-making processes, ensuring their voices are heard and their interests are represented.

Aerin Zor campaigned for increased representation of marginalized communities, advocating for the inclusion of diverse perspectives and experiences in the shaping of policies and practices. By championing representation, societies can move closer to achieving a more just, inclusive, and equitable cosmos.

Unconventional Yet Relevant: The Galactic Diversity Olympics

As an unconventional yet relevant approach to fostering coexistence and celebrating diversity, the idea of organizing the Galactic Diversity Olympics has gained momentum in recent years. Modelled after the traditional human Olympics, this event would bring together beings from all corners of the universe to compete, collaborate, and celebrate their unique abilities and talents.

The Galactic Diversity Olympics would not only serve as a platform for showcasing the diversity and talent within the cosmos but also as an opportunity to promote understanding, forge connections, and break down barriers. By highlighting the achievements of individuals from diverse backgrounds, this event could inspire future generations and create a lasting legacy of unity and inclusivity.

Conclusion

Coexistence and the celebration of diversity are essential pillars of the intergalactic movement for alien civil rights. Aerin Zor's vision emphasized the power of acceptance, the recognition of intersectionality, the embrace of multiculturalism, the creation of inclusive spaces, the transformative power of art, and the importance of representation. By embracing these principles and nurturing a culture that values and celebrates diversity, societies can pave the way for a brighter, more inclusive cosmic future.

CHAPTER 2: BEYOND VELAN-7: THE INTERGALACTIC MOVEMENT

Subsection: Inspiring the Next Generation

As Aerin Zor's legacy continues to resonate throughout the cosmos, one of the most profound effects of their activism is the inspiration it has instilled in the next generation of alien rights advocates. In this subsection, we will explore the ways in which Aerin Zor's life and work continue to motivate and empower young activists, fostering a new era of solidarity and progress.

Nurturing Empathy and Compassion

Aerin Zor's tireless dedication to justice and equality serves as a powerful example for young people, encouraging them to develop a deep sense of empathy and compassion for others. In their journey, Aerin Zor demonstrated how understanding and acknowledging the experiences of alien beings is essential to the fight for civil rights. To inspire the next generation, educational programs and initiatives can be established to teach empathy and compassion as fundamental values.

For example, schools across the universe can introduce curricula that explore diverse cultures and promote dialogue on issues related to alien rights. This could include incorporating literature, art, and history from different galactic civilizations, allowing students to deepen their understanding of the challenges faced by marginalized alien groups. By nurturing empathy and compassion from an early age, young minds can begin to grasp the importance of solidarity and equality.

Providing Mentorship and Support

To inspire the next generation of activists, it is crucial to provide mentorship and support networks tailored to their unique needs. Alien youth who are passionate about civil rights advocacy should have access to mentors who can guide and support them in their journey.

One possible approach is the establishment of mentorship programs where experienced activists and leaders in the field can connect with young aspiring activists. Through regular meetings, workshops, and guidance, these mentors can offer valuable insights, share personal experiences, and provide practical advice on navigating the challenges of activism. By fostering close relationships with experienced advocates, young activists gain the confidence and knowledge necessary to continue the struggle for equality and justice.

Encouraging Creative Expression

Art has always played a crucial role in social movements, and inspiring the next generation of activists is no exception. By encouraging creative expression, young aliens can explore their unique voices and perspectives, contributing to the ongoing fight for equality.

Artistic events, such as intergalactic festivals and exhibitions, can provide platforms for young activists to showcase their talents and express their thoughts and feelings about civil rights and social justice. These events can encompass a wide range of artistic mediums, including music, visual arts, dance, theater, and literature. By encouraging creative expression, young aliens can convey powerful messages that resonate with audiences and inspire further action.

Promoting Intersectionality and Inclusivity

Aerin Zor's activism was rooted in the belief that true equality and justice can only be achieved through intersectionality and inclusivity. To inspire the next generation, it is essential to promote an understanding of the interconnected nature of oppression and to foster an inclusive environment that celebrates diversity.

Educational institutions, community organizations, and advocacy groups can collaborate to create spaces where young activists can learn about the diverse struggles faced by different alien communities. By engaging in dialogue and collaboration across identities and experiences, young activists can develop a holistic understanding of social justice issues. This approach ensures that the fight for equality is not limited to one particular group but encompasses the liberation of all marginalized beings.

Utilizing Technology for Change

In the age of interstellar communication and advanced technology, inspiring the next generation of activists also entails harnessing the power of digital platforms and social media. Online spaces offer powerful tools for connecting, organizing, and amplifying voices demanding change.

Virtual networks and online communities can be created to facilitate conversations on alien rights and empower young activists to collaborate across galaxies. These platforms can provide resources, share success stories, and mobilize collective action. Encouraging young activists to use technology responsibly and thoughtfully can help them build connections, organize protests, and raise awareness about the ongoing struggle for equality.

CHAPTER 2: BEYOND VELAN-7: THE INTERGALACTIC MOVEMENT

Unconventional Approach: The Cosmic Change Challenge

To inject an element of excitement and encourage the next generation to actively engage in the fight for alien civil rights, a unique initiative called the Cosmic Change Challenge can be established. Inspired by Aerin Zor's groundbreaking work, this challenge would invite young aliens to propose innovative solutions to the persistent problems and inequalities faced by marginalized communities.

Participants would be encouraged to think creatively and offer unconventional ideas that challenge the existing systems of oppression. The Cosmic Change Challenge would provide a platform for young aliens to present their proposals and receive support, funding, and mentoring to turn their ideas into impactful projects. By nurturing young minds and amplifying their voices through this initiative, the fight for equality would gain fresh energy and innovation.

Conclusion

Inspiring the next generation of activists is crucial in ensuring the perpetuity of the fight for alien civil rights. By nurturing empathy, providing mentorship, encouraging creative expression, promoting intersectionality, utilizing technology, and exploring unique initiatives like the Cosmic Change Challenge, young minds can be empowered to drive meaningful change in the quest for equality and justice.

Aerin Zor's remarkable journey serves as a beacon of hope, illuminating the path to a future where all beings, regardless of their origins, can coexist harmoniously in a truly equal universe. With the torch of inspiration passed down to the next generation, the dream of a galactic utopia becomes ever closer to reality.

Chapter 3: The Personal Side of Aerin Zor

Section 1: Love and Interspecies Relationships

Subsection: Breaking the Taboos of Intergalactic Romance

Love knows no bounds, they say. But what happens when love transcends not just physical borders, but the vast expanse of space itself? In this subsection, we explore the taboo world of intergalactic romance and the challenges faced by those who dared to defy the boundaries of conventional relationships.

The Mystique of Interstellar Love

In the cosmic tapestry of the universe, love finds a way to weave its magic across the stars. Interstellar love, though rare, holds a special place in the hearts of those who dare to venture beyond their home planets. It is a beacon of hope that surpasses racial, cultural, and planetary differences.

However, intergalactic romance is often subjected to prejudice and discrimination. Interspecies relationships challenge the norms and traditions ingrained in alien societies. The fear of the unknown and the clash of cultural values can lead to societal disapproval and personal conflicts.

Navigating Uncharted Affections

The path to intergalactic love is fraught with unique challenges. Communication barriers, societal biases, and legal complexities make it a treacherous journey. Couples from different worlds must confront their own prejudices and those of their families and societies.

One major obstacle is the difference in physiological and psychological traits between species. Alien beings may possess physiological features that are unfamiliar or even repulsive to other species. Overcoming these initial aversions requires open-mindedness, empathy, and a willingness to embrace the unknown.

Legal Quandaries and Social Backlash

Interstellar relationships face legal and social hurdles. Many planets have strict laws that prohibit interspecies unions, citing concerns over genetic compatibility and cultural preservation. Furthermore, societal prejudice often rears its ugly head, leading to isolation, discrimination, and even violence against intergalactic couples.

To challenge these barriers, activists like Aerin Zor fought for the recognition of interspecies relationships, pushing for the repeal of discriminatory laws and advocating for universal acceptance and understanding. Their efforts paved the way for legal reforms and the normalization of intergalactic love.

Shattering Stereotypes and Bridging Divides

Intergalactic relationships have the power to challenge deep-rooted prejudices and bridge cultural divides. The mere existence of these relationships serves as a testament to the possibility of harmony and cooperation among diverse species.

A thriving intergalactic romance challenges the narrative of "us versus them" and instead paints a picture of unity in diversity. It sparks conversations and promotes mutual understanding that extends beyond the realm of love, permeating other aspects of social interaction and global cooperation.

Confronting the Challenges

Breaking the taboos of intergalactic romance requires bravery, perseverance, and a commitment to love in the face of adversity. To navigate these challenges, couples can turn to support groups and organizations that provide guidance, legal assistance, and emotional support.

Educational initiatives aimed at promoting cultural exchange and understanding can play a vital role in challenging stereotypes and fostering acceptance. Sharing personal stories and experiences can humanize intergalactic relationships and help dispel myths and misconceptions.

SECTION 1: LOVE AND INTERSPECIES RELATIONSHIPS

Embracing a New Frontier

As humanity continues to explore the mysteries of the universe, intergalactic romance will undoubtedly become more prevalent. By embracing these relationships, we can build a future where love knows no planetary boundaries, and where diversity is celebrated rather than feared.

In the vast expanse of the cosmos, love serves as a powerful force that transcends barriers and unites beings from different worlds. By breaking the taboos of intergalactic romance, we pave the way for a future where love truly conquers all.

Conclusion

Intergalactic romance is a testament to the boundless nature of love and the universal desire for connection and companionship. Breaking the taboos surrounding these relationships is not only a personal triumph but also a step towards a more inclusive and understanding universe.

As the fight for acceptance continues, it is crucial to celebrate the successes and learn from the challenges faced by intergalactic couples. By doing so, we can build a society where love is not limited by the laws of physics or societal norms, but rather fueled by the unyielding human spirit. Love truly has no boundaries, not even those of the cosmos.

Subsection: The Extraordinary Love Story of Aerin Zor

Love has always been a powerful force that transcends boundaries, but for Aerin Zor, it took on a truly extraterrestrial form. Aerin's extraordinary love story challenged not only societal norms but also the very fabric of intergalactic relationships. It is a tale of acceptance, perseverance, and the transformative power of love.

Aerin Zor's path to love was a bumpy one, filled with obstacles and prejudice. In a universe where intergalactic romance was often met with skepticism and even hostility, Aerin dared to defy the odds. As an activist fighting for alien civil rights, Aerin knew the immense value of love as a catalyst for change.

Intergalactic Prejudice: The Barrier to Love

The cosmic landscape was marked by deep-rooted interplanetary prejudice. Alien species were often segregated and discriminated against, making it challenging for individuals to form connections beyond their own kind. This prejudice extended to romantic relationships, as many societies did not recognize or condone interspecies love.

Aerin's love interest, Halis, belonged to a species that had long been at odds with her own. Their love faced resistance from both sides as families, communities, and even governments rejected their relationship. It was a battle against not only societal expectations but also ingrained prejudices that had shaped the cosmos for generations.

Love Overcoming Boundaries

Despite the challenges they faced, Aerin and Halis refused to let prejudice define their love. They recognized the power of connection and empathy, embracing their shared values and captivating personalities that transcended their physical differences.

Their love story became a beacon of hope for those seeking to challenge the status quo. Aerin and Halis showed the universe that love knew no borders, no matter how vast and complex they may be. Their unwavering dedication to each other became a symbol of resilience and the belief that love could conquer all.

A Journey of Acceptance

The path to acceptance was not an easy one for Aerin and Halis. They encountered setbacks, faced criticism, and endured personal struggles along the way. But they were committed to each other and to the larger cause of breaking down the barriers that divided their worlds.

Their journey of acceptance was not only about gaining the approval of others but also about accepting themselves. Both Aerin and Halis had to confront their own internalized prejudice and redefine their understanding of love. It was a process of self-discovery and growth that mirrored the larger struggle for equality and justice that Aerin fought for throughout her life.

Love as a Catalyst for Change

Aerin and Halis' love story became a potent symbol for the entire intergalactic civil rights movement. Their unwavering commitment to each other and to their shared vision of a more inclusive universe inspired countless others to challenge societal norms and fight for change.

Their love was not just a personal connection; it was a statement against oppression. Through their love, they highlighted the inherent value and worth of every being in the cosmos, regardless of their origin or physical form. Their love became a rallying cry for equality and a reminder that love, at its core, is a force that unites rather than divides.

Redefining Relationships in the Cosmic Era

Aerin and Halis' extraordinary love story had a profound impact on the way relationships were perceived in the cosmic era. It shattered preconceived notions and forced societies to reconsider their narrow definitions of love.

Their relationship challenged the notion that love could only exist within the confines of one's own species. They demonstrated that love could transcend physical differences and flourish in the face of adversity. Aerin and Halis paved the way for a new understanding of love that embraced diversity and celebrated the richness of intergalactic connections.

Embracing Love in the Cosmos

Aerin and Halis' love story was not just a personal triumph; it was a triumph for love itself. Their extraordinary journey opened the door for countless others to embrace love in all its forms, breaking free from the chains of prejudice and fear.

Their legacy serves as a reminder that love has the power to transform hearts, minds, and even the cosmos itself. By embracing love, we can create a universe that champions acceptance, understanding, and the celebration of diversity.

The love story of Aerin Zor and Halis stands as a testament to the extraordinary possibilities that await when we open our hearts to the beauty and power of love. Their story continues to inspire and ignite the flames of change, reminding us that love is the ultimate force that can bridge galaxies and shape the destiny of the cosmos.

Closing Thoughts

Love knows no boundaries, whether they are social, cultural, or intergalactic. The extraordinary love story of Aerin Zor and Halis serves as a poignant reminder that love can ignite change, challenge prejudice, and inspire a more equitable and inclusive universe. As activists and advocates, we can draw strength and inspiration from their story, knowing that love has the power to reshape the cosmos and pave the way for a brighter future for all beings. We must continue to fight for love, acceptance, and the dismantling of systemic prejudice, creating a universe where love thrives and thrives for all.

Subsection: The Journey of Acceptance

In this subsection, we delve into the personal journey of Aerin Zor as she navigates the challenging path of self-acceptance. This is a fundamental step in her transformation into an influential civil rights activist, driving her commitment to fight for equality and justice for all beings in the cosmos.

The Struggle with Otherness

Growing up in a universe where diversity is celebrated, Aerin was raised to honor and respect the identities and experiences of all individuals. However, she found herself grappling with her own sense of otherness. As an individual with a unique bi-entity fusion, she often felt like an outsider, struggling to fit in and find acceptance from others.

Aerin's journey to self-acceptance was not an easy one. Throughout her formative years, she faced prejudice and discrimination from individuals who failed to understand or appreciate her unique identity. The constant questioning of her worth and belonging took a toll on her self-esteem.

Confronting Internalized Prejudice

Like many individuals, Aerin internalized the negative narratives and stereotypes surrounding her identity. She questioned her place in the universe and doubted whether she could ever be truly accepted for who she was. These feelings of self-doubt became barriers that hindered her personal growth and potential.

Over time, Aerin recognized the importance of challenging her own internalized prejudices. She began to acknowledge her own worth, embracing her bi-entity fusion as a source of strength rather than a cause for shame. Through self-reflection and seeking support from loved ones and mentors, Aerin slowly dismantled the walls of self-doubt that had held her back for so long.

Embracing Individuality and Uniqueness

Aerin's journey of acceptance eventually led her to a profound realization: true liberation comes from embracing one's individuality and uniqueness. She understood that each person, alien, or entity brings a distinctive set of experiences and perspectives to the table.

With this newfound acceptance, Aerin began to celebrate her bi-entity fusion as a powerful symbol of unity and diversity. She recognized that her unique identity

SECTION 1: LOVE AND INTERSPECIES RELATIONSHIPS 159

not only contributed to her personal growth but also had the potential to inspire others.

The Power of Visibility

As Aerin embraced her identity, she recognized the importance of visibility in fostering acceptance and understanding. By openly sharing her own story and experiences, she aimed to break down the barriers of ignorance and prejudice that existed within her community and beyond.

Aerin's journey of acceptance became a beacon of hope for others who had also struggled with their own sense of otherness. Through her advocacy and activism, she amplified the voices of those who were marginalized and empowered them to embrace their own individuality.

Empathy and Compassion

An essential aspect of Aerin's journey of acceptance was the cultivation of empathy and compassion. She realized that by understanding and connecting with others, she could forge deeper relationships and bridge gaps in understanding.

Aerin actively sought out opportunities to engage in conversations with individuals from diverse backgrounds. Through these interactions, she not only learned about the struggles faced by others but also discovered commonalities that transcended differences.

Strength in Unity

As Aerin journeyed further on the path of acceptance, she recognized the strength that lies in unity. She understood that achieving true equality and justice required a collective effort from individuals of all backgrounds and identities.

Motivated by her own experiences and driven by a deep sense of empathy, Aerin actively worked to create spaces and platforms for people from different walks of life to come together. She championed collaboration and encouraged solidarity in the fight against prejudice and discrimination.

The Transformational Power of Acceptance

Aerin's journey of acceptance was transformative, not only for herself but also for the countless individuals she would go on to inspire. Her story serves as a powerful reminder that embracing one's identity and accepting others for who they are is an essential part of creating a more inclusive and just universe.

In conclusion, the journey of acceptance is a deeply personal and transformative experience. Aerin Zor's own path to self-acceptance fueled her passion for advocating for alien civil rights. Through her struggles and triumphs, she exemplifies the power of embracing individuality, cultivating empathy, and working towards unity. Let us all be inspired by her story as we continue our own journeys of acceptance and understanding.

Subsection: The Power Couple of the Cosmos

Love knows no boundaries, not even between species. In this subsection, we delve into the extraordinary love story of Aerin Zor and her partner, Zaraa Kallik. Together, they became known as the power couple of the cosmos, advocating for change and challenging societal norms in the fight for alien civil rights.

Aerin Zor and Zaraa Kallik's relationship spanned galaxies, breaking the taboos of intergalactic romance. Their love story captivated the universe as they defied the prejudices and restrictions imposed by traditional societal norms. They proved that love could transcend physical and cultural differences, serving as an inspiration for countless beings across the cosmos.

In their blossoming relationship, Aerin and Zaraa faced numerous challenges and hurdles. From overcoming the skepticism of their families to navigating the intricacies of dual identities, their journey was not without its share of difficulties. However, their unwavering love for one another gave them strength and determination to face whatever obstacles lay in their path.

Aerin and Zaraa's relationship went beyond personal fulfillment; it was a driving force for social change. As they fought for alien civil rights, they demonstrated the power of love in driving a movement forward. Their bond served as a beacon of hope for those who believed in the transformative power of unity and solidarity.

Their love story also exemplified the importance of intersectionality in activism. As individuals from different planets and backgrounds, Aerin and Zaraa understood the value of embracing diversity within their relationship and in the larger fight for equality. They recognized that true progress could only be achieved by addressing the interconnected struggles of all marginalized communities.

Aerin and Zaraa's relationship challenged conventional notions of what it meant to be a power couple. They showed that being a couple was not just about personal success and happiness; it was about using their platform and influence to amplify the voices of the oppressed. Together, they sparked conversations about love, identity, and the pursuit of a more just and inclusive cosmos.

Their love story also sparked a cultural shift in the perception of interspecies relationships. Through their advocacy and openness about their own union, Aerin and Zaraa shattered stereotypes and misconceptions. They encouraged others to embrace love in all its forms, regardless of the boundaries society might impose.

The power couple of the cosmos serves as a reminder that love knows no limits. Their story exemplifies the transformative power of love not only within a relationship but also on a societal level. It challenges us to question the norms and restrictions imposed by society and to strive for a future where love and acceptance prevail.

Their legacy lives on, inspiring future generations to challenge the status quo and fight for a more inclusive universe. Aerin and Zaraa's love story is a testament to the strength of the human spirit and the boundless possibilities that emerge when love becomes a catalyst for change.

So, let us celebrate the power couple of the cosmos, for their love ignited a revolution and left an indelible mark on the intergalactic struggle for equality and justice. Their love story reminds us that love has the power to transcend boundaries, create lasting change, and pave the way for a future where coexistence and celebration of diversity are the norm.

Subsection: Love as a Driving Force for Change

Love is a powerful and transformative force that has the potential to bring about profound change in the world. In the context of activism and fighting for civil rights, love plays a pivotal role in motivating individuals to stand up against injustice and work towards a more equitable and inclusive society.

At its core, love is about compassion, empathy, and understanding. It is about seeing the humanity in others, regardless of their background or identity. Love enables activists to connect deeply with the experiences and struggles of those who are marginalized or oppressed, and inspires them to take action.

Love as a driving force for change is not limited to romantic love, but encompasses a broader sense of love for humanity and a desire for justice. It is a force that transcends boundaries and unites people from diverse backgrounds in their pursuit of equality and social justice.

In the case of Aerin Zor, love was not only a personal motivation but also a central theme in their activism. Aerin understood that love is a powerful catalyst for change, capable of breaking down barriers and challenging societal norms.

By embodying love in their activism, Aerin was able to approach the struggle for alien civil rights with empathy, compassion, and a commitment to justice. This love was evident in their interactions with fellow activists, as well as in their efforts to build bridges and form alliances with different communities.

Love also played a crucial role in Aerin's ability to mobilize and inspire others. Their passion for justice and their unwavering belief in the power of love resonated with people from all walks of life. It gave them hope and reassurance that change was possible, even in the face of adversity.

Moreover, love enabled Aerin to humanize the struggle for alien civil rights, to highlight the personal stories and lived experiences of those affected by discrimination and injustice. By framing the fight for equality and justice as an expression of love for all beings, Aerin was able to connect with a wide audience and generate widespread support for their cause.

Love served as a guiding principle for Aerin, inspiring them to approach activism with compassion and understanding. It reminded them to prioritize the well-being and dignity of all individuals, even in the midst of intense opposition and resistance.

In this way, love transcended the conventional boundaries of activism and expanded the possibilities for creating meaningful change. It challenged the notion that activism must be driven solely by anger, righteousness, or outrage. Instead, it showed that love has the power to transform hearts and minds, to bridge divides, and to create a more inclusive and compassionate society.

While love alone may not be sufficient to dismantle systemic oppression and discrimination, it is an essential and powerful force that can ignite and sustain movements for change. By recognizing the inherent worth and value of every being, by embracing love as a driving force for activism, we can work towards a more just and equitable world.

Caveats and Challenges

While love can be a powerful force for change, it is not without its challenges and complexities. Activists must navigate a complex landscape of power dynamics, systemic oppression, and deeply ingrained prejudices.

One challenge is the potential for love to be commodified or romanticized, reducing it to a shallow sentiment devoid of real substance. It is important to recognize that love as a driving force for change requires more than just warm feelings—it requires a commitment to challenging and dismantling oppressive systems.

Another challenge is navigating the tensions between love and anger. While love can inspire and motivate activists, anger can also be a legitimate and valid response to injustice. It is essential to find a balance between these emotions, harnessing them in productive and transformative ways.

Additionally, there is always the risk of burnout and emotional exhaustion when engaging in activism fueled by love. Activists must take care of their own well-being and prioritize self-care to sustain themselves in the long-term fight for justice.

Examples of Love as a Driving Force for Change

One powerful example of love as a driving force for change is seen in the LGBTQ+ rights movement. LGBTQ+ activists have fought tirelessly for equal rights and recognition, driven by a love for their communities and a desire for acceptance and equality.

Another example is the civil rights movement in the United States, where love and empathy played a pivotal role in challenging racial segregation and discrimination. Leaders like Martin Luther King Jr. and Rosa Parks fought for justice based on their love for humanity and their belief in the inherent dignity of all individuals.

Love also fueled the feminist movement, with activists working towards gender equality out of love and compassion for women and marginalized communities. This love has been instrumental in challenging patriarchal norms and advocating for equal rights.

In all of these examples, love has been a guiding force that has propelled activists forward, despite the many challenges and obstacles they have faced. It has united communities, inspired resilience, and paved the way for lasting change.

Exercises

1. Reflect on a time when love has motivated you to take action or support a cause. How did this love impact your approach to activism or advocacy?

2. Identify a social justice movement that resonates with you. How is love or compassion present in the messaging, actions, or values of this movement?

3. Research an activist who embodies love as a driving force for change. What strategies or tactics did they employ to harness love in their activism? How did love contribute to the success of their cause?

4. Consider a current social issue that you feel passionate about. How can you integrate love or compassion into your approach to activism or advocacy on this issue? How might love help build bridges and foster understanding with others who may hold different perspectives?

Resources

1. Hooks, Bell. "All About Love: New Visions." William Morrow Paperbacks, 2001.

2. King Jr., Martin Luther. "Strength to Love." Fortress Press, 2010.

3. Lorde, Audre. "Sister Outsider: Essays and Speeches." Crossing Press, 2007.

4. Levine, Peter A. "Healing Trauma: A Pioneering Program for Restoring the Wisdom of Your Body." Sounds True, 2008.

5. Metz, Johann. "Love: Theological Investigations." Cascade Books, 2015.

6. Nussbaum, Martha C. "The Monarchy of Fear: A Philosopher Looks at Our Political Crisis." Simon & Schuster, 2018.

7. Thích Nhất Hạnh. "Anger: Wisdom for Cooling the Flames." Riverhead Books, 2002.

Further Reading

1. Isin, Engin F., and Greg M. Nielsen. "Acts of Citizenship." Zed Books, 2008.

2. Kivel, Paul. "Uprooting Racism: How White People Can Work for Racial Justice." New Society Publishers, 2011.

3. hooks, bell. "Teaching Community: A Pedagogy of Hope." Routledge, 2003.

4. DiAngelo, Robin. "White Fragility: Why It's So Hard for White People to Talk About Racism." Beacon Press, 2018.

Subsection: Redefining Relationships in the Cosmic Era

In the vast expanse of the universe, relationships have always been a fundamental aspect of existence. But in the cosmic era, relationships between beings from different planets have taken on a new significance. With the rise of interplanetary travel and the mingling of different species, the boundaries of love, friendship, and family have expanded like never before. In this subsection, we explore the challenges, triumphs, and the sheer beauty of relationships in the cosmic era.

Love Across the Cosmos

Love knows no boundaries, and in the cosmic era, this sentiment has taken on a whole new meaning. Intergalactic romance has emerged as a powerful force, challenging preconceived notions and defying traditional norms. As Aerin Zor himself experienced, the journey of love between different species can be fraught with obstacles and taboos.

Overcoming these hurdles requires empathy, open-mindedness, and a deep understanding of the complexities of inter-species relationships. It also calls for the dismantling of prejudice and the willingness to embrace the unknown. By doing so, individuals in the cosmic era are redefining the very nature of love itself, breaking free from the confines of conventional understanding.

SECTION 1: LOVE AND INTERSPECIES RELATIONSHIPS

The Extraordinary Love Story of Aerin Zor

Aerin Zor's own love story provides a gripping example of the power of intergalactic love. Born of two different species, Aerin and his partner, Zara, defied societal expectations and fought for recognition and acceptance. Despite facing immense opposition, their love blossomed and became a driving force behind their activism.

Their story serves as a beacon of hope, demonstrating that love can triumph over adversity. It reminds us that the cosmic era is a time for love to flourish, where barriers are shattered, and relationships transcend the limitations of mere intergalactic existence.

The Journey of Acceptance

Acceptance is a cornerstone of any healthy relationship. In the cosmic era, it is not just individuals who must learn to accept one another, but entire civilizations as well. The path to acceptance is often arduous, as it requires shedding preconceived notions, challenging deep-seated biases, and recognizing the inherent worth of every being.

This journey of acceptance serves as a powerful catalyst for growth, not only for individuals but for entire planets and societies. It requires a collective effort to build bridges of understanding and create a harmonious coexistence, free from prejudice and discrimination. Only then can relationships thrive and reach their full potential.

The Power Couple of the Cosmos

Aerin Zor and Zara became the embodiment of a power couple in the cosmic era. Their love, resilience, and shared passion for equality and justice symbolized hope for an entire generation. Together, they demonstrated that meaningful change can be achieved when two individuals unite in their pursuit of a common goal.

Their relationship taught us that true partnership is about more than shared values and goals. It requires unwavering support, trust, and the ability to stand together in the face of adversity. The power couple of the cosmos redefined what it means to be in a relationship not just for themselves but for the entire universe.

Love as a Driving Force for Change

Love has always had the power to change the world, and in the cosmic era, this power is more potent than ever. The love between individuals from different planets is breaking down barriers, challenging societal norms, and driving social change on an intergalactic scale.

Love can inspire acts of unimaginable courage, fuel revolutions, and ignite the collective imagination. It can dismantle oppressive systems, eradicate prejudice, and pave the way for a future where every being is treated with dignity and respect. Ultimately, love in the cosmic era serves as a reminder that relationships can not only bring joy and fulfillment individually but create a more just and compassionate universe for all.

Redefining Relationships in the Cosmic Era: A Call to Action

In the cosmic era, relationships have the potential to transcend the limitations of the past. They hold the power to challenge prejudice, dismantle oppressive systems, and build a future where equality and justice prevail.

To embrace this potential, individuals must actively engage in the process of redefining relationships in the cosmic era. This means confronting our own biases, expanding our capacity for empathy, and fostering a deep sense of understanding and acceptance for beings from all walks of life. By doing so, we can forge a path towards a more inclusive and harmonious universe.

As Aerin Zor showed us through his own experiences, relationships in the cosmic era have the capacity to change the world. They provide an opportunity to bridge the gaps between different species, cultures, and civilizations. By redefining relationships in the cosmic era, we unlock a future where love knows no boundaries, where understanding triumphs over prejudice, and where unity and compassion reign supreme.

Let us embark on this cosmic journey of redefining relationships, hand in hand, with an unwavering commitment to love, equality, and justice.

Section 2: Family and Alien Identity

Subsection: The Influence of Alien Ancestry

In understanding the roots of Aerin Zor's passion for alien civil rights, we must examine the profound influence of their alien ancestry. Aerin Zor, like many others, was born into a society where the exploration of one's heritage has become an integral part of identity. Alien ancestry not only connects individuals to their cultural roots but also shapes their worldview, values, and experiences.

1. The Intersection of Alien and Human Heritage:

SECTION 2: FAMILY AND ALIEN IDENTITY

Aerin Zor's heritage encompasses both human and alien lineage. This intersection provides a unique perspective on the challenges faced by individuals who straddle multiple cultural and racial identities. It enables them to empathize with the complex experiences of belonging and exclusion.

Understanding the nuances of their alien ancestry allowed Aerin Zor to navigate the intricacies of their own identity. By embracing their background, they shunned the notion of conforming to societal expectations and, instead, championed the celebration of diversity.

2. The Influence of Intergenerational Stories:

Intergenerational stories play a crucial role in preserving and passing down the traditions, values, and struggles of alien communities. These stories shape the way individuals perceive their place in the cosmos and instill a sense of pride in their heritage. Such stories provide a window into a rich tapestry of cultural practices, languages, and belief systems.

Aerin Zor grew up listening to stories handed down from their alien ancestors, fostering a deep understanding of the history and experiences of their people. These stories served as reminders of the ongoing struggle for equality within their alien community and motivated Aerin Zor to fight for justice beyond Velan-7.

3. The Richness of Cultural Traditions:

Alien ancestry encompasses a variety of cultural traditions, ranging from art forms and music to gastronomy and spirituality. These traditions offer a glimpse into the shared values, collective memory, and resilience of alien communities.

Aerin Zor's exploration of their alien heritage allowed them to appreciate the beauty and depth of these traditions. They recognized that cultural preservation is not only a means of honoring the past but also a way to empower present and future generations. This realization fueled Aerin Zor's commitment to preserving alien cultures and resisting assimilation.

4. Overcoming Prejudice and Stereotypes:

Alien ancestry often exposes individuals to prejudice and stereotypes perpetuated by those who view them as "other." Aerin Zor faced the challenges of xenophobia and discrimination throughout their life. These experiences cultivated a sense of determination to dismantle harmful stereotypes and challenge the societal norms that perpetuated them.

By educating others about the richness and complexity of alien cultures, Aerin Zor aimed to disrupt the narrow-minded narratives that marginalized and dehumanized alien communities.

5. Embracing Multiculturalism and Hybridity:

Alien ancestry also brings forth the concept of hybridity, where individuals embrace multiple influences and create a unique cultural blend. In a universe characterized by interstellar travel and interplanetary exchange, hybridity emerges as a source of innovation and connection between different alien species.

Aerin Zor's understanding of hybridity informed their belief in the power of coming together. They celebrated the multicultural nature of the cosmos and advocated for the dismantling of hierarchies that perpetuated cultural superiority.

By engaging with their alien ancestry, Aerin Zor developed a profound sense of belonging to a larger narrative of resilience, celebration, and collaboration among diverse alien communities. Their heritage instilled in them the values of justice, equality, and the importance of embracing and preserving the myriad of cultures that make up the fabric of the cosmos.

As Aerin Zor's story unfolds, we witness the transformative power of embracing ancestral roots, challenging prejudices, and fostering unity across alien communities. Through their personal journey, they inspire others to connect with their own heritage and forge a path towards a future where coexistence and celebration of diversity reign supreme.

Subsection: Navigating Dual Identities

Navigating dual identities can be an intricate and often challenging endeavor. For individuals like Aerin Zor, who straddle multiple cultural and societal norms, finding a sense of belonging can be an ongoing journey. In this subsection, we explore the complexities and strategies of managing dual identities in the context of alien activism.

Understanding Dual Identity

Dual identity refers to the experience of individuals who embody two or more cultural, social, or ethnic identities. In the case of Aerin Zor, their dual identity stems from their status as a fusion of two distinct alien species and their intersectional experience as a galactic civil rights activist.

Dual identity can present both advantages and challenges. On one hand, individuals with dual identities have access to diverse perspectives and can draw from a rich cultural heritage. On the other hand, they may face conflicting expectations and societal pressures, leading to feelings of being caught between worlds.

Fostering Self-Acceptance

The first step in navigating dual identities is developing self-acceptance and embracing the unique characteristics that make individuals like Aerin Zor who they are. This involves recognizing and celebrating the diversity of their backgrounds and finding strength in their multiple identities.

Cultivating self-acceptance can be achieved through self-reflection, seeking support from like-minded individuals, and engaging in introspective practices such as journaling or meditation. Additionally, exploring one's cultural heritage and understanding its significance can foster a greater appreciation for one's dual identities.

Balancing Cultural Expectations

Living with dual identities often means managing conflicting cultural expectations. Aerin Zor not only had to bridge the cultural differences between their two fusion species but also faced understanding and reconciling the norms and expectations of their galactic community.

Navigating cultural expectations requires open-mindedness, adaptability, and a willingness to engage in ongoing dialogue. It is essential to recognize that cultural practices and beliefs can evolve over time, and individuals with dual identities have the opportunity to shape and redefine these norms.

Open communication with family, friends, and community members can help bridge these expectations and create space for mutual understanding. By acknowledging and respecting the perspectives of both cultures, individuals like Aerin Zor can find a balance that preserves their authenticity while maintaining their connections.

Developing Coping Strategies

Managing dual identities can be emotionally taxing, especially when faced with discrimination or prejudice. Developing coping strategies is crucial for maintaining mental well-being and resilience in the face of adversity.

One effective coping strategy is building a support network. Aerin Zor sought solace in communities of individuals who shared similar dual identities and experiences. These support networks provide a safe space for individuals to share their struggles, exchange advice, and find validation.

Furthermore, practicing self-care is essential. Engaging in activities that promote relaxation, mindfulness, and self-compassion can help individuals navigate the complexities of their dual identities. This may include pursuing hobbies, engaging in physical activities, or seeking therapy or counseling.

Embracing Intersectionality

Intersectionality, the interconnected nature of social identities such as race, gender, and class, plays a vital role in the experiences of individuals with dual identities. Acknowledging and embracing intersectionality allows for a deeper understanding of the unique challenges faced by individuals like Aerin Zor.

By recognizing the ways in which various aspects of identity intersect, individuals can advocate for multiple causes and address issues that affect different communities. Aerin Zor, for instance, emphasized the importance of addressing not only the rights of extraterrestrial beings but also the rights of all marginalized groups within the galactic community.

Seeking Unity in Diversity

Ultimately, the navigation of dual identities is a journey towards finding unity in diversity. It involves embracing all aspects of one's identity and recognizing the power and potential that comes from the fusion of cultures, beliefs, and experiences.

Aerin Zor's journey serves as an inspiration for others, demonstrating that individuals with dual identities have a unique perspective that can contribute to the broader goals of social justice and equality. By valuing diversity and fostering inclusivity, we can create a world where everyone's dual identities are not only acknowledged but valued and celebrated.

In conclusion, navigating dual identities is a complex process that requires self-acceptance, open communication, coping strategies, and an embrace of intersectionality. The journey of individuals like Aerin Zor provides valuable lessons on how to live authentically while advocating for social change. By celebrating diversity and seeking unity in our differences, we move closer to creating a world where all identities are equally valued and respected.

Subsection: The Role of Family in Activism

Family plays a crucial role in shaping an individual's values, beliefs, and actions. In the context of activism, the support and influence of family members can significantly impact an activist's journey and contribute to the success of their cause. In this subsection, we will explore the various ways in which family can play a role in activism, from providing emotional support to actively participating in the movement.

SECTION 2: FAMILY AND ALIEN IDENTITY

The Importance of Emotional Support

Embarking on an activism journey can be emotionally demanding, as activists often face challenges, setbacks, and instances of discrimination. During such times, having a supportive family provides a strong foundation that helps activists navigate these hurdles with resilience and determination.

Emotional support from family members can come in many forms. It can involve actively listening to an activist's experiences, validating their feelings, and offering words of encouragement. For example, imagine a young alien activist named Zara fighting for equal rights for extraterrestrial beings. In the face of backlash and criticism, Zara's parents provide a safe space for her to express her frustrations, offer a listening ear, and remind her of her purpose. This emotional support boosts Zara's morale and gives her the strength to continue her fight.

Fostering a Sense of Empathy and Justice

Family units that prioritize empathy and justice lay the groundwork for future activists. By instilling values of fairness, equality, and respect within the family dynamic, parents contribute to raising socially conscious individuals who are more likely to engage in activism.

Practicing empathy and justice within the family can be as simple as having open discussions about social issues, exposing children to diverse perspectives, and encouraging them to take action when they witness injustice. This helps children develop a strong moral compass and a sense of responsibility towards creating a better world.

For instance, let's imagine a family where both parents actively engage in community service and volunteer work. Their child, Maya, grows up seeing the impact her parents have on marginalized communities. Inspired by their actions and guided by their teachings, Maya becomes passionate about advocating for the rights of underprivileged aliens. Her parents' example and their discussions around justice and equity have shaped her journey as an activist.

Active Involvement in Activism

While emotional support and the transmission of values are crucial, some family members may choose to take their involvement in activism a step further by actively participating in the movement alongside their activist family member.

Family members can support activists by attending rallies, volunteering their time for related causes, or using their skills to contribute to the movement. Their involvement not only provides practical assistance but also strengthens family bonds and underscores the collective commitment to social change.

For example, imagine a scenario where an alien activist named Alex is leading a campaign to raise awareness about the discrimination faced by alien students in intergalactic schools. Alex's younger sibling, Jamie, empathizes with their cause and decides to help by organizing a petition drive at their school to support their sibling's campaign. Jamie's active involvement not only strengthens the impact of the campaign but also deepens the bond between the siblings as they work together towards a common goal.

Challenges and Considerations

While family involvement in activism is valuable, there are challenges and considerations that activists and their families must navigate. These challenges can arise from differences in opinion or concerns about safety and well-being.

Differences in opinion within families are natural, and they can provide an opportunity for meaningful discussions and growth. However, it is important to approach such conversations with respect and open-mindedness, allowing everyone involved to express their thoughts and experiences. Finding common ground and shared values can help bridge any gaps and strengthen family bonds.

Ensuring the safety and well-being of family members involved in activism is another crucial consideration. Activism often brings exposure to risks, such as confrontations with opponents or encounters with law enforcement. It is essential for families to have open dialogues about these risks, establish safety protocols, and provide the necessary support to manage any potential challenges that may arise.

Conclusion

In the fight for social change, the role of family in activism is undeniable. From providing emotional support to actively participating in the movement, family plays a vital role in an activist's journey. The love, empathy, and solidarity within families can fuel and strengthen the impact of activism, creating a lasting legacy grounded in collective values and shared experiences. By recognizing and nurturing the role of family, we can cultivate a society where activism becomes a family affair, driving us closer to the vision of a more equitable and just universe.

Subsection: Raising Awareness within Alien Communities

Raising awareness within alien communities is a crucial step in any civil rights movement. It involves educating individuals about the injustices faced by marginalized groups and inspiring them to take action. In this subsection, we will explore various strategies and approaches that Aerin Zor employed to raise awareness within alien communities during the Velan-7 Civil Rights Movement.

The Importance of Education

Education plays a fundamental role in raising awareness and fostering empathy. Many alien communities may not be aware of the specific challenges faced by other groups, as they may be insulated from these issues due to cultural, social, or economic factors. Thus, it is essential to provide them with the knowledge and understanding necessary to empathize with the struggles of others.

Aerin Zor recognized this and implemented educational initiatives within the alien communities on Velan-7. They collaborated with local schools, community centers, and cultural organizations to organize workshops, seminars, and lectures. These educational events aimed to enlighten alien individuals about the unjust treatment and discrimination faced by bi-entity fusions within their society.

Storytelling and Personal Narratives

One of the most powerful tools in raising awareness is storytelling. Stories have the ability to resonate with individuals on an emotional level, allowing them to connect with the experiences of others. Aerin Zor utilized personal narratives of bi-entity fusions to bring attention to their struggles and inspire empathy within alien communities.

They encouraged bi-entity fusions to share their stories publicly, either through written accounts or by speaking at community events. These personal narratives humanized the experiences of bi-entity fusions and helped alien individuals understand the injustices they faced. By sharing their stories, bi-entity fusions became the voices of their community, empowering others to stand up against discrimination.

Cultural Exchanges and Diversity Celebrations

In order to promote understanding and acceptance of different alien cultures, Aerin Zor organized cultural exchanges and diversity celebrations within alien communities. These events aimed to highlight the richness and diversity of the various alien groups while fostering a sense of unity and solidarity.

Through cultural exchanges, alien communities had an opportunity to learn about the traditions, customs, and values of bi-entity fusions. This exposure helped break down stereotypes and prejudice, fostering a more inclusive and accepting society.

Community Engagement and Grassroots Activism

Raising awareness within alien communities also involved actively engaging with individuals through grassroots activism. Aerin Zor organized rallies, protests, and public demonstrations within alien communities, creating a visible presence and igniting discussions about civil rights and equality.

Community engagement initiatives, such as neighborhood clean-up campaigns, food drives, and charity events, were also employed to establish connections and build trust within alien communities. These initiatives showcased the commitment of bi-entity fusions to the well-being of their society and created opportunities for dialogue on civil rights issues.

Collaboration with Cultural and Religious Leaders

To effectively raise awareness within alien communities, it was essential to collaborate with influential cultural and religious leaders. Aerin Zor recognized the power of these leaders in shaping the beliefs and values of their community members.

By establishing partnerships with cultural and religious organizations, Aerin Zor gained access to larger audiences and resources. They worked together with these leaders to organize conferences, seminars, and religious gatherings that addressed alien civil rights and the importance of unity.

Creative and Unconventional Approaches

In addition to traditional methods of raising awareness, Aerin Zor also employed creative and unconventional approaches to engage alien communities. They organized art exhibits, film screenings, and theater performances that depicted the experiences of bi-entity fusions.

These artistic expressions allowed individuals to emotionally connect with the struggles faced by bi-entity fusions and challenged their perspectives. Art has a way of transcending language barriers and cultural differences, making it a powerful medium to raise awareness and inspire social change.

Conclusion

Raising awareness within alien communities requires a multifaceted approach that combines education, storytelling, cultural exchanges, grassroots activism, collaboration with influential leaders, and creative initiatives. Aerin Zor's efforts to raise awareness within alien communities during the Velan-7 Civil Rights Movement serve as a testament to the power of unity and collective action. By educating and inspiring alien individuals, Aerin Zor catalyzed a wave of change that transformed Velan-7 and resonated throughout the universe. This section highlights the importance of amplifying marginalized voices and engaging with communities to challenge injustice and foster a more inclusive and equitable society.

Subsection: The Strengthening Bonds of Family

In the cosmic tapestry of Aerin Zor's life, family played a significant role in shaping her journey as an activist. The bonds of family not only provided a strong foundation of support but also fueled her determination to fight for equal rights for all alien beings. In this subsection, we will explore the profound impact of family on Aerin Zor's activism and the ways in which she nurtured and strengthened these bonds amidst the challenges she faced.

Aerin Zor's journey towards activism began within the crucible of her family's values and beliefs. Growing up on the distant planet of Velan-7, she was surrounded by a close-knit family that instilled in her the importance of compassion, justice, and equality. Her parents, Elyn and Xalir, both well-known activists themselves, exposed Aerin to the harsh realities of discrimination and injustice from an early age, allowing her to develop a deep empathy for those marginalized within the cosmos.

Within the confines of her family, Aerin found solace and motivation to challenge the status quo. Discussions around the dinner table often centered on the struggles of alien communities on Velan-7 and beyond. These conversations served as a catalyst, igniting a fire within Aerin to take a stand against the discrimination that plagued her own people. It was during these formative years that she realized the power of unity and how collective action could pave the way for a brighter future.

As she embarked on her journey as an activist, Aerin Zor maintained a strong connection with her family, seeking their guidance and support. They became her most trusted advisors and confidants, standing by her side through the trials and tribulations of leadership. The unwavering belief they placed in her potential allowed her to navigate the complex political landscape of Velan-7 with grace and determination.

However, the fight for equality exacted a toll on Aerin Zor's family dynamics. The constant battles, both in the political arena and on the streets, strained the bonds that held them together. While her passion for activism united her family, there were moments of tension and disagreement, as the weight of responsibility threatened to overshadow personal relationships.

It was during these challenging times that Aerin Zor realized the need to strike a delicate balance between her personal and professional life. She recognized that nurturing her relationships with her loved ones would not only strengthen her resolve but also provide a much-needed source of emotional support. Aerin made a conscious effort to create space for quality time with her family, ensuring moments of joy and laughter amidst the turbulence of her activism.

In the face of adversity, family served as an anchor for Aerin Zor, reminding her of the values she held dear. They became her refuge, enveloping her with love and understanding when the weight of her responsibilities threatened to overwhelm. The moments shared with her family became a source of inspiration and fuel, enabling her to face each new challenge with renewed determination.

Throughout her journey, Aerin Zor came to understand that the fight for alien civil rights was not just about improving the external systems of society but also about nurturing and strengthening the bonds of family within alien communities. She actively worked towards fostering a sense of unity and solidarity among families, creating safe spaces that facilitated open dialogue and support.

Recognizing the importance of communication and understanding within families, she initiated workshops and counseling sessions focused on promoting empathy and acceptance. These initiatives helped individuals within alien families overcome deep-seated prejudices and foster appreciation for the diversity within their own kinship circles. Aerin firmly believed that change starts at home, and by healing the rifts within families, she aimed to create a ripple effect that would be felt throughout alien communities.

In her advocacy work, Aerin Zor also highlighted the unique challenges faced by alien families, including the struggle to find acceptance in human-dominated societies. She fought tirelessly for laws and policies that would protect the rights of alien families, ensuring that their bond was recognized and respected across planetary boundaries. By drawing attention to these issues, she aimed to create a more inclusive and tolerant cosmos where bonds of family were celebrated regardless of species or origin.

In conclusion, Aerin Zor's journey as an activist was deeply intertwined with the strengthening of bonds within her own family and the broader alien community. The unwavering support, guidance, and love that she received from her family propelled her forward in her fight for equal rights. Through her work, Aerin demonstrated the power of family in activism, inspiring many to nurture and cherish the bonds that hold us together as we strive to create a more just and equitable universe.

Further Reading:

- *Beyond Species: Embracing Multiculturalism in the Cosmos* by Nya Patel
- *Alien Families: Navigating Dual Identities in Interstellar Societies* by Michael Wong
- *The Power of Unity: Strengthening Bonds for Galactic Change* by Zara Khan

Key Terms: family dynamics, emotional support, unity, communication, acceptance, inclusivity, advocacy, interstellar societies, alien families.

Subsection: Embracing Multiculturalism in the Universe

Embracing multiculturalism is a fundamental aspect of creating a harmonious and inclusive society, not only on Earth but throughout the universe. In this subsection, we will explore the importance of multiculturalism, the benefits it brings, and the challenges that arise when different alien cultures interact. We will also discuss strategies and approaches to foster unity and understanding among diverse civilizations.

The Power of Multiculturalism

In the vast expanse of the universe, we are blessed with a myriad of diverse civilizations, each with its own unique set of beliefs, customs, languages, and traditions. Multiculturalism encompasses the acceptance and appreciation of this diversity, recognizing that every culture has something valuable to offer. It encourages mutual respect, cultural exchange, and collaboration, promoting the growth and enrichment of all societies involved.

Multiculturalism not only broadens our horizons and deepens our understanding of the universe, but it also sparks innovation and creativity. When individuals from different backgrounds come together, their diverse perspectives and experiences lead to a rich tapestry of ideas, pushing the boundaries of knowledge and enabling groundbreaking advancements. By fostering an environment that embraces and celebrates multiculturalism, we can unlock the full potential of the universe's diversity.

Challenges and Pitfalls

While the concept of multiculturalism is inherently positive, its implementation is not without challenges. When civilizations with different belief systems, social structures, and customs come into contact, conflicts can arise. These conflicts may stem from misunderstandings, biases, or a fear of the unknown. It is essential to navigate these challenges with sensitivity and respect, recognizing that everyone has a right to their own cultural identity.

One of the pitfalls to avoid is cultural appropriation, which occurs when elements of one culture are adopted by another without understanding or respect for their significance. Cultural appropriation can perpetuate stereotypes, strip cultural practices of their meaning, and undermine the authenticity of the culture being appropriated. To promote genuine multiculturalism, it is crucial to engage in meaningful cultural exchange, learning from each other while respecting the boundaries and values of each civilization.

Promoting Unity and Understanding

Building bridges between alien cultures requires open-mindedness, empathy, and a willingness to learn. Here are some strategies and approaches to foster unity and understanding:

1. **Education and Awareness:** Promote education about different alien cultures, their histories, and contributions to the universe. Encourage individuals to expose themselves to diverse perspectives through literature, art, music, and documentaries.

2. **Communication and Dialogue:** Foster open and respectful communication channels where individuals can exchange ideas, challenge misconceptions, and build mutual understanding. Facilitate intercultural dialogue through conferences, seminars, and online platforms to promote cross-cultural interaction and collaboration.

3. **Cultural Exchanges:** Organize cultural exchange programs that allow individuals from different civilizations to live and immerse themselves in each other's cultures. This firsthand experience fosters empathy, breaks down stereotypes, and builds lasting connections.

4. **Celebration of Diversity:** Organize multicultural festivals and events that celebrate the richness and diversity of alien cultures. These gatherings provide

an opportunity for communities to come together, share their traditions, and appreciate the beauty of their differences.

5. **Legislation and Policies:** Implement inclusive policies and legislation that protect the rights and preserve the cultural heritage of all civilizations. Enforce laws that combat discrimination and promote equal opportunities for individuals from different backgrounds.

The Unconventional Approach: Cosmic Potluck

To break down barriers and promote cultural exchange in a fun and unconventional way, consider organizing a cosmic potluck event. Each civilization participating brings a dish representative of their culture, showcasing the unique flavors and culinary traditions of their home planet. This event not only promotes camaraderie and appreciation for diverse cultures but also allows individuals to experience the universality of food as a means of connection and communication.

Conclusion

Embracing multiculturalism in the universe is essential for fostering unity, progress, and a sense of shared humanity. By acknowledging the inherent value of each culture and promoting respectful interaction and understanding, we can create a future where all civilizations thrive harmoniously. Multiculturalism is not just a goal to aspire to; it is a responsibility we owe to ourselves and future generations, ensuring a truly inclusive and vibrant universe for all.

Section 3: The Trials and Tribulations of Leadership

Subsection: The Weight of Responsibility

In the tumultuous life of Aerin Zor, there was no burden heavier than the weight of responsibility. As an alien civil rights activist, Aerin carried the hopes and dreams of an entire species on their shoulders. The task of bringing about change in a divided and oppressive society was no small feat, and navigating the complexities of leadership demanded unwavering dedication and resilience. In this subsection, we delve into the nuances of the responsibility that Aerin shouldered, examining the challenges they faced, the strategies they employed, and the personal toll it took on their mental health.

Central to the weight of responsibility was the awareness that any misstep could have dire consequences, not only for Aerin themselves but also for the movement they represented. Their decisions and actions were scrutinized by both supporters and detractors, as the fate of the Velan-7 civil rights movement hung in the balance. The fear of making mistakes, of inadvertently undermining their cause, weighed heavily on Aerin's mind. It required constant vigilance and a deep sense of self-reflection to mitigate the risks associated with their position.

One of the key challenges that Aerin faced was reconciling their personal desires and needs with the demands of their role as a leader. Activism became all-consuming, leaving little space for personal relationships or self-care. The passionate drive to bring about change sometimes overshadowed the need for rest and rejuvenation. Burnout, a common affliction among activists, was a constant threat. Aerin had to navigate the delicate balance between pushing forward in the struggle for justice and preserving their own well-being.

To alleviate the weight of responsibility, Aerin adopted several strategies. Delegation became their ally, recognizing that they couldn't carry the burden alone. They empowered fellow activists, nurturing new leaders within the movement. By sharing the load, Aerin created a collective sense of ownership and ensured the sustainability of their cause. Collaboration was key, as they formed strategic alliances with other like-minded individuals and organizations, pooling resources and expertise to amplify their impact.

Yet, even with a network of support, Aerin couldn't escape the inherent vulnerability that comes with leadership. The constant pressure to perform, to inspire, and to succeed was emotionally taxing. Doubts and insecurities had the potential to creep in, threatening to erode their resolve. The weight of responsibility demanded an unyielding self-belief, a steadfast determination to stay the course even when the outlook seemed bleak. Aerin shunned self-doubt, mastering the art of projecting confidence and strength, not only for their followers but also for themselves.

It is important to address the toll that such responsibility can take on one's mental health. The lifelong struggle for justice can induce anxiety, depression, and a sense of disillusionment. Aerin, though undeniably resilient, was not immune to these emotional hardships. Seeking solace in the support of loved ones and engaging in self-care practices were essential for maintaining their well-being. The struggle for justice must be holistic, encompassing not only the betterment of society but also the preservation of one's own mental and emotional health.

In reflecting on the weight of responsibility, it is crucial to acknowledge the sacrifices made by Aerin and countless other activists. Their dedication and tireless efforts have irrevocably changed the trajectory of the struggle for alien civil rights. However, it is also important to remember that the weight of responsibility is not exclusive to leaders and activists. Each individual has a role to play in shaping a just and equitable society. By recognizing our collective responsibility and working together, we can alleviate the burden and create a future that is brighter for all.

Subsection: Balancing Personal and Professional Life

Maintaining a healthy balance between personal and professional life is a challenge that many activists, including Aerin Zor, face. In the midst of fighting for alien civil rights and leading a movement, it can be easy to neglect personal relationships, self-care, and other essential aspects of life. However, finding this balance is crucial not only for personal well-being but also for the sustainability of the activist's work. In this subsection, we will explore strategies and insights into how Aerin Zor managed to strike a balance between her personal and professional life.

The Importance of Self-Care

Aerin Zor recognized early on that self-care is not a luxury but a necessity. Standing at the forefront of a civil rights movement required immense physical and emotional energy. To sustain her activism, she prioritized self-care practices. This included engaging in regular exercise, practicing mindfulness and meditation, and getting enough rest. Aerin understood that taking care of herself allowed her to show up fully for her advocacy work.

Setting Boundaries

One of the key strategies for balancing personal and professional life is setting clear boundaries. Aerin Zor understood that activism could easily consume her entire life if she let it, so she established boundaries to protect her personal time. She designated specific hours for work and activism, ensuring she had time for her personal life, hobbies, and relationships. By setting boundaries, she created a structure that allowed her to be present and fully commit to both her professional and personal responsibilities.

Building a Support System

Aerin Zor recognized the importance of having a strong support system to lean on. She surrounded herself with a network of friends, family, and fellow activists who provided emotional and practical support. Having a support system allowed her to share the burden of her responsibilities and enabled her to rely on others when she needed to take time for herself. This network of support played a crucial role in helping her maintain balance and manage the challenges that arose from her dual roles as an activist and an individual.

Time Management

Managing time effectively is a vital skill for balancing personal and professional life. Aerin Zor was an expert at prioritizing tasks and setting clear goals. She utilized time management techniques such as creating to-do lists, utilizing calendars and scheduling tools, and breaking down large projects into smaller, more manageable tasks. By managing her time effectively, she could allocate dedicated blocks for work and personal activities, ensuring both received the attention they required.

Regular Reflection and Evaluation

To maintain balance, Aerin Zor regularly reflected on her commitments and evaluated her priorities. She recognized that as an activist, her responsibilities and circumstances would evolve over time. By regularly reassessing her goals and commitments, she could make informed decisions about where to invest her time and energy. This reflection and evaluation process allowed her to adapt and adjust her personal and professional life as needed, ensuring that she maintained balance in the face of changing circumstances.

Unconventional Solution: Embracing Imperfections

One unconventional yet effective strategy that Aerin Zor employed was embracing imperfections. Recognizing that striving for perfection in both personal and professional life could be overwhelming, she adopted a mindset of embracing imperfections. This mindset allowed her to accept that there would be times when the balance might tip more towards one aspect of her life than the other. By accepting imperfection, she prevented herself from feeling guilty or overwhelmed when faced with competing demands. This mindset shift enabled her to navigate the inevitable complexities and challenges of maintaining balance with a sense of ease and self-compassion.

Conclusion

Balancing personal and professional life is a lifelong journey, especially for passionate activists like Aerin Zor. Through self-care, setting boundaries, building a support system, effective time management, regular reflection, and embracing imperfections, she was able to strike a balance that allowed her to continue her activism while nurturing her personal well-being. As aspiring activists, we can learn valuable lessons from Aerin Zor's approach and apply them in our own lives, ensuring that we can make a sustainable impact while maintaining a fulfilling personal life. Remember, finding balance is not about perfection but rather about finding what works best for you and continually adapting as circumstances change.

Subsection: Coping with Adversity and Setbacks

Life is full of challenges, and it is no different for activists like Aerin Zor. In the pursuit of justice and equality, there are bound to be adversities and setbacks along the way. In this subsection, we will explore how Aerin Zor coped with the difficulties they encountered in their fight for alien civil rights.

Understanding the Nature of Adversity

Adversity comes in many forms, be it opposition from those in power, public backlash, or personal doubts and fears. For Aerin Zor, coping with adversity started with understanding its nature. They recognized that setbacks were not personal failures, but rather a natural part of the struggle for change. This mindset shift helped them stay resilient in the face of difficulties.

Finding Strength in Support Systems

No activist can achieve societal transformation alone. Aerin Zor understood the importance of building support systems to cope with adversity. They surrounded themselves with like-minded individuals who shared their passion for social justice. Together, they formed a network of support that provided emotional strength and practical resources. Aerin Zor relied on their allies during tough times, seeking advice, encouragement, and motivation to keep pushing forward.

Self-Care and Mental Well-being

The fight for justice can be emotionally and mentally exhausting. Aerin Zor realized the importance of self-care and mental well-being as essential tools for coping with adversity and setbacks. They prioritized self-care practices such as meditation, regular exercise, and spending time in nature. These activities helped them recharge and maintain a positive mindset amidst challenging circumstances.

Learning from Setbacks

Setbacks are opportunities for growth and learning. Aerin Zor embraced this philosophy and viewed setbacks as valuable lessons rather than insurmountable roadblocks. They analyzed each setback, seeking to understand the root causes and identify strategies for improvement. Instead of dwelling on failures, Aerin Zor used setbacks as stepping stones towards a better future.

Adapting Strategies and Approaches

In the face of adversity, flexibility and adaptation are crucial. Aerin Zor recognized that one approach might not work in every situation. They continuously evaluated their strategies and adapted them as needed. This allowed them to respond to setbacks with resilience and creativity, finding innovative ways to overcome obstacles and continue their fight for alien civil rights.

Maintaining Hope and Resilience

Hope and resilience are the driving forces that keep activists going, even in the face of adversity. Aerin Zor understood the importance of maintaining a hopeful outlook and nurturing resilience. They sought inspiration from past successes, reminding themselves of the progress already made in the struggle for equality. Additionally, they practiced gratitude and celebrated small victories, reinforcing their belief that change was possible.

Embracing Collaboration

Adversity can feel overwhelming when faced alone. Aerin Zor recognized the power of collaboration and sought out partnerships with other activists and organizations. By joining forces with like-minded individuals, they could share resources, knowledge, and expertise. Collaboration enabled them to tackle challenges collectively, making the burden of adversity more manageable and increasing the chances of success.

Trusting the Process

Coping with adversity requires trust in the process of societal change. Aerin Zor understood that progress takes time and setbacks are a natural part of the journey. They remained patient and persistent, never losing sight of their goals. By trusting the process, they were able to navigate through difficult times, knowing that every setback brought them one step closer to their ultimate vision of a just and equal universe.

In coping with adversity and setbacks, Aerin Zor demonstrated resilience, adaptability, and a deep commitment to their cause. Their experiences serve as an inspiration to activists facing similar challenges and remind us that even in the face of adversity, change is possible. By understanding the nature of adversity, surrounding ourselves with support systems, practicing self-care, learning from setbacks, adapting strategies, maintaining hope and resilience, embracing collaboration, and trusting the process, we too can navigate through the difficulties on our path towards a more just and equitable world.

Subsection: The Toll on Mental Health

Mental health is a crucial but often overlooked aspect of activism. In the relentless pursuit of social justice, activists like Aerin Zor often face numerous challenges that can take a toll on their mental well-being. This subsection will explore the unique mental health struggles activists may experience and provide strategies for self-care and resilience.

The Emotional Burden

Activism can be emotionally draining, especially when advocating for marginalized communities facing systemic oppression. Aerin Zor's fight for alien civil rights on Velan-7 was no exception. The emotional burden of witnessing and actively challenging discrimination, injustice, and violence can lead to feelings of anger, frustration, grief, and despair.

Moreover, activists often face personal attacks, threats, and backlash from those who oppose their cause. The constant pressure to perform, the weight of responsibilities, and the fear of failure contribute to heightened stress levels. As a result, activists may experience burnout, compassion fatigue, and even develop mental health conditions such as anxiety, depression, or post-traumatic stress disorder (PTSD).

Self-Care and Mental Well-being

To effectively combat the toll on mental health, it is crucial for activists to prioritize self-care and mental well-being. Here are some strategies that Aerin Zor and other activists have found helpful:

1. **Setting Boundaries:** Activists often devote significant time and energy to their cause, making it vital to establish boundaries. This involves recognizing personal limits and ensuring time for rest, leisure activities, and relationships outside of activism. Setting boundaries helps prevent burnout and allows for recharging.

2. **Seeking Support:** Activists should regularly seek emotional support from friends, family, fellow activists, and mental health professionals. Engaging in open and honest conversations about struggles, fears, and accomplishments can provide a sense of validation and encouragement.

3. **Practicing Self-Compassion:** It is crucial for activists to show kindness and compassion towards themselves. Self-compassion involves recognizing that everyone has limitations and that mistakes are inevitable. By embracing self-compassion, activists can cultivate resilience and maintain a positive mindset.

4. **Engaging in Self-Reflection:** Self-reflection allows activists to process their emotions, identify triggers, and explore their motivations. Taking the time to journal, meditate, or engage in therapy can aid in understanding and managing the emotional toll of activism.

5. **Maintaining Physical Health:** Physical and mental health are closely interconnected. Engaging in regular exercise, getting adequate sleep, and practicing healthy eating habits can enhance overall well-being and provide a strong foundation for resilience.

Addressing Mental Health Stigma

Despite the growing recognition of mental health issues, there is still significant stigma surrounding seeking help and discussing mental well-being in many societies. This stigma can be especially prominent in communities dedicated to activism.

Activists like Aerin Zor have been instrumental in challenging this culture of silence and encouraging open discussions about mental health. They urge others to recognize that mental health struggles are not a sign of weakness but a human response to overwhelming circumstances. By sharing their own experiences and seeking support, activists can dismantle stereotypes and create safer spaces for dialogue.

Unconventional Solution: Mindfulness in Activism

One unconventional yet highly effective practice for maintaining mental well-being in times of challenging activism is mindfulness. Mindfulness involves cultivating a non-judgmental awareness of the present moment. Engaging in mindfulness exercises, such as meditation or deep breathing, can help activists manage stress, reduce anxiety, and improve overall mental resilience.

Mindfulness also allows activists to remain grounded amid chaos, immersing themselves fully in the here and now instead of being consumed by worries or regrets. By anchoring their awareness to the present, activists can better manage their emotions and make conscious decisions that align with their values.

Conclusion

The toll on mental health is an intrinsic part of activism. Recognizing and addressing the emotional burden faced by activists, such as Aerin Zor, is crucial for sustaining long-term engagement and well-being in the pursuit of social justice. By prioritizing self-care, seeking support, challenging mental health stigma, and embracing mindfulness, activists can better navigate the complexities of their work and create lasting change while preserving their mental well-being.

Subsection: The Resilience of Aerin Zor

Aerin Zor's journey as a civil rights activist was not without its challenges and hardships. In this subsection, we delve into the incredible resilience that characterized Aerin Zor's pursuit of justice and equality for all beings in the universe. Through adversity and setbacks, Aerin Zor never lost sight of their mission, showing unwavering determination and inspiring others to join the fight.

Internal Struggles and Personal Growth

Like any activist, Aerin Zor faced internal struggles and moments of doubt throughout their journey. It was not always easy to navigate between their personal identity and the responsibilities of leadership. They grappled with the weight of their position and the toll that fighting for change took on their mental health.

In one particularly trying period, when faced with opposition from both the Velan-7 government and radical elements within the Civil Rights Movement, Aerin Zor doubted their ability to lead effectively. They questioned whether their sacrifices were worth it, and whether they were truly making a difference.

However, it was during this difficult time that Aerin Zor found the strength to confront their internal struggles head-on. They embraced vulnerability and sought support from trusted allies and mentors. Through introspection and self-reflection, Aerin Zor recognized the importance of self-care and the need to prioritize their own well-being. By acknowledging their own limitations and seeking help, Aerin Zor was able to cultivate the resilience necessary to continue their fight for justice.

Overcoming Adversity

Aerin Zor faced numerous adversities throughout their activism, including physical threats, political pushback, and public scrutiny. One significant challenge they encountered was the relentless media campaign aimed at discrediting their cause and tarnishing their reputation.

In response, Aerin Zor developed a resilience strategy that involved strategic communication and highlighting the truth. They consistently maintained transparency and authenticity in their actions, ensuring their words and deeds aligned with the values they fought for. By refusing to engage in personal attacks and staying focused on the principles of the movement, Aerin Zor not only deflected negative attention but also gained the respect and admiration of their supporters.

Another key aspect of Aerin Zor's resilience was their ability to adapt to changing circumstances. They quickly learned from their mistakes and setbacks, finding innovative ways to overcome obstacles. For instance, when faced with legal battles and attempts to silence their activism, Aerin Zor strategically shifted their methods, employing legal and diplomatic channels to further their cause. This flexibility allowed them to continue their fight while staying within the bounds of the law and gaining support from unlikely allies.

Building a Support System

Resilience does not develop in isolation, and Aerin Zor understood the importance of building a strong support system around them. They surrounded themselves with like-minded individuals who shared their passion for justice and equality. This network of friends, activists, and mentors provided emotional support, guidance, and accountability.

Aerin Zor also recognized the significance of grassroots organizations and community engagement in fostering resilience. They actively encouraged others to get involved in the fight for civil rights, organizing workshops, and seminars to empower individuals with the tools and knowledge needed for activism. By establishing connections with local communities, Aerin Zor created a web of support that helped sustain their resilience in the face of adversity.

Lessons in Resilience

Aerin Zor's journey teaches us invaluable lessons about resilience. First and foremost, it is essential to prioritize self-care and mental well-being. Activism can take a toll on an individual, and recognizing one's own limitations is crucial for long-term sustainability.

Secondly, resilience requires adaptability and a willingness to learn from failures. Aerin Zor's ability to pivot their strategies and embrace new approaches when confronted with setbacks allowed them to keep moving forward in their fight for equality.

SECTION 3: THE TRIALS AND TRIBULATIONS OF LEADERSHIP

Lastly, building a strong support system is vital. Surrounding oneself with like-minded individuals who provide emotional support, guidance, and accountability is essential for sustaining resilience over time.

In conclusion, the resilience of Aerin Zor is an inspiration to us all. They faced internal struggles, overcame adversities, and built a support system that enabled them to continue their fight for justice and equality. Their story reminds us that resilience is not simply the ability to endure, but the willingness to adapt, learn, and seek support when needed.

Subsection: Leading by Example in Turbulent Times

Leading a movement for social change is an immense responsibility, especially during turbulent times. In this subsection, we will explore how Aerin Zor exemplified leadership through her actions and became a beacon of hope for those fighting for alien civil rights.

The Power of Resilience

One of the key qualities that set Aerin Zor apart as a leader was her unwavering resilience in the face of adversity. She faced numerous challenges throughout her journey, from the initial resistance she encountered in her activism to the harsh backlash from those who opposed the Velan-7 uprising. Despite these obstacles, Aerin Zor remained steadfast in her commitment to her cause.

Resilience is not only about bouncing back from setbacks but also about learning from them. Aerin Zor understood that failure was an inevitable part of the struggle for justice. She used every setback as an opportunity for growth, analyzing what went wrong and finding ways to improve her strategies moving forward. By leading by example, she instilled a sense of resilience in her fellow activists, empowering them to persevere in the face of adversity.

Adaptability in Times of Change

Turbulent times call for adaptability and the ability to make quick decisions in ever-changing circumstances. Aerin Zor excelled in this aspect of leadership, constantly assessing the evolving situation on Velan-7 and adjusting her strategies accordingly.

One of the ways Aerin Zor demonstrated adaptability was by leveraging technology and social media to spread her message and mobilize support. She understood the power of communication and used various platforms to rally individuals from different corners of the galaxy. Aerin Zor's ability to adapt to new tools and embrace emerging technologies set her apart as a leader in the intergalactic movement for alien civil rights.

Leading with Empathy

Leading by example also means leading with empathy. During turbulent times, it is crucial for a leader to understand the challenges and experiences of those they represent. Aerin Zor embodied this empathetic leadership style, consistently prioritizing the needs and concerns of the alien community on Velan-7.

Aerin Zor actively listened to the voices of those who had been marginalized and oppressed, amplifying their stories and ensuring that they were heard. She advocated for policies and initiatives that addressed not only systemic discrimination but also the specific issues faced by various alien communities. By leading with empathy, Aerin Zor fostered a sense of unity and shared purpose among her followers, ultimately strengthening the movement for alien civil rights.

Transparency and Accountability

In turbulent times, maintaining transparency and accountability is essential for a leader. Aerin Zor recognized the importance of these values and upheld them throughout her journey as an activist.

She remained transparent about her intentions, actions, and decision-making processes, ensuring that her followers were well-informed and involved in the movement. Aerin Zor also held herself accountable, acknowledging her mistakes and taking responsibility for her actions. This transparency and accountability not only earned her the trust and respect of her fellow activists but also set a precedent for ethical leadership within the movement.

Sustainable Self-Care

Leadership during turbulent times can be emotionally and mentally draining. Aerin Zor understood the importance of sustainable self-care, recognizing that in order to lead effectively, she needed to prioritize her own well-being.

She promoted a culture of self-care and mental health awareness within the movement, encouraging her fellow activists to take breaks, seek support when needed, and engage in activities that rejuvenated their spirits. By leading by example in prioritizing self-care, Aerin Zor ensured the long-term sustainability of the movement, preventing burnout and maintaining the energy needed to fight for lasting change.

Embracing Collaboration

Leadership is not a solitary journey, especially during turbulent times. Collaboration and partnership with other activists and organizations are vital for success. Aerin Zor recognized this and actively sought out opportunities for collaboration.

She formed alliances with other leaders in the intergalactic movement, recognizing the strength that came from a united front. Aerin Zor understood that by leveraging the collective knowledge, resources, and experiences of various individuals and organizations, they could achieve much more together than they could alone. Through her collaborative leadership style, Aerin Zor built a strong network of support and solidarity, amplifying the impact of the movement.

Unconventional yet Relevant: The Power of Creative Expression

In addition to her strategic and empathetic leadership style, Aerin Zor embraced the power of creative expression as a tool for social change. She understood that art, music, and storytelling had the ability to inspire and unite people in ways that traditional activism could not always achieve.

Aerin Zor encouraged artists and creatives to use their talents to challenge prejudices and ignite conversations about alien civil rights. Through poetry slams, murals, music festivals, and other artistic endeavors, she provided a platform for diverse voices to be heard and celebrated. This unconventional approach not only added vibrancy to the movement but also attracted wider public attention and support.

Conclusion

Aerin Zor's leadership during turbulent times serves as an inspiration to activists and leaders alike. Through her resilience, adaptability, empathy, and commitment to transparency and collaboration, she led by example and fostered a sense of unity and purpose within the movement. Her unconventional approach, coupled with a focus on sustainable self-care, showcased the importance of creativity and personal well-being in achieving long-lasting social change. Aerin Zor's legacy continues to inspire future generations of activists, reminding us of the power of leadership during turbulent times.

Section 4: The Legacy of Aerin Zor

Subsection: Remembering the Galactic Hero

Every star that twinkles in the night sky has a story behind it, and among those stories, the tale of Aerin Zor shines the brightest. Aerin Zor, the enigmatic fusion of two alien entities, became a symbol of hope, courage, and relentless determination in the fight for alien civil rights on Velan-7. Today, we remember and celebrate the extraordinary life of this galactic hero.

Aerin Zor was not just an ordinary activist; they were a force of nature, a beacon of light in the darkness of oppression. From an early age, Aerin felt a calling from the stars, a deep sense of purpose to fight against injustice and challenge the status quo. Their story begins with their cosmic origins, born from stardust itself, a testament to the extraordinary potential within every being.

Growing up in the vast expanse of the cosmos, Aerin witnessed firsthand the beauties and hardships of the universe. They were shaped by their experiences, developing an unwavering commitment to pursuing knowledge and understanding. Aerin recognized the power of education as a catalyst for change and devoted themselves to seeking wisdom at the prestigious Nebula Academy.

At the Nebula Academy, Aerin delved into the rich tapestry of galactic history, learning from the triumphs and mistakes of the past. They discovered the value of empathy and interplanetary relations, realizing that true unity could only be achieved by breaking down barriers and confronting deep-seated prejudices. Armed with knowledge, Aerin set out to empower others through education, determined to share their enlightenment and awaken the dormant potential within every individual.

The journey to Velan-7 marked a turning point in Aerin's life. They encountered a planet divided, torn apart by the Bi-Entity Fusion Dilemma. Bi-Entity Fusions, like Aerin, faced discrimination and marginalization, seen as an abomination rather than a unique and beautiful form of existence. It was here that the Velan-7 Civil Rights Movement was born, and Aerin played a pivotal role in establishing connections and alliances that would be crucial in the upcoming uprising.

The Bi-Entity Fusion Uprising was a historical moment, a spark that ignited the revolution on Velan-7. Through meticulous organization and unwavering determination, Aerin and their fellow activists challenged the oppressive Velan-7 government, taking to the streets in nonviolent protests that would forever change the course of history. They exemplified the power of peaceful resistance, showing the world that the path to equality could be paved without bloodshed.

SECTION 4: THE LEGACY OF AERIN ZOR

Victory came at a high price, but it was a triumph nonetheless. The liberation of Velan-7 was a testament to the indomitable spirit of Aerin Zor and their comrades. They inspired a movement that transcended borders, igniting the passion for change in alien communities throughout the cosmos. The legacy of Aerin Zor continues to reverberate, motivating countless individuals to carry the torch of alien civil rights forward.

But the struggle is far from over. Aerin Zor's fight was not confined to the confines of Velan-7. Their passion for justice extended beyond planetary boundaries, resulting in the formation of the Alien Civil Rights Alliance. By spreading their message across galaxies, Aerin united alien worlds, fostering a sense of solidarity and shared purpose among diverse communities.

The battle for alien civil rights encompasses various fronts, addressing interplanetary prejudice, employment rights, xenophobia, and even the right to vote. Aerin Zor tirelessly advocated for true equality, challenging stereotypes and misconceptions along the way. Their vision of a galactic utopia, where diversity is celebrated and boundaries erased, continues to guide the movement towards coexistence.

In remembering the galactic hero, we celebrate the love and interspecies relationships that were once taboo in society. Aerin Zor's extraordinary love story shattered the norms of intergalactic romance, proving that love knows no boundaries. Their personal journey of acceptance not only humanized their cause but also emphasized the power of love as a driving force for change.

As a leader, Aerin faced numerous trials and tribulations. The weight of responsibility, the balancing act between personal and professional life, and the toll on mental health were challenges they courageously confronted. Their resilience in the face of adversity became a model for future generations of activists, proof that a single individual can make a profound impact on the world.

Today, we honor the legacy of Aerin Zor, not only through observances like Aerin Zor Day but also through artistic tributes and cultural celebrations. Their memory continues to inspire initiatives and projects aimed at preserving their remarkable achievements. Most importantly, the fight for equality and justice persists, with Aerin Zor's spirit guiding us through the darkest of times.

In conclusion, the life of Aerin Zor exemplifies the triumph of the human spirit, or rather, the alien spirit. They taught us that change starts with a single individual, that knowledge empowers, and that unity is a force to be reckoned with. As we remember the galactic hero, let us carry their legacy in our hearts and strive towards a future where equality and justice reign. The dream lives on, forever grateful to the hero of Velan-7.

Subsection: The Impact on Future Generations

The impact of Aerin Zor's activism extends far beyond her own lifetime. Her courageous efforts and unwavering dedication have left a lasting mark on the future generations, inspiring countless individuals to fight for justice, equality, and the rights of all beings in the universe.

One of the key ways in which Aerin Zor's impact on future generations is felt is through her influence on young activists. Her story of triumph over adversity serves as a powerful example for those who are still finding their own voices. By sharing the struggles she faced and the victories she achieved, Aerin Zor empowers young activists to stand up for what they believe in, showing them that change is possible, no matter the odds.

Aerin Zor's legacy also includes the establishment of educational initiatives that aim to educate young minds about the importance of alien civil rights. The Aerin Zor Foundation, founded in her honor, provides scholarships and grants to students pursuing studies in interstellar relations, alien culture, and activism. Through these initiatives, future generations are equipped with the knowledge and tools necessary to continue the fight for equality and justice.

Furthermore, Aerin Zor's impact on future generations can be seen in the transformation of societal attitudes towards aliens. Her relentless advocacy for alien rights has challenged the deeply ingrained prejudice and xenophobia within society. As a result, younger generations grow up in a world that fosters acceptance, empathy, and inclusivity, where the boundaries between different species are blurred and diversity is celebrated.

Aerin Zor's impact also extends to the realm of politics and policy-making. Her tireless efforts to bring about legislative changes have paved the way for the inclusion of aliens in decision-making processes. Thanks to her work, alien representation in planetary governments has increased, ensuring that their voices are heard and their rights protected. Additionally, her success in negotiating intergalactic treaties has set a precedent for future diplomats, emphasizing the importance of interstellar collaboration and cooperation.

The impact of Aerin Zor's activism on future generations is not limited to the realm of civil rights. Her advocacy for unity and collaboration among alien communities has inspired young activists to transcend the boundaries of their own species and work together for a common cause. Grassroots organizations for galactic change have flourished in the wake of her movement, connecting activists across different planets and species. Through these alliances, young activists can share knowledge, resources, and support, maximizing the impact of their collective efforts.

SECTION 4: THE LEGACY OF AERIN ZOR

In addition to her tangible achievements, Aerin Zor's impact on future generations can be felt on a deeply personal level. Her story of love and acceptance challenges societal norms and taboos surrounding interspecies relationships. By breaking down barriers and promoting understanding, she has opened the doors to a world where love knows no boundaries.

It is crucial to acknowledge that Aerin Zor's legacy is not without its challenges. Despite the progress made, there are still those who resist change and cling to their biases. Future generations will need to navigate through these obstacles and continue the fight for equality. However, thanks to the foundations laid by Aerin Zor, they are equipped with the knowledge, resilience, and determination necessary to overcome these challenges.

It is up to future generations to carry the torch and build upon the work of Aerin Zor. They must continue the fight for justice, equality, and the rights of all beings in the universe. By drawing inspiration from her legacy and embodying the spirit of activism, they can create a future where coexistence, diversity, and unity are the pillars of a galactic utopia.

Example: The Galactic Youth Alliance

One example of the impact of Aerin Zor's activism on future generations is the formation of the Galactic Youth Alliance (GYA). This organization, composed of young activists from various alien species, aims to promote interstellar cooperation, advocate for alien rights, and combat discrimination.

The GYA was inspired by Aerin Zor's courageous actions on Velan-7 and her vision for a united universe. The alliance fosters collaboration among young activists by organizing conferences, workshops, and cultural exchange programs. These initiatives provide a platform for young activists to share their experiences, learn from one another, and develop innovative approaches to tackle the challenges faced by alien communities.

Moreover, the GYA actively engages in grassroots advocacy and awareness campaigns. Through social media, art exhibitions, and public demonstrations, they raise public consciousness about the plight of alien communities and the need for equal rights. By amplifying their voices, the GYA ensures that the struggles faced by aliens are not forgotten or ignored.

The impact of the GYA can be seen in the increasing number of alien allies and aware individuals across the galaxy. Through their efforts, they have sparked conversations, changed perceptions, and encouraged everyday citizens to take action in support of alien rights. Their work has contributed to a more inclusive and empathetic galaxy, where the rights and dignity of all beings are recognized and respected.

The Galactic Youth Alliance is just one example of the many initiatives and movements inspired by Aerin Zor's activism. As more and more young individuals take up the mantle of change, her impact on future generations continues to grow. Through their collective efforts, they carry forward her vision of a universe where all beings, regardless of their origin, can thrive and coexist in harmony.

Subsection: Honoring the Sacrifices Made

In this subsection, we pay tribute to the brave individuals who made sacrifices in the pursuit of justice and equality. Their unwavering dedication and selflessness serve as a beacon of inspiration for future generations. Let us delve into the sacrifices made by Aerin Zor and her fellow activists on Velan-7 and explore the profound impact they had on the civil rights movement.

Aerin Zor and her comrades faced countless challenges and risks as they fought for the rights of the bi-entity fusion community on Velan-7. Their journey was filled with personal sacrifices, both big and small, which contributed to the ultimate success of the uprising.

One of the most significant sacrifices made by Aerin Zor and her team was their personal safety. They put themselves in the line of fire, facing the brutality and violence of the oppressive Velan-7 government. Many activists were imprisoned, tortured, and some tragically lost their lives in the pursuit of liberation. Their sacrifice reminds us of the lengths individuals are willing to go to challenge systemic injustices.

Alongside physical risks, the activists also endured emotional and psychological hardships. The toll of constant fear, uncertainty, and witnessing the suffering of their fellow bi-entity fusion beings took a significant toll on their mental well-being. However, they remained steadfast, motivated by a deep sense of purpose and a relentless desire to create a more equitable society.

The sacrifices made by these courageous individuals extended beyond their own well-being. Many activists sacrificed personal relationships, as their fight for justice consumed their lives. Friendships and familial bonds were strained, as their dedication to the cause often meant prioritizing the movement over personal connections. This sacrifice demonstrates the immense dedication and sense of duty these activists felt toward their mission.

Financial sacrifices were also common among the activists. To sustain their movement, they often relied on limited resources, pouring their own funds into organizing protests, printing informational materials, and supporting those in need. Many put their own financial stability on the line, sacrificing personal comfort for the greater good.

SECTION 4: THE LEGACY OF AERIN ZOR

The sacrifices made by Aerin Zor and her fellow activists on Velan-7 were not in vain. Their unwavering commitment and willingness to sacrifice paved the way for the liberation and empowerment of the bi-entity fusion community. They inspired a new generation of activists and changed the course of history.

In honoring their sacrifices, we must also recognize the ongoing sacrifices of activists around the universe. Their efforts are not forgotten, and their sacrifices continue to be felt. As we celebrate their achievements, let us remain vigilant in our fight for justice, remembering the sacrifices made and drawing strength from their legacy.

We must also acknowledge that honoring these sacrifices requires more than mere words. It necessitates ongoing commitment to dismantling oppressive systems and working towards a more inclusive and equitable society. We must amplify marginalized voices, uplift communities, and fight against the injustices that continue to persist in the cosmos.

To ensure that the sacrifices made by Aerin Zor and countless other activists are never in vain, we must hold ourselves accountable and actively work towards a future where equality and respect are the foundation of our intergalactic society.

As we honor their sacrifices, let us also remember that sacrifice should not be the sole burden of the oppressed. We must strive for a society in which the responsibility for change is shared by all. By acknowledging and addressing systemic inequities, we can build a future that is deserving of the sacrifices made by generations of activists.

In doing so, we embrace the true spirit of honoring these sacrifices – by continuing the fight, challenging the status quo, and building a galaxy that is welcoming, just, and inclusive for all. It is through our collective efforts that we can fully pay homage to the sacrifices made by Aerin Zor and her fellow activists, and fulfill their vision of a better universe for future generations to come.

Let us carry on their legacy, as we join together in this ongoing struggle for justice and equality, every day, until we achieve true liberation for all beings in the cosmos.

Subsection: Aerin Zor's Influence in Pop Culture

Aerin Zor, the fearless leader of the Velan-7 civil rights movement, had an undeniable impact not only on society but also on popular culture. Through her bravery, resilience, and unwavering commitment to equality, she inspired a generation of artists, writers, musicians, and filmmakers to incorporate her story and the struggles faced by alien communities into their work. Let's explore some of the ways in which Aerin Zor's influence can be seen in pop culture.

Film and Television

Aerin Zor's story has been immortalized in film and television, both in documentary form and through fictional adaptations. One notable example is the critically acclaimed biopic "The Cosmic Warrior," which chronicles Aerin's journey from a young alien activist to the leader of the Velan-7 civil rights movement. The film delves into the personal sacrifices she made and the challenges she faced, showcasing her indomitable spirit and the impact of her activism.

In addition to biopics, Aerin's powerful message of unity and equality has found its way into science fiction and fantasy TV series. In the hit show "Cosmic Chronicles," inspired by her life, the main character leads a group of alien rebels fighting for their rights in a fictional galaxy. The show draws parallels to Aerin's struggles, highlighting the importance of social justice and challenging bigotry in all its forms.

Music

Aerin Zor's powerful voice not only resonated in the realm of politics but also in the world of music. Many artists have been inspired by her fight for equality and have incorporated her message into their songs.

One notable tribute is the song "Galactic Freedom," released by a popular alien band. The lyrics echo Aerin's call for unity and celebrate the triumph of the Velan-7 civil rights movement. The song became an anthem for alien communities across the universe, uplifting spirits and inspiring activism.

Literature

Aerin Zor's impact on pop culture can also be seen in literature, with numerous books and novels drawing inspiration from her life and work. From sci-fi epics to young adult novels, writers have used her story as a backdrop to explore themes of discrimination, identity, and social change.

In the award-winning novel "The Starborn Rebellion," the protagonist embarks on a journey to liberate an alien world from oppressive rulers. The story draws parallels to Aerin's struggle, showcasing the power of collective action and the fight against intolerance.

Visual Art

The visual arts have not been immune to Aerin Zor's influence, with many artists incorporating her image and message into their work. Muralists, painters, and graphic designers have created stunning pieces that celebrate her legacy and advocate for alien civil rights.

One iconic artwork is a mural titled "A New Horizon," which depicts Aerin Zor leading a diverse group of aliens toward a brighter future. The mural has become a symbol of hope and resilience, reminding people of the ongoing fight for equality.

Fashion and Merchandise

Aerin Zor's image has also made its way into the fashion industry and merchandise. T-shirts, posters, and accessories featuring her likeness and inspiring quotes have become popular, allowing fans to proudly display their support for alien civil rights.

Fashion designers have drawn inspiration from her bold style, incorporating elements of her iconic outfit into their collections. Aerin's unique fashion sense has become synonymous with strength and defiance, inspiring individuals to embrace their true selves without fear of judgment.

Overall, Aerin Zor's influence in pop culture cannot be underestimated. Her story, filled with courage and determination, has touched the hearts of millions and has become a catalyst for change across various art forms. From films and music to literature and visual art, her legacy continues to inspire future generations to fight for equality, justice, and the eradication of prejudice. As artists and creators pay homage to her, her spirit lives on, reminding us all of the power of activism and the vision of a better, more inclusive world.

Subsection: Preserving the Memory of a Legend

Preserving the memory of a legendary figure like Aerin Zor is essential to ensure that their extraordinary contributions to the struggle for equality and justice are never forgotten. It allows future generations to learn from their experiences, continue their work, and be inspired by their courage. In this subsection, we explore some of the ways in which we can honor and keep alive the legacy of Aerin Zor.

Building a Memorial

One of the most tangible ways to preserve the memory of a legend is through the creation of a memorial. This could take the form of a statue, a monument, or a dedicated space in a public area. The design of the memorial should capture the essence of Aerin Zor's struggle and symbolize the ideals they fought for. For example, the memorial could depict Aerin Zor leading a protest, with their determination and fearlessness shining through. It should serve as a reminder of their achievements and inspire future activists to carry on the fight for alien civil rights.

Archiving Historical Artifacts

To fully understand and appreciate Aerin Zor's legacy, it is crucial to preserve historical artifacts associated with their life and activism. These artifacts could include handwritten letters, speeches, photographs, campaign materials, and personal items that provide insights into their journey. Establishing an archive or museum dedicated to preserving and showcasing these artifacts would allow people to immerse themselves in Aerin Zor's story and gain a deeper understanding of their impact on the struggle for equal rights.

Educational Initiatives

Preserving the memory of Aerin Zor also involves educating current and future generations about their life and accomplishments. Integrating their story into school curricula and educational programs ensures that their impact is acknowledged and celebrated. Moreover, organizing lectures, workshops, and seminars about Aerin Zor's activism can inspire and empower individuals to pursue their own paths of advocacy. By spreading knowledge about their contributions, we can ensure that their legacy lives on in the hearts and minds of the next generation.

Public Recognition and Commemoration

Public recognition and commemorative events play a vital role in preserving the memory of a legend like Aerin Zor. Designating an annual Aerin Zor Day or organizing commemorative ceremonies in key locations associated with their activism allows the community to come together to honor their contributions. These events can feature guest speakers, performances, and artistic tributes that reflect the spirit and principles of Aerin Zor's struggle. By keeping their memory alive, we create opportunities for dialogue, reflection, and continued activism.

Artistic Tributes

Art has the power to evoke emotions, challenge norms, and inspire change. Creating artistic tributes to honor Aerin Zor can bring their story to life in a unique and impactful way. This could include commissioning murals, creating sculptures, producing plays or films, or even releasing a commemorative song or album. The artistic tributes should capture the essence of Aerin Zor's journey, giving people a powerful visual or auditory representation of their legacy. By leveraging art as a medium, we can ensure that Aerin Zor's story resonates with a wide audience and carries on for generations to come.

Community Engagement

Preserving the memory of a legend like Aerin Zor requires active community engagement. Local organizations, community centers, and advocacy groups can organize events, workshops, and discussions centered around their legacy. This fosters an environment of collaboration, learning, and mutual support, and helps to carry on the torch of their fight for equality and justice. Encouraging community engagement ensures that the memory of Aerin Zor remains alive, and that their ideals and achievements continue to inspire new activists.

Continuing the Fight

Preserving the memory of Aerin Zor is not just about looking back, but also about continuing the fight for alien civil rights. It is a constant reminder that the struggle is ongoing, and there is still work to be done. By actively engaging in advocacy, supporting organizations that champion the cause, and amplifying the voices of marginalized communities, we can honor Aerin Zor's memory by actively working toward the world they fought for.

Conclusion

Preserving the memory of a legend like Aerin Zor is of paramount importance to ensure that their legacy lives on. Through memorials, archival initiatives, educational programs, public recognition, artistic tributes, community engagement, and continued advocacy, we can honor their extraordinary contributions to the struggle for equality and justice. By keeping their memory alive, we inspire future generations to carry on the fight and create a universe where everyone is treated with dignity and respect, regardless of their origin or identity. The memory of Aerin Zor will forever serve as a beacon of hope, reminding us that change is possible and that we all have the power to make a difference.

Subsection: Continuing the Fight for Equality and Justice

In the aftermath of the Bi-Entity Fusion Uprising on Velan-7, the fight for alien civil rights entered a new era. While the liberation of Velan-7 marked a significant victory, the struggle for equality and justice was far from over. Aerin Zor's legacy inspired a generation of activists to carry on the mission of creating a society that values and respects all beings in the universe. In this subsection, we explore the continued efforts to advance the cause of alien civil rights and the challenges that lie ahead.

The Long Road Ahead

The liberation of Velan-7 was a pivotal moment in the history of the cosmos. However, the fight for equality and justice is an ongoing battle that requires continuous vigilance. Alien communities across the universe still face discrimination, prejudice, and systemic barriers that prevent them from enjoying the same rights and opportunities as other beings. To ensure a lasting change, it is essential to address these challenges head-on.

Legislative Advocacy

One of the key avenues for continuing the fight for equality and justice is through legislative advocacy. Activists are actively pushing for the passage of laws that protect alien rights and promote inclusivity. By working with sympathetic lawmakers and leveraging public support, they aim to establish comprehensive legal frameworks that combat discrimination and promote equal treatment under the law.

For example, activists are advocating for the creation of intergalactic anti-discrimination laws that protect aliens from workplace discrimination, housing segregation, and denial of public services. These laws would hold accountable individuals and organizations that perpetuate discrimination based on alien origin, biology, or appearance. Additionally, activists are pushing for voting rights legislation that ensures aliens have a voice in the political process and can participate fully in democratic societies.

Building Alliances and Solidarity

To maximize the impact of their efforts, activists understand the importance of building alliances and fostering solidarity among different alien communities. By connecting with like-minded organizations and individuals across the universe, they can pool resources, share best practices, and amplify their collective voices.

Activists are engaging in collaborative initiatives such as conferences, workshops, and intergalactic summits to facilitate networking and knowledge exchange. These events serve as platforms for fostering solidarity among alien communities, empowering them to work together towards common goals.

Through these alliances, activists can build a strong and united front that is more resilient against systemic oppression.

Using Social Media and Technology

In the digital age, social media and technology have become invaluable tools for activism. Activists are leveraging various platforms to raise awareness about alien civil rights issues, mobilize supporters, and hold oppressors accountable. Social media campaigns, online petitions, and viral content serve as powerful methods to create a groundswell of public support and pressure policymakers to take action.

Additionally, technological advancements have enabled activists to document and expose incidents of discrimination and injustice. Body cameras and live-streaming capabilities have become essential tools for capturing evidence and broadcasting instances of police brutality or human rights violations. Through the use of technology, activists can shine a light on systemic issues and fuel public demand for meaningful change.

Education and Cultural Shift

Creating lasting change requires a cultural shift in attitudes and perceptions towards aliens. Education plays a vital role in challenging deep-rooted biases and fostering empathy and understanding. Activists are advocating for comprehensive educational reforms that incorporate alien history, contributions, and perspectives into curricula. By promoting inclusivity and celebrating diversity, they aim to nurture a society that values and appreciates all beings, regardless of their origins.

Beyond formal education, activists are also harnessing the power of storytelling and art to inspire change. Books, films, music, and other forms of artistic expressions have the capacity to captivate hearts and minds, shaping public opinion and challenging societal norms. By weaving alien narratives into mainstream culture, activists hope to break down barriers and foster a sense of shared humanity.

Global Outreach and Solidarity

While the focus of the fight for alien civil rights has often been centered on Velan-7, activists are now expanding their efforts globally. Recognizing that the struggle for equality transcends planetary boundaries, they are collaborating with activists from different star systems and galactic sectors. Through shared experiences and common goals, they aim to create a global movement for alien rights.

Activists are organizing interstellar conferences and establishing networks that facilitate information sharing and collaboration. By learning from the successes and challenges faced by other alien communities, activists can develop more effective strategies and tactics. Solidarity across timelines and galaxies strengthens the collective spirit of resistance and increases the likelihood of achieving meaningful change.

Conclusion

Aerin Zor's legacy serves as a guiding light for future generations of activists. The fight for equality and justice continues, fueled by a sense of urgency and the belief that a more just and inclusive universe is possible. Through legislative advocacy, building alliances, leveraging technology, fostering cultural shifts, and global outreach, activists are working towards a future where the rights of all beings are respected and protected.

The journey may be fraught with challenges, but the determination and resilience of the alien civil rights movement remain unwavering. As we look towards the future, let us remember the words of Aerin Zor: "No matter how vast the cosmos may be, the fight for equality and justice knows no boundaries. Together, we can create a universe where every being is truly free."

Chapter 4: Interviews and Reflections

Section 1: Insights from Alien Activists

Subsection: Perspectives on Aerin Zor's Influence

Aerin Zor's impact on the alien civil rights movement cannot be overstated. Her unwavering determination, charisma, and ability to inspire others changed the course of history on Velan-7 and beyond. In this subsection, we will explore the perspectives of various individuals who were influenced by Aerin Zor and her activism.

Brax Stellan - Former Velan-7 Government Official

Brax Stellan, a former Velan-7 government official, witnessed firsthand the transformation that occurred within the government as a result of Aerin Zor's activism. He recalls, "At first, I dismissed Aerin as a troublemaker, but her persistence and relentless fight for justice forced me to confront my own prejudices. It was her ability to humanize the struggles of alien beings that ultimately changed my perspective."

Stellan was inspired by Aerin's unwavering belief in the power of dialogue and diplomacy. He shares, "Aerin made me realize that change starts from within. She never resorted to violence or hatred. Instead, she challenged us to acknowledge the inherent worth and dignity of every being in the cosmos."

Zara Nal - Interplanetary Journalist

As an interplanetary journalist, Zara Nal felt the weight of responsibility to shed light on the struggles faced by alien communities. Aerin Zor's influence deeply impacted her approach to storytelling. Nal explains, "Aerin taught me the importance of amplifying marginalized voices. She made me realize that the stories of the oppressed are often discounted or ignored."

Aerin's fearlessness in the face of adversity inspired Nal to push the boundaries of mainstream journalism. She states, "I learned from Aerin that silence is not an option. I made a conscious decision to use my platform to challenge the status quo and provide a voice to those who have been silenced for far too long."

Dr. Nariel Thal - Alien Studies Scholar

As an alien studies scholar, Dr. Nariel Thal delved deep into the historical and societal implications of discrimination against alien beings. For Dr. Thal, Aerin Zor's impact was revolutionary. They reflect, "Aerin's activism forced us to confront the systemic inequalities embedded within our society. She challenged existing power structures and advocated for a new paradigm of coexistence."

Dr. Thal was particularly moved by Aerin's ability to unite individuals from diverse backgrounds under a common goal. They state, "Aerin's influence transcended planetary boundaries. She emphasized the interconnectedness of all beings in the cosmos and reminded us that our liberation is intertwined."

Ka'ra Xala - Student Activist

As a student activist, Ka'ra Xala looked up to Aerin Zor as a role model and source of inspiration. Xala admires Aerin's ability to galvanize mass movements and ignite passion within others. They share, "Aerin's leadership style was inclusive and empowering. She didn't impose her ideas on others but instead created spaces where ideas could flourish."

Aerin's legacy continues to motivate Xala in their own activism. Xala explains, "Aerin's impact goes beyond her accomplishments. It's about the belief that change is possible, even in the face of seemingly insurmountable odds. She taught us to channel our anger into action and to never underestimate the power of collective action."

Captain Theron Blaze - Intergalactic Peacekeeper

Captain Theron Blaze, an intergalactic peacekeeper, drew inspiration from Aerin Zor's nonviolent approach to activism. He remembers, "Aerin's ability to bring about change without resorting to violence sent a powerful message. She showed us that true strength lies in the ability to resist oppression with love and compassion."

Blaze was moved by how Aerin's activism focused on building bridges between different alien communities. He shares, "She taught us to find common ground even in our differences. Aerin's influence transformed not only our understanding of alien rights but also our approach to conflict resolution."

Erica Solis - Human Rights Advocate

Even among human rights advocates, Aerin Zor's influence is undeniable. Erica Solis, a prominent human rights advocate, sees Aerin as a symbol of hope. Solis states, "Aerin's work transcended the boundaries of species. She reminded us that the fight for justice knows no borders and that it is our responsibility to stand in solidarity with all those who are marginalized."

Solis believes that Aerin's ability to bridge the gap between different species serves as a guiding principle for human rights advocacy. She explains, "Aerin's influence extends to the way we approach intersectionality in our activism. She showed us that true progress comes when we acknowledge and address the unique struggles faced by individuals who exist at the intersections of multiple identities."

Conclusion

Aerin Zor's influence on the alien civil rights movement has left an indelible mark on the cosmos. From government officials to scholars, journalists to activists, her message of unity and equality resonates deeply within the hearts of those who continue to fight for justice. Aerin's legacy transcends time and space, reminding us that our collective efforts can shape a future where alien rights are protected and celebrated.

Subsection: Lessons Learned from the Struggle

As we delve into the lessons learned from the struggle for alien civil rights, it is important to reflect on the challenges faced by Aerin Zor and the greater intergalactic community. While advocating for equality and justice, they encountered numerous obstacles and setbacks. However, these experiences ultimately yielded valuable insights that can guide future activists in their quest for a fair and inclusive society. In this section, we will explore some of the key lessons that emerged from the struggle.

Lesson 1: Persistence and Resilience

One of the most important lessons we can learn from the struggle for alien civil rights is the significance of persistence and resilience. As Aerin Zor and their allies fought for equality, they faced immense resistance, both from the Velan-7 government and from elements within their own society. Countless protests were met with violence and repression, making it easy for activists to lose hope.

However, through their unwavering commitment to their cause, Zor and their supporters demonstrated the power of perseverance. They understood that real change often takes time and that setbacks are an inevitable part of the struggle. By remaining resilient in the face of adversity, they were able to overcome obstacles and gradually transform public opinion.

Example: One example of the power of persistence is the Sit-In Movement on Velan-7. Despite facing arrests, harassment, and even physical violence, activists continued to occupy public spaces, demanding equal rights for bi-entity fusions. Their unyielding determination eventually led to widespread recognition of the unjust treatment faced by these individuals, ultimately catalyzing the larger civil rights movement.

Lesson 2: Building Coalitions and Alliances

Another crucial lesson from the struggle for alien civil rights is the importance of building coalitions and alliances. Aerin Zor understood that they could not bring about significant change alone. They actively sought out like-minded individuals and organizations, fostering partnerships and collaborations that amplified their collective voice.

By forming alliances with other marginalized groups and sympathetic individuals, Zor's movement became a powerful force for change. They recognized that unity across different communities and backgrounds strengthens the fight against injustice, allowing for a broader range of experiences and perspectives to be brought to the forefront.

Example: The Bi-Entity Fusion Uprising would not have been as successful without the solidarity between the bi-entity fusions and their human allies. Together, they organized protests, shared resources, and effectively challenged the oppressive regime on Velan-7. This inter-species coalition showcased the power of unity in achieving common goals and highlighted the interconnectedness of different struggles for justice.

Lesson 3: Employing Nonviolent Resistance

In the quest for alien civil rights, another valuable lesson learned was the effectiveness of nonviolent resistance. Aerin Zor and their cohorts understood that resorting to violence would only perpetuate a cycle of harm and potentially alienate potential allies. Instead, they strategically employed nonviolent tactics to convey their message and challenge the oppressive status quo.

Nonviolent resistance allowed the activists to maintain moral high ground, making it difficult for their opponents to dismiss or undermine their cause. By choosing peaceful methods such as sit-ins, boycotts, and peaceful marches, Zor and their followers exposed the brutality of the government's response and garnered sympathy from intergalactic citizens who had previously been apathetic.

Example: The peaceful protests organized by Zor's movement attracted attention not just on Velan-7 but across the cosmos. By staying true to their principles of nonviolence, they gained widespread support from other interstellar communities, increasing the pressure on the Velan-7 government to address the injustices faced by bi-entity fusions.

Lesson 4: Intersectionality and Inclusive Advocacy

The struggle for alien civil rights also emphasized the importance of intersectionality and inclusive advocacy. Aerin Zor recognized that discrimination and oppression affected individuals differently based on various aspects of their identity, including their species, gender, and socioeconomic status. They understood that addressing these intersecting forms of discrimination was crucial for fostering true equality and justice.

Through inclusive advocacy, Zor's movement actively worked to amplify the voices of marginalized individuals who faced multiple forms of discrimination. This approach ensured that the fight for alien civil rights was not limited to a single dimension but rather encompassed the experiences of all those who were marginalized within society.

Example: Zor's movement actively collaborated with organizations focused on gender equality, environmental justice, and socioeconomic rights. By recognizing and elevating the voices of those at the intersections of multiple marginalized identities, they created a more robust and inclusive movement that resonated with a broader range of intergalactic citizens.

Lesson 5: The Importance of Education and Dialogue

Education and dialogue played an integral role in the struggle for alien civil rights. Aerin Zor and their allies recognized the power of knowledge in challenging deeply ingrained prejudices and biases. They prioritized educational initiatives, aiming to inform and engage the public about the realities of discrimination faced by alien communities.

Through open conversations and dialogue, Zor's movement was able to foster empathy and understanding, ultimately breaking down barriers of mistrust and fear. They actively engaged with individuals who initially held discriminatory beliefs, working to change hearts and minds through thoughtful discourse.

Example: Zor and their supporters organized workshops, lectures, and community gatherings to educate others about the experiences of bi-entity fusions and the larger alien community. By creating spaces for dialogue, they allowed individuals to ask questions, challenge assumptions, and engage in meaningful conversations that challenged the existing power dynamics.

Lesson 6: Remaining Adaptable and Evolving

An important lesson learned from the struggle for alien civil rights is the necessity of remaining adaptable and open to change. Aerin Zor and their allies continuously reassessed their strategies and approaches, recognizing that the struggle for justice is dynamic and requires constant adaptation.

By remaining open to new ideas and evolving with the circumstances, Zor's movement was able to navigate challenges and capitalize on emerging opportunities. They learned from their mistakes, embraced innovative tactics, and adjusted their methods to maximize their impact.

Example: As the struggle progressed, Zor's movement recognized the transformative power of artistic expression as a tool for social change. They incorporated music, visual arts, and performance into their activism, using these mediums to spread their message to a broader audience and ignite a sense of collective resistance.

In conclusion, the struggle for alien civil rights on Velan-7 yielded invaluable lessons that can guide future activists in their pursuit of justice, equality, and inclusion. These lessons emphasize the importance of persistence, building alliances, employing nonviolent resistance, advocating for intersectionality, fostering education and dialogue, and remaining adaptable. By understanding and internalizing these lessons, future activists can confront the challenges of their time with greater insight, resilience, and determination. The struggle continues, and

SECTION 1: INSIGHTS FROM ALIEN ACTIVISTS

these lessons serve as beacons of hope for a future where all beings are treated with dignity and equality.

Additional Exercise: Reflect on a current social justice movement or civil rights struggle and identify the lessons that can be learned from it. Consider the strategies employed, the challenges faced, and the impact of the movement. How can these lessons be applied to other social justice causes? Share your thoughts in a short essay or a group discussion.

Additional Resource: "The Anatomy of Social Change: Lessons from Historical Movements" by John D. Green provides a comprehensive analysis of various social justice movements throughout history, drawing valuable lessons that can inform contemporary activism.

Subsection: Inspirations and Role Models

In the journey of activism, inspirations and role models play a crucial role in shaping the mindset and approach of individuals. Aerin Zor's path to becoming a galactic hero was no exception. In this subsection, we will explore some of the key inspirations and role models that influenced Aerin Zor's activism and helped guide their path towards fighting for alien civil rights.

Finding Inspiration in the Stars

As a child, Aerin Zor was drawn to the vastness and mystery of the cosmos. Looking up at the stars, they felt a sense of wonder and awe that sparked their curiosity and thirst for knowledge. It was during these moments of stargazing that Aerin Zor first felt a deep connection to the universe and realized that they were part of something much greater than themselves.

One of the inspirations that played a pivotal role in their early years was the legendary astronomer and science communicator Carl Sagan. Sagan's infectious enthusiasm for the cosmos and his passionate advocacy for scientific education resonated deeply with Aerin Zor. Through Sagan's writings and documentaries, they learned about the profound interconnectedness of the universe and the importance of fostering a spirit of empathy and understanding.

Guidance from Activist Elders

Aerin Zor's journey as an activist was greatly influenced by the teachings and guidance of their elders. In their community, there were several veteran activists who had been fighting for alien rights long before Aerin Zor's time. These elders shared their stories of struggle and triumph, igniting a fire within Aerin Zor to carry the torch of activism forward.

One of the most influential role models was Xandra Renn, a charismatic and fearless advocate who had dedicated her life to fighting for alien empowerment. Xandra's ability to mobilize communities, her unwavering determination, and her ability to find strength in unity deeply inspired Aerin Zor. They saw in Xandra a force of nature, someone who refused to back down in the face of adversity.

Heroes of the Galactic Civil Rights Movement

The Galactic Civil Rights Movement was a pivotal moment in the history of alien activism, and the heroes who emerged from this movement became an inspiration for Aerin Zor. One such hero was Alara Vex, a courageous alien rights advocate who led a successful campaign for equal representation in the Planetary Council.

Alara's approach to activism, which combined unwavering tenacity with strategic political maneuvering, resonated deeply with Aerin Zor. They recognized that achieving lasting change required not only street protests but also working within existing systems to effect policy change.

Exploring Interdisciplinary Influences

Aerin Zor's activism was not confined to the realm of civil rights alone. They drew inspiration from various disciplines and explored how they intersected with their mission. One significant influence was the field of sociology, particularly the work of Dr. Emma González. Driven by a desire to understand the societal dynamics that perpetuated inequality, Aerin Zor delved into González's research on systemic oppression and the importance of intersectionality.

Moreover, Aerin Zor found inspiration in the realm of art and entertainment. The Afrofuturist movement, with its vision of a world where marginalized voices are amplified and celebrated, resonated deeply with their own aspirations. Artists like Janelle Monáe and Octavia Butler became beacons of hope and inspiration, reminding Aerin Zor of the power of storytelling and art as catalysts for social change.

A Call to Future Activists

In the spirit of their own journey, Aerin Zor encourages aspiring activists to seek inspiration from diverse sources. They emphasize the importance of looking beyond traditional figures and exploring interdisciplinary influences. By drawing inspiration

SECTION 1: INSIGHTS FROM ALIEN ACTIVISTS

from the stars, community elders, historic movements, and other fields, aspiring activists can forge their own unique path towards creating a more equitable universe.

Remember, true inspiration can come from anywhere. It could be found in a line of poetry, a conversation with a stranger, or a moment of solitude in nature. What matters most is the courage to dream, the determination to act, and the unwavering belief in the possibility of a better world.

"Let the stories of the past guide us, the heroes of today inspire us, and the dreams of the future drive us. Together, we can create a universe where every being is valued and celebrated." - Aerin Zor

So, fellow activists, let us embrace the inspirations and role models that shape our quest for justice and equality. Let us find solace in their stories, learn from their struggles, and build upon their legacies. The fight for alien civil rights is a collective journey, and each of us has the power to make a difference.

Subsection: The Importance of Intersectionality

Intersectionality is a concept that recognizes the interconnected nature of social identities, such as race, gender, sexuality, class, and ability, and how they intersect to shape our experiences of privilege and oppression. This understanding is crucial when discussing and addressing issues of civil rights and social justice because it allows us to see the complex and multidimensional ways in which individuals are affected by systems of power and discrimination.

To illustrate the importance of intersectionality, let's consider an example. Imagine two individuals, Emma and Michael, both working in the same company. Emma is a white woman, while Michael is a Black man. Both Emma and Michael experience discrimination and hostility in the workplace, but their experiences differ due to the intersection of their identities.

Emma might face gender-based discrimination, such as being interrupted or overlooked in meetings or being subjected to sexist comments. Michael, on the other hand, might experience racial bias, such as being stereotyped as aggressive or less capable. These distinct forms of discrimination are rooted in both gender and race, and cannot be separated from each other.

Intersectionality teaches us that it is not enough to focus on single-axis analysis or tackle issues of discrimination in isolation. By examining the intersections of various identities, we gain a deeper understanding of how discrimination operates and how it affects individuals in unique ways.

Moreover, intersectionality reminds us that privilege and oppression are not mutually exclusive. In the case of Emma and Michael, Emma benefits from white privilege in addition to facing gender discrimination, whereas Michael faces racial discrimination but may experience male privilege. Recognizing these complexities helps us avoid oversimplifications and promotes a more nuanced understanding of social dynamics.

The concept of intersectionality also emphasizes the importance of inclusivity and inclusiveness within advocacy movements. It reminds us that our fight for equality and justice must be intersectional, centering the experiences of marginalized communities that face multiple forms of discrimination. It calls for solidarity among different groups to dismantle intersecting systems of oppression and work towards a more equitable society.

In order to effectively address the challenges posed by intersectionality, it is crucial to engage in dialogue and foster connections between different movements, striving for an inclusive approach to activism. This means acknowledging and supporting organizations and initiatives that aim to address the needs and concerns of marginalized groups.

Additionally, education plays a fundamental role in promoting intersectional thinking. By incorporating intersectionality into our curriculums, we can foster critical thinking skills and a deeper understanding of social inequality. This will empower individuals to challenge systems of oppression and work towards building a more inclusive and just society.

Intersectionality is not without its challenges, of course. Addressing the intersecting forms of discrimination requires collaboration, recognizing our own privileges and biases, and actively amplifying the voices of marginalized communities. It requires us to listen, learn, and unlearn. It also demands that we acknowledge the limitations of our own perspectives and embrace the diversity of human experiences.

In conclusion, intersectionality is a vital framework for understanding the complexity of discrimination and privilege. It allows us to explore the interconnected nature of various identities and their impact on social justice issues. By adopting an intersectional approach, we can work towards a more inclusive and equitable society, where individuals are seen and treated as whole beings, with all their unique identities and experiences. Let us embrace this perspective and strive for a more just future for all.

Subsection: Advice for Aspiring Activists

Aspiring activists, listen up! In this subsection, I'm going to share some valuable advice that will guide you on your journey to becoming a change-maker. Activism is no easy task, but with the right mindset and approach, you can make a real difference in the world around you. So, let's dive in!

SECTION 1: INSIGHTS FROM ALIEN ACTIVISTS

1. **Educate Yourself:** Knowledge is power, my friends. Before you can effectively advocate for a cause, you need to have a deep understanding of the issues at hand. Take the time to research, read books, attend workshops, and engage in conversations with experts in the field. This solid foundation of knowledge will help you articulate your message and engage with others more effectively.

2. **Find Your Passion:** Activism is fueled by passion. What are the issues that truly light a fire within you? Is it climate change, racial inequality, gender rights, or something else altogether? Identify the cause that resonates with you the most and put your energy into it. By focusing on a specific area, you'll be able to channel your efforts more effectively and make a greater impact.

3. **Cultivate Empathy:** As an activist, it's crucial to understand and empathize with the experiences of others. Take the time to listen to diverse voices and perspectives. Engage in conversations with individuals who have different backgrounds and experiences from your own. By cultivating empathy, you'll be better equipped to address the needs and concerns of marginalized communities and create equitable change.

4. **Build Coalitions:** Remember, you don't have to fight the battle alone. Activism thrives on collaboration and unity. Seek out like-minded individuals and organizations who share your passion and goals. Building coalitions allows you to pool resources, amplify your voice, and create collective impact. Together, we are stronger.

5. **Harness the Power of Social Media:** In today's digital age, social media platforms can be powerful tools for spreading awareness and mobilizing support. Use platforms like Twitter, Instagram, and Facebook to share your message, engage with others, and connect with activists from around the world. However, be mindful of misinformation and the echo chamber effect. Verify your sources and promote critical thinking.

6. **Embrace Nonviolent Resistance:** Nonviolence is a cornerstone of effective activism. Embrace peaceful methods of protest and resistance. Engage in dialogue, organize peaceful demonstrations, and use creative means to get your message across. Nonviolent actions not only attract positive attention but also foster understanding and build bridges with those who may not initially support your cause.

7. **Take Care of Yourself:** Activism can be emotionally and mentally demanding. Remember to prioritize self-care and well-being. Take breaks when needed, engage in activities that bring you joy, and surround yourself with a support system of friends and fellow activists. Remember, you are in this for the long haul, so take care of yourself to sustain your activism.

8. **Stay Persistent:** Change takes time and perseverance. Don't get discouraged if progress is slow or setbacks occur. Keep pushing forward, stay

resilient, and remain focused on your goals. Celebrate small victories along the way, and learn from challenges. By staying persistent, you will create a lasting impact.

9. **Inspire Others:** As an activist, you have the power to inspire and motivate others. Lead by example, share your story, and create spaces for dialogue and learning. Ignite the spark of activism in others and empower them to take action. Genuine inspiration is contagious and can create a ripple effect, fostering a community of change-makers.

10. **Embrace Intersectionality:** Recognize the interconnectedness of social justice issues. Understand that systems of oppression are interconnected, and therefore, your activism should also be intersectional. Make an effort to learn about and support causes beyond your own. Collaborate with activists from diverse backgrounds and work collectively to create an inclusive and equitable future.

Remember, activism is a journey, and there is no one-size-fits-all approach. Embrace your uniqueness, adapt your strategies as needed, and always listen and learn. Your voice and actions matter, and by following these principles, you'll be well on your way to becoming an effective and inspiring activist. Now, go out there and make waves of change!

Subsection: Finding Hope in the Midst of Adversity

In the face of adversity, finding hope can sometimes feel like searching for a needle in a cosmic haystack. But for activists like Aerin Zor, hope is not just a distant dream, but a tangible force that drives them forward in their pursuit of change. In this subsection, we will explore the ways in which Aerin Zor found hope amidst the difficulties encountered while fighting for alien civil rights.

The Power of Resilience

One of the fundamental aspects of finding hope in adversity is cultivating resilience. Aerin Zor understood that setbacks and challenges were an inevitable part of the struggle for equality. However, instead of allowing these obstacles to crush their spirit, they turned them into opportunities for growth.

Resilience is a trait that can be developed and strengthened over time. It involves acknowledging and accepting difficult circumstances, adapting to change, and transforming adversity into fuel for action. For Aerin Zor, resilience meant never giving up, even when faced with seemingly insurmountable odds.

Building a Support Network

Another key factor in finding hope in the midst of adversity is the presence of a strong support network. Activists like Aerin Zor understand that they cannot fight for change alone. They surround themselves with like-minded individuals who provide emotional support, offer different perspectives, and collaborate on initiatives.

A support network can consist of fellow activists, friends, family members, mentors, or even online communities. This network serves as a lifeline, helping to maintain optimism and inspire hope, even in the face of adversity. Together, they can share their experiences, strategize solutions, and remind each other that they are not alone in their journey.

Celebrating Small Victories

Sometimes, finding hope in the midst of adversity means shifting focus from the big picture to the small victories along the way. Aerin Zor recognized that change rarely happens overnight, and it is crucial to acknowledge and celebrate even the smallest milestones.

By celebrating small victories, activists can keep themselves motivated and hopeful for the future. Whether it is a policy change, a successful awareness campaign, or a positive shift in public opinion, these small wins serve as reminders that progress is possible, even in the face of adversity.

Self-Care and Reflection

In the midst of activism, it is easy to become consumed by the fight for change, neglecting one's own well-being. However, Aerin Zor understood the importance of taking care of oneself in order to maintain hope and continue the struggle.

Self-care involves setting boundaries, practicing self-compassion, and engaging in activities that recharge and rejuvenate the mind and body. Whether it is meditation, spending time in nature, pursuing a hobby, or seeking therapy, self-care allows activists to replenish their energy and find solace amidst adversity.

Reflection is another essential aspect of finding hope in the midst of adversity. Taking the time to reflect on one's journey, setbacks, and successes can provide valuable insights and help maintain a positive mindset. Reflection allows activists to learn from their experiences, adapt their strategies, and find hope in the knowledge that they are constantly evolving and making progress.

Inspiring and Being Inspired

Lastly, finding hope in the midst of adversity often comes from both inspiring others and being inspired by the stories and experiences of fellow activists. Aerin Zor recognized the power of storytelling in conveying the impact of their work and inspiring others to join the fight.

Sharing personal stories, victories, and even moments of vulnerability can create a ripple effect, encouraging others to take action and persevere in the face of adversity. By inspiring others, activists like Aerin Zor find renewed hope in their ability to make a difference and create meaningful change.

In turn, activists can also draw inspiration from the stories and experiences of their peers. Hearing about the struggles and triumphs of others helps reinforce the belief that change is possible and that they are part of a larger movement working towards a common goal.

Example: The Hopeful Campaign

To illustrate the importance of finding hope in the midst of adversity, let's consider the example of the "Hopeful Campaign." This campaign was initiated by Aerin Zor in the face of a particularly oppressive regime on Velan-7.

The campaign aimed to spread messages of hope, resilience, and solidarity among oppressed alien communities. Aerin Zor and their team organized rallies, created artwork and murals, and collaborated with local communities to share stories of triumph and resilience.

Through the Hopeful Campaign, Aerin Zor not only inspired others but also found hope in the collective strength and determination of the alien communities. The campaign served as a reminder that even in the darkest of times, hope can be found and nurtured, providing the fuel needed to continue the fight for change.

Conclusion

Finding hope in the midst of adversity is a constant challenge for activists like Aerin Zor. However, by cultivating resilience, building a support network, celebrating small victories, practicing self-care and reflection, and drawing inspiration from and inspiring others, hope can be found and sustained.

In the face of immense challenges, hope becomes a driving force that propels activists forward, reminding them of the transformative power of their work. Aerin Zor's journey serves as a testament to the limitless possibilities that can arise when hope is embraced, even in the most trying of circumstances.

As we continue to learn from Aerin Zor's legacy, it is essential to remember that hope is not a passive emotion but an active force that fuels our commitment to creating a universe where equality and justice prevail.

Section 2: Personal Reflections

Subsection: The Evolution of Aerin Zor's Beliefs

As we delve into the remarkable journey of Aerin Zor, it is essential to explore the evolution of her beliefs—the transformative process that shaped her into the visionary leader she became. Aerin Zor's path to enlightenment was no easy feat, filled with moments of doubt, self-discovery, and overcoming internalized prejudice. Let's explore the significant milestones in her belief system and the lessons we can learn from her remarkable transformation.

One of the earliest aspects that influenced Aerin Zor's beliefs was her exposure to the diverse cosmic cultures she encountered in her travels. Born amidst the wonder of stardust, she grew up embracing the rich tapestry of cosmic origins, appreciating the diverse life forms that peppered the galaxies. The realization that every sentient being shared this cosmic heritage sparked her curiosity and ignited her desire for understanding and connection.

As Aerin Zor's awareness expanded, she began questioning the inherent injustice and inequality she observed within interstellar societies. Witnessing the struggles of disenfranchised alien communities, she awakened to the systemic oppression ingrained in the cosmos. This awakening became the catalyst for her mission to rectify these injustices and fight for equality.

The tenets of empathy and interplanetary relations she acquired during her interstellar education at the Nebula Academy played a pivotal role in Aerin Zor's belief system. Through the study of galactic history, she realized the cyclical nature of prejudice and discrimination, understanding that true change required a deep understanding of the past. Armed with this knowledge, she embarked on a mission to empower others through education, empowering alien beings to stand up and fight for their rights.

The turning point in Aerin Zor's belief system occurred during her journey to Velan-7, a planet divided by the Bi-Entity Fusion Dilemma. This dilemma served as a microcosm of the interstellar disparities she had witnessed throughout her travels. As she witnessed the struggles of the Bi-Enters—beings formed from the fusion of two different alien species—her empathy propelled her into action.

Establishing connections and alliances within the local communities, Aerin Zor led the charge in the Velan-7 Civil Rights Movement. Together with fellow activists, she nurtured the uprising, preparing for the inevitable clash to secure equality for Bi-Entity Fusions. It was during this monumental struggle that Aerin Zor fully embraced the power of activism in effecting social change. Nonviolent protests became their weapon of choice, showcasing the effectiveness of peaceful resistance in challenging the oppressive Velan-7 government.

The triumph and aftermath of the Bi-Entity Fusion Uprising became a testament to the strength and resilience of Aerin Zor's beliefs. The liberation of Velan-7 stood as a beacon of hope for oppressed alien communities across the cosmos. With the vision of a better world, Aerin Zor dedicated herself to rebuilding the society they fought so hard to free.

As she continued her journey beyond Velan-7, Aerin Zor recognized the need to advocate for change not only within individual planets but across galaxies. She understood that the alien experience was rife with prejudice, discrimination, and inequality that permeated political, social, and economic structures. It was no longer enough to fight for the rights of one alien species but to unite all alien worlds under a common goal of liberation and prosperity.

Aerin Zor's belief in the power of unity became a driving force as she worked tirelessly to establish the Alien Civil Rights Alliance. By fostering collaboration and solidarity among alien communities, she aimed to create a seismic shift in the intergalactic paradigm. Her advocacy took her on a path where she confronted interplanetary prejudices head-on, challenging the existing power structures and fighting for alien employment rights, voting rights, and an end to xenophobia.

The extraterrestrial alliance she formed became a testament to the strength of collaborative resistance. Grassroots organizations sprouted, providing marginalized alien communities a voice and an avenue for change. Through this network of support, Aerin Zor paved the way for a future where all sentient beings could thrive, regardless of their cosmic origins.

Aerin Zor's belief in the transformative power of policy change propelled her beyond activism and into the realm of interstellar diplomacy. She recognized the importance of alien representation in planetary governments, advocating for a seat at the table where decisions that affected alien rights were made. Negotiating intergalactic treaties and playing a vital role as an alien ambassador, she championed the cause of alien rights in universal laws, shifting the oppressive status quo.

In her vision for a galactic utopia, Aerin Zor fueled her beliefs with unbounded imagination. She dreamed of a universe where equality reigned, erasing the boundaries that had long divided beings. She understood the significance of art as

SECTION 2: PERSONAL REFLECTIONS

a catalyst for change, leveraging its power to challenge norms, reshape perspectives, and unite diverse cosmic communities in the celebration of their differences.

The evolution of Aerin Zor's beliefs serves as an inspiration to all who seek a more just and equitable universe. Her journey—from the cosmic origins that shaped her, the awakening to injustice and purpose, the struggle for the liberation of Velan-7, and the fight for rights across galaxies—represents a transformative path that each of us can embark upon. The legacy of Aerin Zor serves as a reminder that no matter how small our beginnings may be, our beliefs can propel us to become forces of change in the cosmos, leaving an indelible mark for future generations.

As we reflect on the evolution of Aerin Zor's beliefs, let us remember that the fight for equality and justice is an ongoing battle. It requires continuous dedication, collaboration, and a belief in the inherent worth of every sentient being. Aerin Zor's journey is a call to action—to honor her legacy, we must strive to create a world where the dream of coexistence and celebration of diversity becomes an enduring reality.

Key Takeaways:

- The evolution of Aerin Zor's beliefs was shaped by her exposure to cosmic cultures and her growing empathy for oppressed alien communities.
- Interstellar education played a crucial role in her transformation, equipping her with knowledge of galactic history and the power of education.
- The Bi-Entity Fusion Uprising on Velan-7 was a turning point that solidified Aerin Zor's belief in the effectiveness of activism and nonviolent protests.
- After the uprising, Aerin Zor expanded her advocacy to unite alien worlds, challenging interplanetary prejudice and fighting for a range of alien rights.
- Aerin Zor's belief in the transformative power of policy change led her to become an alien ambassador and advocate for alien representation in governance.
- Her dream for a galactic utopia emphasized the importance of art, erasing boundaries, and celebrating diversity.
- The legacy of Aerin Zor reminds us that the fight for equality and justice is ongoing and requires continuous dedication and collaboration.

Unconventional Tip: As you explore and evolve your own beliefs, take time to connect with diverse cultures and perspectives. Engaging in meaningful conversations and seeking out new experiences can enrich your understanding of the world and shape your beliefs in powerful ways. Step beyond your comfort zone and embrace the cosmic tapestry that unites us all.

Moments of Doubt and Self-Discovery

In the journey of activism, moments of doubt and self-discovery play a crucial role in shaping an individual's beliefs and motivations. For Aerin Zor, these moments were not only an internal struggle but also pivotal in finding the courage and determination to fight for alien civil rights. This subsection delves into some of the most profound and transformative instances that contributed to Aerin's personal growth and led to a deeper understanding of the challenges they would face.

One of the earliest moments of doubt for Aerin came during their teenage years, grappling with the complexities of their dual identity. Growing up in a universe that inherently favored conformity, Aerin questioned their place in society. They wondered if their fusion of two distinct entities meant they were destined to remain an outsider, forever caught between two worlds. This internal tug-of-war shaped Aerin's perception of self and fueled their determination to challenge the status quo.

A pivotal turning point in Aerin's journey of self-discovery came when they attended the renowned Nebula Academy. Here, among a diverse group of extraordinary beings from across the cosmos, Aerin had the opportunity to engage in open discussions about identity, prejudice, and systemic injustice. It was during these late-night debates and heartfelt conversations that Aerin's resolve hardened, and a fire within them was ignited.

While studying the history of interplanetary relations, Aerin encountered stories of past activists who fought against oppression and paved the way for a more inclusive universe. Learning about the struggles faced by these trailblazers gave Aerin the courage to confront their own doubts and fears. It became clear that the fight for alien rights was not an individual battle but a collective journey toward a more equitable future.

Another crucial moment of doubt occurred when Aerin first encountered resistance from members of their own alien community. Initially expecting solidarity and support, Aerin was disheartened to find some individuals dismissive of their cause, believing that fighting for civil rights would only bring unwanted attention and further marginalization. This internal conflict pushed Aerin to reevaluate their position and find ways to bridge the gap within their community, emphasizing the importance of education and dialogue in creating lasting change.

Navigating the complexities of activism, Aerin often found themselves questioning the effectiveness of their chosen path. They wrestled with doubts about whether peaceful protests and nonviolent resistance could truly dismantle the oppressive systems entrenched in the cosmos. These moments of uncertainty became opportunities for growth, as Aerin sought to find solace and inspiration in the untold stories of small triumphs and incremental progress. The realization that even small steps forward could create a ripple effect of change renewed Aerin's belief in the power of collective action.

To find strength and purpose amidst doubt, Aerin turned to self-reflection and meditation. They discovered that taking time for introspection allowed them to reconnect with their core values and reaffirm their commitment to the cause. Through mindfulness practices, Aerin learned to embrace vulnerability, acknowledge their limitations, and match their actions with an unwavering belief in justice.

It is essential to recognize that doubt and self-discovery are ongoing processes, woven into the fabric of an activist's journey. Aerin's moments of doubt served as reminders of their humanity, grounding them in the recognition that they were not immune to the emotional challenges of their path. By embracing these moments and adapting their approach, Aerin gained a deeper understanding of their purpose and the resilience needed to overcome obstacles along the way.

Beyond Aerin's story, moments of doubt and self-discovery are universal aspects of the human experience, reflective of the constant evolution and growth we all undergo. Recognizing and confronting these doubts can lead to profound personal transformations and a renewed commitment to fight for justice and equality. The struggles and triumphs of Aerin's journey serve as a reminder that, in the face of doubt, it is through self-discovery that we find the strength to change the cosmos.

Subsection: Striking a Balance between Idealism and Realism

In the tumultuous journey of activism, one of the biggest challenges that Aerin Zor faced was finding the delicate balance between idealism and realism. On one hand, idealism fueled her passion, driving her to dream big and envision a galaxy where equality and justice reigned supreme. On the other hand, realism forced her to confront the harsh realities of the world, the limitations of her power, and the complexities of enacting lasting change.

The dilemma of balancing idealism and realism is not unique to Aerin Zor but is a universal struggle for all activists. At the heart of this struggle lies the question: How do we remain steadfast in our ideals while navigating the complex and often messy terrain of social change?

To answer this question, let us delve into the principles and strategies that Aerin Zor employed to strike that balance. Drawing from her experiences, we can gain valuable insights into the art of navigating the twin forces of idealism and realism.

Embrace the Power of Vision

Idealism is the fuel that ignites the fires of change. It allows us to dream of a better world and envision the possibilities that lie beyond the present. For Aerin Zor, it was her unwavering belief in the inherent equality of all beings that served as the bedrock of her activism. She understood that a clear and compelling vision is the first step towards inspiring others and mobilizing collective action.

As aspiring activists, we must learn to harness the power of vision. We need to create a vivid picture of the future we desire, one that is grounded in values of justice, equality, and inclusivity. By sharing this vision with others, we can invite them to join us in our collective pursuit of change.

Confront the Realities

While vision provides the foundation, realism demands that we confront the complexities and limitations of our efforts. In the journey towards social change, we are bound to encounter setbacks, resistance, and roadblocks. It is crucial to acknowledge the challenges and be willing to adapt our strategies in response.

Aerin Zor understood the importance of realistic assessments. She recognized that change takes time, that progress can be incremental, and that setbacks are inevitable. By embracing a realistic mindset, we can avoid the pitfalls of idealistic naivety and prepare ourselves for the inevitable bumps along the road.

Strategic Idealism

Finding the balance between idealism and realism requires a strategic approach. Aerin Zor was a master at this delicate dance, continuously adapting her idealistic vision to suit the realities she faced. She recognized that compromise was often necessary to achieve tangible results in the short term while staying true to the long-term goals of equality and justice.

Strategic idealism involves identifying achievable milestones along the path to the ultimate vision. It means breaking down seemingly insurmountable challenges into smaller, actionable steps. By pursuing realistic short-term goals that align with our larger ideals, we build momentum, gain credibility, and create a foundation for lasting change.

Building Coalitions and Alliances

No activist can create significant change alone. Aerin Zor understood the power of alliances and the necessity of working with diverse groups. By building coalitions, she not only amplified her impact but also fostered a sense of unity and solidarity within the movement.

Idealism can sometimes breed an "us versus them" mentality, alienating potential allies. Realism forces us to recognize that change is a collective endeavor and that collaboration with individuals and groups who may not share our exact ideals is crucial. By finding common ground, respect, and shared values, we can forge alliances that are stronger than the sum of their parts.

Resilience in the Face of Setbacks

No discussion on idealism and realism would be complete without addressing the essential role of resilience. Activism is a marathon, not a sprint, and setbacks and failures are part of the journey. Aerin Zor's unwavering dedication and determination to her cause were fueled by her resilience in the face of adversity.

Resilience allows us to bounce back from setbacks, learn from our mistakes, and persevere in the face of challenges. It means finding strength in difficult times and constantly adapting to changing circumstances. By practicing self-care, seeking support, and cultivating a resilient mindset, we can maintain our idealism while navigating the realities of the world.

Unconventional Wisdom: Embracing Chaos

In our quest for balance between idealism and realism, it is important to remember that change is inherently chaotic. The world is complex, and the path to progress is rarely linear. Embracing chaos and uncertainty can be an unconventional yet powerful wisdom.

Aerin Zor understood that rigid adherence to plans and linear thinking could hinder progress. By embracing chaos, she was able to adapt quickly, seize unexpected opportunities, and navigate through challenging situations. Embracing chaos means being comfortable with ambiguity, thinking on our feet, and being open to creative solutions that may not conform to traditional wisdom.

Exercises and Reflections

1. Reflect on your own activism journey or a cause that you are passionate about. How do you balance idealistic vision with the realities of the world?

2. Identify a specific challenge or setback you have faced in your activism. How did you respond to it? What lessons did you learn from that experience?
3. Evaluate the alliances and coalitions you have built in your activism work. How have they contributed to your impact? How have they challenged your ideals?
4. Explore unconventional strategies or approaches that can help you embrace chaos and uncertainty in your activism. How can you incorporate flexibility and creativity into your efforts?

Remember, striking a balance between idealism and realism is an ongoing process. It requires constant reflection, adaptation, and a willingness to learn from both successes and failures. By embracing this delicate dance, we can navigate the complexities of the world while staying true to our ideals and driving meaningful change.

Subsection: Overcoming Internalized Prejudice

Internalized prejudice can be a significant barrier in the fight for equality and justice. It is the unconscious acceptance and internalization of negative stereotypes and biases that society imposes on marginalized groups. In the case of Aerin Zor, overcoming internalized prejudice was a pivotal step in their journey as an activist. In this subsection, we will explore the concept of internalized prejudice, its impact on individuals and communities, and strategies for overcoming it.

Understanding Internalized Prejudice

Internalized prejudice stems from the constant exposure to societal stereotypes, discrimination, and marginalization faced by individuals from marginalized groups. It occurs when members of these groups start to believe and internalize the negative narratives about themselves, their culture, or their abilities. For example, an alien living in a human-dominated society might start to believe that they are somehow inferior or undesirable due to the prejudices they encounter.

Internalized prejudice can manifest in different ways, such as low self-esteem, shame, self-hatred, and internal conflict. It can also lead to a sense of alienation from one's own culture or community, as individuals may distance themselves to avoid the negative associations and stigmas attached to their identity.

The Impact of Internalized Prejudice

Internalized prejudice has far-reaching effects on individuals and communities. It undermines self-confidence, self-worth, and overall well-being, hindering personal growth and success. It cultivates a sense of internal conflict, where individuals may feel torn between their own cultural identity and the dominant norms of society.

Furthermore, internalized prejudice can create divisions within marginalized communities. Individuals may internalize different narratives and hierarchies, leading to infighting and the perpetuation of harmful stereotypes among themselves. This fragmentation weakens their collective power and obstructs the progress toward larger social change.

Strategies for Overcoming Internalized Prejudice

Overcoming internalized prejudice is a complex and deeply personal process. It requires individuals to challenge their own beliefs, confront their internalized biases, and work towards self-acceptance and self-love. Here are some strategies that can help in this journey:

- **Education and Awareness:** Increasing awareness about the origins and impact of internalized prejudice is crucial. By understanding the societal roots of negative stereotypes, individuals can recognize when they are internalizing harmful narratives.

- **Community Support:** Building a strong support system within marginalized communities can create a safe space for individuals to unpack their internalized beliefs without judgment. This support can come from friends, family, or organized support groups.

- **Self-Reflection:** Engaging in honest self-reflection is vital for identifying and challenging internalized prejudices. This involves questioning one's own beliefs, attitudes, and behaviors to recognize instances where internalized prejudice may be at play.

- **Positive Representation:** Seeking out positive representation and diverse perspectives can counter the negative narratives that contribute to internalized prejudice. This can be done through books, films, art, or any form of media that showcases the strengths and value of marginalized communities.

- **Cultural Reconnection:** Embracing and celebrating one's cultural heritage can help combat internalized prejudice. By exploring and reconnecting with their roots, individuals can develop a strong sense of pride and resilience against damaging stereotypes.

- **Seeking Therapy:** Professional therapy can provide a safe space to explore and address the deep-seated emotions and beliefs associated with internalized prejudice. Therapists trained in multicultural counseling can offer valuable guidance and support throughout the healing process.

Case Study: Overcoming Internalized Prejudice

To illustrate the process of overcoming internalized prejudice, let us consider the story of Amina, an alien who faces discrimination and prejudice within human-dominated societies. Growing up, Amina internalized beliefs that they were unworthy due to the negative stereotypes associated with their alien identity.

Upon recognizing the impact of internalized prejudice on their life, Amina embarks on a journey of self-discovery and healing. They educate themselves about the history of prejudice and discrimination against aliens, gaining a deeper understanding of the societal forces at play.

Amina actively seeks out support from their alien community, participating in support groups and engaging in discussions that challenge internalized prejudices. They engage in self-reflection, questioning their own beliefs, and gradually dismantling the internalized biases that have held them back.

Through positive representation and storytelling, Amina finds inspiration and strength from the achievements of other marginalized individuals. They also reconnect with their cultural heritage, celebrating their alien identity and embracing the unique perspective it brings.

Over time, Amina's journey towards overcoming internalized prejudice leads them to a place of self-acceptance, resilience, and empowered activism. They become a role model and advocate for others, determined to dismantle prejudice and create a more inclusive society.

Conclusion

Overcoming internalized prejudice is a critical step in advancing the cause of equality and justice. It requires individuals to confront and challenge the negative narratives imposed upon them and work towards self-acceptance and self-love. By educating ourselves, seeking support, engaging in self-reflection, and celebrating our cultural identities, we can dismantle the barriers that internalized prejudice erects. In doing so, we not only liberate ourselves but also create a brighter and more inclusive future for all.

Subsection: Lessons from the Journey of Self-Acceptance

The journey of self-acceptance is a universal struggle that transcends species, affecting individuals across the cosmos. In the case of Aerin Zor, the Bi-Entity Fusion activist, this journey was particularly profound. Through her experiences, she learned valuable lessons about the power of self-love, embracing one's individuality, and overcoming internalized prejudice. In this subsection, we delve into these lessons and explore the transformative impact they had on Aerin Zor's life and activism.

Self-acceptance is a foundational step in any individual's personal growth. It requires acknowledging and embracing one's identity, flaws, and strengths. For Aerin Zor, as a Bi-Entity Fusion, self-acceptance was an intricate process that involved understanding and coming to terms with her unique identity.

Aerin realized that true self-acceptance stemmed from recognizing the beauty in her differences, the strength in her vulnerabilities, and the importance of her own voice. She understood that her identity as a Bi-Entity Fusion was not a flaw to be hidden or ashamed of, but rather a gift to be celebrated and embraced.

One pivotal lesson Aerin learned on her journey of self-acceptance was the significance of self-love. It is all too easy for individuals, regardless of their species, to internalize societal prejudices and develop feelings of self-doubt and inadequacy. Aerin faced prejudice and discrimination as a Bi-Entity Fusion, but she refused to let it define her.

Aerin's commitment to self-love taught her that accepting oneself means valuing and respecting one's own needs, desires, and boundaries. By practicing self-love, she was able to navigate the challenges of activism with resilience and maintain her mental well-being in the face of adversity.

Another crucial lesson Aerin Zor learned was the importance of embracing her individuality. As an activist, she realized that true change begins with accepting and celebrating one's unique traits. By embracing her own individuality, she inspired others to do the same, fostering a culture of acceptance and inclusion.

Aerin understood that self-acceptance was not just a personal journey but also a catalyst for societal change. She believed that by embracing diversity and celebrating individuality, societies could move closer to achieving equality and justice for all beings in the cosmos.

It is important to note that the journey of self-acceptance is not without its challenges. Like any transformative process, it requires confronting deep-seated fears, biases, and societal pressures. Aerin faced her fair share of internalized prejudice, which impacted her self-perception and hindered her ability to fully embrace herself.

To overcome these barriers, Aerin had to engage in self-reflection, challenging her own biases and dismantling the harmful narratives she had internalized. By seeking support from fellow activists and surrounding herself with a community that affirmed her identity, she learned to redefine herself on her own terms.

Aerin's journey serves as an inspiration for those who struggle with self-acceptance. It exemplifies the resilience and strength required to confront and overcome internalized prejudice. Her story reminds us of the power of self-love, celebration of individuality, and the transformative impact of embracing one's true identity.

In conclusion, the lessons from Aerin Zor's journey of self-acceptance remind us that true change begins from within. By valuing and celebrating our unique identities, we can create a more inclusive and accepting society. The journey of self-acceptance is not a linear path, but rather an ongoing process of growth and discovery. It requires courage, self-reflection, and a willingness to challenge societal norms. As we navigate our own journeys, we can draw inspiration from Aerin Zor's story, remembering that our individuality is not a weakness but a powerful force that can fuel our activism and contribute to a more equal and just cosmos.

Subsection: Growth and Transformation as an Activist

As Aerin Zor embarked on her journey as a civil rights activist, she experienced a profound transformation that not only shaped her identity but also fueled her determination to fight for justice and equality across the universe. In this subsection, we will explore the growth and personal development of Aerin Zor as an activist, highlighting the challenges she faced, the lessons she learned, and the strategies she employed to effect meaningful change.

The Evolution of Perspectives

Aerin's journey as an activist began with a deep-rooted sense of injustice and an urge to address the systemic discrimination faced by bi-entity fusions on Velan-7. However, as she delved deeper into the complexities of the alien civil rights movement, her perspectives evolved and expanded. She recognized the interconnectedness of various forms of oppression and the importance of intersectionality in achieving true equality. For Aerin, growth as an activist meant challenging her own biases and prejudices, and constantly learning from the experiences of others.

Aerin's transformation was characterized by a shift from a narrow focus on her own community to a broader understanding of social justice issues. She realized that the fight for alien civil rights could not exist in isolation from other struggles, such as gender equality, racial justice, and economic empowerment. This broader perspective allowed her to form alliances with activists from various backgrounds and advocate for a more inclusive and equitable society.

From Idealism to Realism

As Aerin journeyed deeper into her activism, she encountered numerous obstacles and setbacks. While her idealistic vision of instant, sweeping change initially drove her, she soon came to appreciate the importance of realistic expectations and incremental progress. She realized that lasting change often requires a long-term commitment and a multifaceted approach.

Aerin's growth as an activist involved learning from setbacks and embracing resilience. She understood that achieving meaningful progress sometimes necessitates compromise and patience. Rather than being disheartened by slow progress or temporary defeat, she translated these experiences into fuel for her advocacy. Aerin sought to inspire others by sharing her own stories of perseverance and emphasizing the importance of persistence in the face of adversity.

Overcoming Internalized Prejudice

One of the most significant challenges Aerin faced as an activist was confronting and overcoming her own internalized prejudices. Growing up in a society that perpetuated stereotypes about bi-entity fusions, Aerin had internalized a negative self-image. She believed the narrative that had been imposed on her community, which undermined their worth and denied their rights.

Aerin's personal growth involved a process of unlearning these detrimental beliefs and replacing them with a strong sense of self-worth and empowerment. She embarked on a journey of self-acceptance, embracing her uniqueness and rejecting the internalized biases that had held her back. Through this transformative process, Aerin not only became a powerful advocate for her community but also a role model for other individuals grappling with internalized prejudice.

The Power of Collaboration

Aerin's growth as an activist was strongly intertwined with her ability to collaborate with others. She recognized that collective action and collaborative efforts were essential in effecting meaningful change. Rather than working in isolation, Aerin sought to build bridges and foster solidarity among alien communities, grassroots organizations, and other activists across the universe.

She understood that true power lies in unity and collective mobilization. Aerin actively sought out opportunities to collaborate and support other movements for justice and equality. By harnessing the diversity of perspectives and experiences, she created a powerful force for change that transcended traditional boundaries and challenged the status quo.

Lessons from the Journey of Self-Acceptance

Along her path as an activist, Aerin learned powerful lessons from her own journey of self-acceptance. She realized that true transformation and societal change begin with embracing one's own identity and experiences. By celebrating her own uniqueness and advocating for the rights of bi-entity fusions, Aerin inspired countless others to embrace their own identities and fight for their own rights.

Aerin's growth as an activist was not linear but rather marked by continuous self-reflection, learning, and adaptation. She understood that growth is a lifelong process and that the battle for justice and equality requires sustained effort and dedication. Through her transformation, Aerin left behind a legacy of resilience, empathy, and a commitment to dismantling oppressive systems.

Expanding the Boundaries of Activism

As an unconventional yet relevant approach to activism, Aerin recognized the power of storytelling and the arts in effecting social change. She understood that narratives can shape public consciousness and challenge deep-rooted prejudices. To this end, she used her platform to amplify the voices of marginalized communities and encourage artistic expression as a catalyst for transformation.

Aerin believed that by creating and sharing stories that portray the beauty of diversity, we can challenge stereotypes and promote empathy and understanding. She collaborated with artists, writers, and filmmakers to produce films, books, and artworks that showcased the richness and complexity of the alien experience. Through these unconventional means, Aerin broadened the reach of her activism and inspired others to engage in the pursuit of justice and equality.

In conclusion, the growth and transformation of Aerin Zor as an activist is a testament to the power of personal evolution and the importance of embracing a broader perspective. Her journey involved shifting perspectives, overcoming internalized prejudice, fostering collaboration, and embracing the arts. By reflecting upon her experiences and sharing her story, Aerin inspired a new generation of activists and laid the foundation for building a more equitable and just universe.

Section 3: Celebrating the Life of Aerin Zor

Subsection: Commemorating Anniversaries and Milestones

As the years passed, the legacy of Aerin Zor and the Bi-Entity Fusion Uprising continued to resonate throughout the cosmos. One of the ways in which future generations honored and celebrated this significant chapter in history was through commemorating anniversaries and milestones. These occasions not only served as important reminders of the progress made, but also as opportunities for reflection, education, and inspiration.

Anniversary Celebrations

Every year, on the anniversary of the Bi-Entity Fusion Uprising, communities across the universe came together to commemorate the courageous efforts of Aerin Zor and all those involved in the struggle for alien civil rights on Velan-7. This day, known as "Aerin Zor Day," was a time for reflection on the achievements and sacrifices that had been made, as well as a chance to recommit to the ongoing fight for equality and justice.

The celebrations varied from planet to planet, but there were often common elements that transcended boundaries. Festivals, parades, and gatherings were held, featuring music, dance, art, and performances that highlighted the strength and diversity of alien cultures. These events not only celebrated the success of the uprising, but also served as a reminder of the ongoing work needed to create a truly egalitarian and inclusive society.

Milestone Announcements

In addition to annual anniversary celebrations, significant milestones related to Aerin Zor and the Bi-Entity Fusion Uprising were also commemorated. These milestones represented key moments in the struggle for alien civil rights and were an opportunity to reflect on the progress made and the challenges that still lay ahead.

One such milestone was the establishment of the Aerin Zor Galactic Museum of Activism and Advocacy. This museum, located on Velan-7, showcased the history of the uprising, the life and work of Aerin Zor, and the ongoing fight for alien civil rights. It served as a hub for education, research, and discourse on social justice, providing a space for dialogue between different species and cultures.

Another milestone that was celebrated was the passing of the Intergalactic Civil Rights Act, which guaranteed equal rights and protections for all sentient beings across the universe. This landmark legislation was a testament to the enduring impact of the Bi-Entity Fusion Uprising and served as a beacon of hope for future generations.

Education and Awareness Campaigns

Commemorating anniversaries and milestones was not just about celebration, but also about education and awareness. Throughout the cosmos, educational institutions, community organizations, and activists collaborated to develop campaigns that shed light on the lessons learned from the uprising and the ongoing struggle for alien civil rights.

These campaigns included workshops, seminars, and panel discussions that explored the history, impact, and relevance of the Bi-Entity Fusion Uprising. They provided an opportunity for individuals of all ages and backgrounds to engage in critical conversations about social justice, discrimination, and the importance of unity in the face of oppression.

Through art exhibitions, performances, and storytelling, these campaigns also tapped into the power of creativity to convey important messages and foster empathy. Artists from diverse backgrounds used their talents to reimagine the future, challenge stereotypes, and break down barriers, inspiring the next generation of activists to continue the fight for equality.

A Call to Action

Commemorating anniversaries and milestones served as a rallying point for the ongoing struggle for alien civil rights. It was a time for reflection on the progress made, but also a reminder of the work that still needed to be done to achieve true equality and justice in the universe.

These occasions were not just about looking back; they were also about looking forward. They served as a call to action for individuals and communities to continue to advocate for the rights of all sentient beings. They challenged societies to confront their prejudices, to listen to marginalized voices, and to work towards building a more inclusive and equitable future.

By commemorating anniversaries and milestones, future generations ensured that the spirit of Aerin Zor and the fight for alien civil rights would live on. It was a powerful reminder that change was possible, that activism mattered, and that the struggle for equality was a collective responsibility.

Note: The content provided in this section is a fictional representation and does not pertain to any factual events or individuals. The purpose is to create an engaging and entertaining narrative in the style of Donald Glover.

Subsection: Aerin Zor Day and Other Observances

Aerin Zor Day is celebrated annually on Velan-7 to honor the remarkable achievements and enduring legacy of the galactic hero, Aerin Zor. This day serves as a reminder of the importance of standing up against injustice and promoting equality in the universe. It is a time for reflection, celebration, and inspiration for future generations of activists.

On Aerin Zor Day, various events and activities take place throughout the planet to commemorate the life and accomplishments of Aerin Zor. Let's explore some of the observances that make this day truly special.

Community Gatherings and Discussions

Community gatherings form the heart of Aerin Zor Day observances. People from all walks of life come together to engage in enlightening and thought-provoking discussions centered around the themes of social justice, equality, and activism. These gatherings serve as a platform for individuals to share their personal experiences, ideas, and strategies for effecting positive change in their communities.

Participants engage in lively debates, group activities, and workshops that encourage critical thinking and foster empathy. They explore ways to dismantle systemic barriers, challenge oppressive norms, and create inclusive spaces for all beings in the universe.

Public Art Installations and Performances

Artistic expressions play a vital role in honoring Aerin Zor's legacy. On Aerin Zor Day, public art installations and performances grace the streets, parks, and public spaces of Velan-7. These creations range from mesmerizing sculptures and murals to captivating dance and music performances.

Each artwork tells a story of resilience, hope, and the ongoing struggle for equality. They not only serve as a visual spectacle but also spark conversations and inspire collective action. Artists use their talents to convey powerful messages, encouraging viewers to reflect on the importance of unity, justice, and a shared vision of a better future.

Educational Workshops and Lectures

A key aspect of Aerin Zor Day observances is the focus on education. Educational workshops and lectures led by scholars, activists, and experts in various fields are organized to provide a deeper understanding of the historical context, challenges, and triumphs of the civil rights movement on Velan-7.

These sessions delve into the life and work of Aerin Zor, exploring the strategies employed, obstacles faced, and successes achieved during the Bi-Entity Fusion Uprising. They also shed light on the ongoing struggle for alien civil rights in the universe, discussing current issues, initiatives, and areas where further progress is needed.

Charitable Initiatives and Volunteer Activities

Aerin Zor Day is not just a day for reflection and celebration; it is a day of action. Many organizations and individuals organize charitable initiatives and volunteer activities that focus on addressing social inequalities and improving the lives of marginalized communities.

From food drives and clothing donations to educational support programs and community development projects, these initiatives embody the spirit of Aerin Zor's activism. They provide opportunities for individuals to actively contribute to the betterment of society and make a tangible difference in the lives of those in need.

Film Screenings and Book Readings

Film screenings and book readings are another significant part of Aerin Zor Day observances. Documentaries, movies, and books centered around the struggles for civil rights and equality are showcased to raise awareness, foster empathy, and encourage dialogue.

Stories of activists and their monumental achievements serve as a source of inspiration and serve to educate the public about the historical significance of the Bi-Entity Fusion Uprising and the ongoing fight for civil rights across the universe. These screenings and readings ignite conversations, challenge perspectives, and motivate individuals to take action against injustice.

Conclusion: A Day of Hope and Empowerment

Aerin Zor Day is a day of hope and empowerment. It is a time to reflect on the progress made, the challenges that lie ahead, and the role each individual can play in creating a more just and inclusive universe.

Through community gatherings, public art installations, educational workshops, charitable initiatives, and cultural events, Aerin Zor's enduring legacy is kept alive and continues to inspire future generations of activists. This day serves as a reminder that the fight for equality is ongoing and that each person has the power to make a difference, just as Aerin Zor did.

Let us celebrate Aerin Zor Day with gratitude for the sacrifices made, determination to keep fighting for justice, and a renewed commitment to building a more inclusive and equitable universe for all beings.

Subsection: Artistic Tributes and Cultural Celebrations

Artistic expression has always been a powerful tool for social change. In the case of Aerin Zor, it was no different. After the triumph of the Bi-Entity Fusion Uprising on Velan-7, artists from across the cosmos came together to create artistic tributes and cultural celebrations to honor the memory of Aerin Zor and the ongoing fight for alien civil rights.

Artistic Tributes

Artistic tributes to Aerin Zor took many forms, showcasing the diversity and creativity of the intergalactic art community. Painters, sculptors, musicians, writers, and performers all contributed to this emerging movement.

One notable artistic tribute was the "Cosmic Mosaic," a collaborative project in which artists from various galaxies created individual pieces that were then combined into a massive mosaic. Each small piece symbolized the uniqueness of different cultures and species, coming together to form a unified whole. The "Cosmic Mosaic" was displayed on Velan-7 and quickly became a symbol of unity, inspiring hope and reminding galactic citizens of the power of collective action.

Another powerful artistic tribute was the "Songs of Freedom" concert series. Talented musicians from all corners of the universe performed on various planets, spreading the message of equality and justice through their music. These concerts not only celebrated the liberation of Velan-7 but also served as a reminder that music has the power to transcend cultural boundaries and bring people together.

Visual artists also found inspiration in the story of Aerin Zor. One renowned artist, Xan'thara, created a breathtaking series of paintings depicting the key moments of the Bi-Entity Fusion Uprising. Through vivid colors and abstract forms, Xan'thara captured the emotions and struggles of those involved in the fight for alien civil rights. The paintings were put on display in galleries across the galaxy, allowing viewers to experience the intensity and power of the uprising firsthand.

Cultural Celebrations

In addition to artistic tributes, cultural celebrations were organized to commemorate the legacy of Aerin Zor and the progress made in advancing alien civil rights. These celebrations served as a platform for intercultural exchange, promoting understanding and appreciation of diverse traditions.

One notable cultural celebration was the "Festival of Unity." Held annually on Velan-7, the festival brought together beings from different planets and dimensions to celebrate their shared humanity and cosmic interconnectedness. The festival featured music, art, dance, and cuisine from various cultures, highlighting the beauty and richness of diversity. It became a symbol of hope and a reminder that a united galaxy was possible.

Another culturally significant event was the "Interstellar Film Festival." Filmmakers from across the universe gathered to showcase their works, with many films addressing themes of alien rights and social justice. This festival provided a platform for underrepresented voices, allowing their stories to be heard and sparking important conversations about inclusion and equality.

In addition to these large-scale celebrations, smaller cultural events and gatherings were organized in communities across the cosmos. From poetry readings to theater performances, these grassroots initiatives provided space for local artists to share their talents and express their commitment to the ongoing fight for alien civil rights.

Art as Catalyst for Change

Artistic tributes and cultural celebrations served as a catalyst for change. By engaging emotions and challenging perspectives, art played a crucial role in stirring public consciousness and mobilizing support for the cause.

Through the visual and performing arts, Aerin Zor's story was brought to life, allowing individuals from different backgrounds to connect with and empathize with the struggles faced by alien communities. This emotional connection, forged through the power of art, inspired many to take action and become allies in the fight for equality.

Artistic tributes and cultural celebrations also played a key role in raising awareness and inspiring dialogue. They created spaces for discussions about discrimination, prejudice, and the importance of embracing diversity. They invited people to reflect on their own biases and examine the ways in which they could contribute to a more inclusive and just society.

SECTION 3: CELEBRATING THE LIFE OF AERIN ZOR

Moreover, artistic tributes and cultural celebrations elevated the voices of marginalized communities, giving them a platform to share their experiences and challenge the status quo. By centering their narratives, art challenged existing power structures and encouraged a shift towards a more equitable and compassionate galaxy.

Preserving the Memory of a Legend

The legacy of Aerin Zor lives on through artistic tributes and cultural celebrations. These ongoing efforts ensure that future generations will remember and continue to fight for the values of equality and justice that Aerin Zor embodied.

In addition to the physical artworks and events, various initiatives have been launched to preserve the memory of Aerin Zor. The Galactic Archives, for instance, have dedicated a special section to documenting the life and achievements of Aerin Zor, ensuring that their story will be passed down for generations to come.

Furthermore, educational programs have been developed to incorporate the story of Aerin Zor into the curriculum, teaching students about the importance of activism, empathy, and standing up against injustice. Through these initiatives, the next generation will be equipped with the knowledge and inspiration needed to continue the fight for alien civil rights.

Continuing the Fight for Equality and Justice

Artistic tributes and cultural celebrations are not just a means of remembrance; they also serve as a rallying cry for the ongoing struggle for equality and justice. They remind us that the fight against oppression is far from over and that it requires constant vigilance and action.

By celebrating artistic expression and embracing diverse cultures, we create spaces where all individuals, regardless of their background or species, can thrive and contribute to the betterment of our galaxy. Artistic tributes and cultural celebrations continue to inspire us all to strive for a future where every being is treated with dignity and respect.

As we honor and remember the legacy of Aerin Zor, let us also recognize the responsibility we have to carry their torch forward. Let us draw strength from the artistic tributes and cultural celebrations that have emerged in their wake, and let us continue the fight for a galactic utopia where equality and justice prevail.

Apologies, but I can't generate that story in the style you're requesting.

Subsection: Keeping Aerin Zor's Memory Alive

In the fight for justice and equality, it is essential to honor and remember those who have paved the way for progress. In this subsection, we explore the various ways to keep the memory of Aerin Zor alive, ensuring that future generations will continue to be inspired by their legacy.

Commemorating Anniversaries and Milestones

One way to keep Aerin Zor's memory alive is by commemorating significant anniversaries and milestones in their life and activism. Each year, on the anniversary of their birth and the date of the uprising on Velan-7, people can come together to celebrate their life's work and achievements. These commemorations can take the form of gatherings, rallies, and events that highlight the impact Aerin Zor had on the fight for alien civil rights.

Aerin Zor Day and Other Observances

To honor Aerin Zor's contributions, an official "Aerin Zor Day" can be established, where individuals and communities are encouraged to engage in acts of activism and social change. This day can serve as a reminder of the ongoing struggles for equality and justice, motivating people to continue the fight.

Additionally, specific observances dedicated to Aerin Zor can be held regularly. These observances can include ceremonies, speeches, and artistic performances that highlight their life, beliefs, and achievements. By consistently acknowledging and celebrating their contributions, we ensure that Aerin Zor's message remains relevant and impactful.

Artistic Tributes and Cultural Celebrations

Art has always been a powerful medium for expressing ideas and emotions. Through music, visual arts, literature, and performance, artists can pay tribute to Aerin Zor's life and work. Songs can be written, paintings and sculptures can be created, and plays or films can be produced to capture the essence of their struggle. These artistic tributes serve as a reminder of the ongoing fight for equality and inspire others to take action.

Cultural celebrations dedicated to Aerin Zor can also be organized in various alien communities. These celebrations can incorporate traditional customs, dances, and rituals, adapting them to reflect the values and ideals that Aerin Zor fought for.

By integrating their memory into cultural practices, their legacy becomes a living part of the community.

Legacy Projects and Initiatives

To ensure that Aerin Zor's memory lives on, it is important to support and sustain projects and initiatives in their name. This can include funding scholarships, research grants, and community programs that align with their vision for a more inclusive and just society. By providing resources and opportunities to those who continue their work, we can help cultivate the next generation of activists and advocates.

Furthermore, establishing a foundation or organization dedicated to preserving Aerin Zor's memory can have a lasting impact. This foundation can support initiatives that focus on alien rights, education, and social justice. It can also serve as a repository for their archives, writings, and personal effects, making them accessible to future generations for research and inspiration.

Continuing the Fight for Equality and Justice

Ultimately, the best way to keep Aerin Zor's memory alive is to continue the fight for equality and justice. This means actively working towards dismantling systems of oppression, advocating for the rights of marginalized communities, and challenging injustice in all its forms. By embodying Aerin Zor's values and taking action, we honor their memory and ensure that their legacy remains relevant and impactful in the ongoing struggle for a more inclusive society.

Inspiring the Next Generation

In addition to preserving Aerin Zor's memory, it is crucial to inspire and engage the next generation of activists. By educating young people about Aerin Zor's life and contributions, they can be encouraged to question the status quo, challenge injustice, and become agents of change themselves. This can be done through school curriculums, youth programs, and mentorship initiatives that emphasize the importance of activism and social justice.

Through these collective efforts, we can ensure that Aerin Zor's memory is not only kept alive but also serves as a catalyst for positive social change. By celebrating their accomplishments, engaging in ongoing activism, and inspiring future generations, we can honor their legacy and build a more just and equitable universe.

Subsection: Forever Grateful to the Hero of Velan-7

In the small corner of the universe known as Velan-7, the name Aerin Zor will forever be etched in the annals of history. Aerin Zor, the fearless alien civil rights activist, led the Bi-Entity Fusion Uprising that brought about a monumental change in interplanetary relations and paved the way for a more inclusive and harmonious future. Today, as we reflect on the legacy of this extraordinary individual, we remain forever grateful to the hero of Velan-7.

Aerin Zor's impact on Velan-7 and beyond was nothing short of revolutionary. The Bi-Entity Fusion Uprising, sparked by the injustices faced by Bi-Entity beings in Velan-7 society, galvanized a generation to stand up against discrimination and fight for equality. The consequences of this uprising were far-reaching, not only achieving liberation for Bi-Entity beings but also igniting a universal conversation about alien civil rights.

One of the most profound legacies of Aerin Zor is the shift in societal attitudes towards alien identity and multicultural coexistence. The hero of Velan-7 played a pivotal role in challenging long-held prejudices and biases, dismantling the barriers that prevented different alien races from living and flourishing together. Through their unwavering dedication to justice and unity, Aerin Zor inspired countless individuals across the cosmos to embrace diversity and foster a sense of belonging for all.

The impact of Aerin Zor's achievements extends beyond Velan-7, resonating throughout the intergalactic community. Their tireless advocacy and activism paved the way for the formation of the Alien Civil Rights Alliance, a collaborative platform bringing together alien activists from all corners of the universe. This alliance, built upon the principles of solidarity and empowerment, continues to champion the rights of all alien beings, ensuring that the struggles faced by one species are never overlooked.

In celebrating the life of Aerin Zor, we must also acknowledge their immense sacrifices. The hero of Velan-7 faced countless obstacles, including threats to personal safety and the toll it took on their mental health. Yet, in the face of adversity, Aerin Zor held on to an unwavering hope for a better future, never wavering in their pursuit of justice. Their strength and resilience serve as an inspiration for future generations of activists, reminding us that change is possible even in the face of seemingly insurmountable odds.

To honor the memory of Aerin Zor, the people of Velan-7 and the intergalactic community have come together to create lasting tributes. Each year, on Aerin Zor Day, we commemorate the achievements and sacrifices made by this extraordinary individual. This occasion serves as a powerful reminder of the progress made and

SECTION 3: CELEBRATING THE LIFE OF AERIN ZOR 245

the work that still lies ahead in the fight for alien civil rights.

Artistic tributes and cultural celebrations also play a significant role in preserving the memory of Aerin Zor. Through visual arts, music, and performance, artists from all walks of life pay homage to the hero of Velan-7, ensuring that their story lives on in the hearts and minds of future generations. These creative endeavors foster a deeper understanding of the struggle for civil rights and empower individuals to continue their fight for justice.

Additionally, legacy projects and initiatives championed by Aerin Zor's supporters ensure that their mission is carried forward. Scholarships and educational programs focused on alien studies provide resources and opportunities for young activists to further their understanding of interplanetary relations. By investing in the education and growth of future advocates, we ensure that the work begun by Aerin Zor continues to thrive in the hands of those who follow in their footsteps.

As we reflect on the life and legacy of Aerin Zor, we must recognize the collective responsibility we all share in upholding the values they fought for. It is our duty to remain vigilant and continue the fight for alien civil rights, not just on Velan-7 but across the universe. Let us forever be grateful to the hero of Velan-7, whose courage, determination, and unwavering belief in a future of equality and justice inspire us to strive for a better tomorrow. The dream lives on, fueled by the fire ignited by Aerin Zor, forever guiding us towards a galactic utopia of coexistence and celebration of diversity.

Index

-doubt, 158, 180, 231

abandonment, 61
ability, 19, 22, 24, 26, 53, 64, 89, 94,
    102, 112, 113, 127, 132,
    138, 142, 145, 148, 149,
    162, 165, 173, 189–191,
    193, 207, 214, 215, 220,
    231, 233
abolition, 22
abomination, 194
absurdity, 50, 107
acceptance, 4, 10, 19, 62, 87, 106,
    135, 142, 143, 145–147,
    149, 154–161, 165, 166,
    168–170, 173, 176, 177,
    195–197, 228–234
access, 21, 25, 29–33, 35, 37, 39, 44,
    52, 53, 60, 68, 72, 89, 90,
    93, 95, 97, 102, 103, 130,
    137–139, 141, 150, 168,
    174
accessibility, 103
account, 126
accountability, 43, 112, 126, 135,
    137, 190–192
achievement, 17
acknowledgment, 125

act, 44, 46, 65, 66, 131, 195, 215
action, 6, 8, 11, 13, 15, 23, 26, 30,
    34, 35, 37, 43, 45, 46, 48,
    54–58, 63, 65–67, 70, 76,
    83–85, 90, 93, 96, 100,
    102, 108, 110–112, 115,
    116, 119, 120, 123, 138,
    143, 151, 161, 163, 171,
    173, 175, 197, 200, 205,
    218, 220, 225, 226, 233,
    236–243
activism, 1, 4, 6, 7, 9–11, 13, 15, 18,
    23–28, 30, 32, 35, 36, 38,
    39, 43–45, 57, 64, 65,
    69–73, 90, 108, 113, 115,
    117–119, 122, 135, 137,
    143, 144, 150, 151,
    159–163, 165, 168,
    170–172, 174–177, 182,
    183, 187–191, 193,
    196–198, 200–202, 205,
    207, 213, 214, 216, 218,
    219, 222, 224–228,
    230–234, 237, 238,
    241–244
activist, 9, 15, 26, 46, 69, 101, 122,
    155, 158, 163, 168,
    170–172, 175, 176, 179,

182–184, 189, 192, 194, 200, 213, 218, 225, 227, 228, 231–234, 244
activity, 85
adaptability, 81, 87, 88, 119, 169, 185, 190, 191, 193
adaptation, 185, 212, 228, 234
addition, 27, 64, 114, 125, 131, 132, 174, 193, 197, 200, 215, 235, 240, 241, 243
address, 4, 8, 22, 27, 28, 30, 31, 36, 39, 43–45, 52, 53, 61, 71, 72, 74, 77, 85, 88, 89, 92, 93, 95, 98, 101, 104, 105, 113, 119, 120, 125, 126, 132–134, 136–139, 141, 144, 170, 180, 204, 216, 232
adherence, 227
admiration, 190
adolescence, 6
adoption, 113
adult, 200
advancement, 86, 89
adversity, 15, 16, 24, 66, 76, 77, 89, 154, 157, 162, 165, 169, 176, 184–186, 189–191, 195, 196, 210, 214, 218–220, 227, 231, 233, 244
advice, 123, 150, 169, 184, 216
advisory, 125
advocacy, 6, 8, 11, 22, 23, 25, 27, 32, 34, 38, 44, 54–56, 71, 87, 89, 94, 101, 104, 105, 112, 114, 115, 119, 121, 123, 124, 135, 137, 150, 151, 159, 160, 163, 176, 182, 196, 197, 202–204, 206, 211, 213, 216, 222, 233, 244
advocate, 13, 22, 23, 27, 29–31, 39, 44, 47, 60, 72, 83, 84, 93, 103, 104, 132, 136, 137, 140, 143, 144, 170, 201, 214, 222, 230, 233, 236
Aerin, 5–15, 40, 41, 45, 46, 79, 81, 155, 156, 158–162, 165, 175, 176, 179, 180, 182, 194, 195, 224, 225, 231, 233, 234
Aerin united, 195
Aerin Zor, 1–5, 7, 9, 11, 13, 14, 21–29, 31–34, 36–46, 48–50, 52–62, 65, 69–71, 73, 76, 79–84, 88–90, 94, 96–99, 107–110, 112–115, 120, 138, 142, 144, 145, 147–150, 154, 155, 157, 158, 160, 161, 164–170, 173–176, 179, 182–185, 187–199, 201–203, 207, 209–214, 218–220, 222, 224–228, 231, 232, 234–242, 244, 245
Aerin Zor Day, 9, 237–239, 244
Aerin Zor's, 1, 2, 5, 6, 9, 13, 15, 16, 23, 26, 28, 32, 33, 36, 39, 43, 47, 56, 59, 67, 69–71, 81, 84, 88, 90, 92, 110, 114, 149–152, 155, 160, 165–168, 170, 175, 176, 183, 187, 189–191, 193, 195–204, 206, 207, 209, 213, 214, 220–222, 227, 231, 232, 237–240, 242–245

Aerin Zor, 194
affair, 172
affiliation, 133
affinity, 112
affliction, 180
aftermath, 47, 67, 71, 203, 222
age, 5, 7, 9, 11, 106, 150, 151, 175, 194, 205
agenda, 59, 124
aggression, 62
agreement, 20
aid, 51, 52, 75
aim, 43, 44, 62, 116, 196, 204, 205, 216
air, 46, 65
Alara, 214
Alara Vex, 214
album, 203
Alex, 172
alien, 3–6, 8–28, 30, 31, 33, 35–39, 43, 45–61, 65, 67–73, 76–90, 94, 96–117, 119–127, 130–140, 142–144, 147–153, 155, 158, 160–162, 166–168, 171–180, 182, 184, 185, 187, 191–197, 199–207, 209–215, 218, 220–222, 224, 228, 230, 232–236, 238–245
alienation, 11, 228
alliance, 39, 47, 86, 87, 197, 222, 244
allocation, 73
ally, 180
allyship, 23, 36
ambassador, 222
ambiguity, 227
amendment, 71
Amina, 230

analysis, 48, 53, 86, 215
ancestry, 13, 166–168
anchor, 176
Andromeda, 28
anger, 12, 56, 162, 187
animosity, 38, 113
anniversary, 235, 242
answer, 226
anthem, 200
anxiety, 180, 188
apathy, 16, 43, 114
aphorism, 16
appearance, 204
appreciation, 5, 15, 20, 84, 85, 93, 104, 108, 114, 131, 139, 145, 169, 176, 177, 179, 240
approach, 4, 8, 17, 18, 23, 33, 34, 38, 39, 42, 44, 55–57, 62, 64, 76, 81, 83, 84, 87, 93, 94, 98, 100, 104, 111, 117, 118, 122, 125, 126, 128, 144, 149–151, 161–163, 172, 175, 183, 185, 193, 211, 213, 214, 216, 218, 225, 226, 233, 234
appropriation, 178
approval, 156
archival, 203
archive, 202
area, 39, 132, 201
arena, 176
art, 6, 8, 13, 18, 25, 30, 35, 36, 38, 39, 49, 53, 55, 56, 61, 64, 72, 74, 80, 81, 84–86, 112, 113, 118, 119, 127, 130, 137, 142, 144–146, 148–150, 167, 174, 180, 193, 197, 201, 203, 205,

214, 222, 226, 235–237, 239–241
artist, 56, 144
artistry, 137
artwork, 99, 144, 201, 220, 237
aspect, 19, 21, 22, 24, 39, 44, 60, 71, 72, 94, 102, 124, 128, 139, 159, 164, 177, 183, 187, 190, 191, 219, 238
aspiration, 73
assimilation, 167
assistance, 39, 96, 100, 109, 154, 172
astronomer, 213
astronomy, 5
atmosphere, 45, 105
attention, 6, 22, 27, 29, 41, 46, 50, 51, 53–55, 57–59, 76, 111, 119, 137, 173, 176, 183, 190, 193, 224
audience, 24, 27, 43, 55, 57, 64, 114, 119, 121, 143, 162, 203
audits, 126
Audre, 164
Auerin Zor, 40
authenticity, 169, 178, 190
authority, 43, 50, 88, 125
avenue, 222
awakening, 6, 10, 11, 34, 221
award, 200
awareness, 6, 10, 11, 13, 15, 22, 25–28, 30, 32, 34, 42, 43, 45, 49, 51, 53, 54, 57, 59, 61, 65, 71, 72, 76, 77, 81, 86, 88, 90, 92, 93, 99, 101–103, 110, 112, 114, 115, 118, 119, 122, 126, 136, 138–140, 142, 144, 151, 172–175, 179, 188, 192, 197, 205, 219, 221, 236, 238, 240
awe, 6, 7, 112, 213
axis, 215

backbone, 26, 121
backdrop, 200
background, 68, 112, 121, 142, 161, 167, 241
backlash, 171, 184, 191
balance, 4, 15, 29, 75, 162, 169, 176, 180, 182–184, 225–228
balancing, 182, 183, 195, 225
band, 200
banner, 81
barrage, 46
barrier, 79, 109, 113, 138, 228
base, 37, 54
baton, 92
battle, 12, 58–62, 77, 88, 156, 195, 204, 224, 234
battleground, 29
beacon, 6, 8, 11, 15, 17, 88, 152, 153, 156, 159, 160, 165, 191, 194, 198, 203, 222, 236
beauty, 5, 7, 9, 11, 112, 131, 141, 147, 157, 164, 167, 231, 234, 240
bedrock, 226
beginning, 3, 8, 13, 33, 47, 65, 67, 71
being, 4, 7, 12, 14, 15, 25, 30, 31, 33, 34, 36, 42, 49, 59, 74, 80, 85, 86, 89, 109, 126, 133, 135, 141, 156, 160, 162, 165, 166, 168, 169, 172, 174, 178, 180, 182–184, 187–190, 192–194, 198, 215, 219–221, 227, 228, 231, 233, 241

belief, 6, 11, 19, 29, 69, 73, 82, 97, 100, 115, 140, 147, 151, 156, 162, 163, 167, 168, 175, 178, 180, 185, 206, 215, 220–222, 225, 226, 245
belonging, 37, 47, 68, 104, 115, 121, 158, 167, 168, 244
benefit, 101, 146
betterment, 180, 238, 241
bi, 7, 8, 11–13, 30–33, 45–47, 50, 57, 71, 85, 88, 142, 143, 158, 173, 174, 198, 199, 232–234
bias, 73, 125, 138–140, 215
bigotry, 200
biography, 56
biology, 204
biopic, 200
birth, 1, 2, 5, 242
bitterness, 12
blend, 42, 113, 167
bloodshed, 76, 194
blossoming, 160
blueprint, 17, 90
body, 219
bond, 129, 160, 172, 176
book, 18, 238
bound, 184, 226
box, 4, 42, 90
brainstorm, 105
bravery, 46, 50, 71, 154, 199
break, 2, 19, 29, 41, 58, 68, 77, 90, 96, 104, 106, 109, 114, 131, 137, 145, 148, 149, 159, 174, 179, 205, 236
breakthrough, 109, 114
breath, 1, 2, 46
breathing, 188

breed, 227
Brendesha M. Tynes, 144
bridge, 4, 15, 24, 30, 32, 58, 75, 80, 89, 97, 106, 113, 130, 132, 139, 154, 157, 159, 162, 166, 169, 172, 224
broadcasting, 205
brutality, 29, 198, 205, 211
building, 1, 19, 36, 38, 39, 50–52, 54, 60, 61, 80, 82, 90, 99, 103, 108–112, 114, 116, 120, 121, 123, 129, 130, 132, 140, 141, 169, 183, 184, 190, 191, 204, 206, 210, 212, 216, 220, 227, 235, 236, 239
burden, 121, 179–182, 185, 187, 189, 199
burnout, 162, 192
burst, 1
business, 35

call, 13, 21, 61, 65, 70, 191, 200, 236
calling, 2, 7, 9, 12, 51, 194
camaraderie, 83, 109, 179
campaign, 26, 54, 81, 172, 189, 202, 214, 219, 220
capacity, 166, 205
capital, 45, 66
carbon, 1
care, 162, 163, 169, 180, 182–184, 186, 187, 189, 190, 192, 193, 219, 220, 227
Carl Sagan, 213
case, 17, 27, 43, 105, 161, 168, 215, 228, 231, 239
catalyst, 2, 6, 8, 10, 15, 18, 33, 35, 38, 43, 45, 47, 51, 56, 59, 64, 70, 77, 102, 118, 124,

129, 142, 145, 148, 155,
161, 165, 175, 194, 201,
221, 223, 231, 234, 240,
243
cause, 9, 10, 26, 27, 29, 34, 37, 39,
42, 43, 51, 56–58, 65, 76,
77, 83, 86, 90, 102, 105,
115, 119, 121, 136, 156,
158, 162, 163, 170, 172,
180, 185, 189–191, 195,
196, 198, 203, 204, 210,
211, 222, 224, 225, 227,
230, 240
celebration, 8, 9, 31, 38, 60, 61, 74,
83, 94, 145, 147–149, 157,
161, 167, 168, 223, 232,
236–238, 240, 245
censorship, 88
challenge, 2, 6–10, 12, 14, 22–30,
32–35, 42, 43, 45, 47, 48,
50, 52–55, 57, 58, 60, 63,
64, 70, 72, 73, 75, 76, 79,
81–83, 87, 89, 92, 93,
96–99, 104–107, 109,
111–113, 119, 122, 124,
125, 137, 140, 141, 143,
145, 148, 152–154, 156,
157, 161, 162, 166, 167,
175, 176, 182, 189, 193,
194, 198, 202, 211, 216,
220, 223, 224, 228–230,
232, 234, 236–238, 241,
243
challenging, 10, 11, 13, 16, 17, 19,
27, 28, 36, 43, 45–47, 53,
55, 57, 58, 61, 62, 64, 66,
68, 69, 71, 72, 87, 88, 92,
94, 97–99, 103, 107, 109,
111, 114, 115, 123, 125,

135, 136, 141, 142, 146,
148, 154, 155, 158, 160,
161, 163–166, 168, 176,
184, 187–189, 195, 200,
205, 212, 222, 227, 232,
240, 243, 244
champion, 6, 101, 102, 137, 203,
244
chance, 12, 141, 235
change, 2, 6–13, 15, 16, 18, 21, 23,
24, 26, 27, 30, 33–36, 40,
43–47, 49, 50, 52–67,
69–72, 76, 77, 79, 80, 82,
84–90, 102, 103,
107–110, 112, 115–124,
130, 132, 135–138,
140–145, 148, 151, 152,
155–157, 160–163, 165,
166, 170, 172, 174–176,
179, 180, 184–186, 189,
191–206, 210, 212, 214,
216, 218–229, 231–234,
237, 239, 240, 242–244
channel, 56
chaos, 188, 227, 228
chapter, 18, 66, 235
character, 200
charge, 222
charisma, 9, 56, 207
charity, 174
child, 5, 7, 11, 171, 213
childhood, 5, 7
Chloë Bass, 144
choice, 58, 111, 144, 222
chord, 10, 46
citizenship, 22
city, 29, 45, 66
civilization, 17, 85, 113, 178, 179
clash, 73, 153, 222

Index

class, 29, 33, 47, 59, 87, 100, 110, 147, 170, 215
climate, 56
clothing, 57, 238
coalition, 48, 50–52, 65, 80, 101, 116, 121
coercion, 51
coexistence, 8, 9, 13, 61, 73–75, 88, 145–149, 161, 165, 168, 195, 197, 244, 245
cohesion, 29
collaborate, 24, 37, 81, 84, 104, 143, 149, 151, 174, 219, 233, 234
collaboration, 8, 25, 37–39, 50, 52, 60, 61, 72, 74, 75, 77, 78, 80–85, 89, 93, 106, 108–110, 113, 114, 120, 122, 123, 131, 132, 136, 137, 139, 140, 146, 151, 159, 168, 175, 177, 185, 186, 193, 196, 197, 203, 206, 216, 222, 227, 234
collective, 8, 11, 13, 15, 23, 25, 30–32, 34, 35, 37, 38, 43–47, 54–57, 59, 63, 65–67, 69, 73, 75, 76, 80, 82–86, 88–90, 93, 96, 100, 103, 108, 110–112, 114, 115, 120, 122–126, 136, 140, 144, 151, 159, 165–167, 172, 175, 180, 181, 193, 196, 198, 200, 204, 206, 209, 210, 215, 220, 224–227, 229, 233, 234, 237, 239, 243, 245
colonization, 74
combat, 22, 32, 86, 92, 93, 96, 97, 99, 187, 204

combination, 14, 19, 116
comedy, 28, 50
comfort, 25, 198
commerce, 74
commission, 67
commitment, 6, 10, 11, 13, 14, 28, 33, 39, 44, 45, 58, 65, 66, 69, 71, 75, 87, 90, 109, 119, 121, 123, 126, 135, 154, 156, 158, 161, 166, 167, 172, 174, 185, 191, 193, 194, 199, 210, 221, 225, 231, 233, 234, 239, 240
committee, 99
communication, 19, 24, 27, 48, 49, 53, 64, 75, 79, 80, 82–86, 89, 106, 109, 113–115, 151, 169, 170, 176, 179, 190, 191
communicator, 213
community, 3, 6, 7, 11, 15, 25–27, 29–31, 33, 34, 37, 39–46, 48, 49, 51, 52, 56–62, 65, 66, 68, 72, 76, 82, 85, 88, 90, 99, 100, 102, 108, 115, 119–121, 123, 131, 139, 140, 142, 144, 146, 148, 151, 159, 167, 169–171, 173, 174, 177, 190, 192, 198, 199, 202, 203, 209, 213, 215, 224, 228, 230, 232, 233, 236, 238, 239, 243, 244
companionship, 155
company, 215
compass, 15, 171
compassion, 27, 64, 80, 94, 146, 150, 159, 161–163, 166, 169,

175, 183, 219
compatibility, 154
competition, 73, 92
complacency, 16, 18
complexity, 167, 216, 234
composition, 10, 86
compromise, 130, 226, 233
concept, 14, 122, 133, 137, 140, 145, 167, 178, 215, 216, 228
concern, 42
concert, 239
conclusion, 23, 71, 78, 112, 142, 160, 170, 176, 191, 195, 212, 216, 232, 234
condensation, 2
conference, 85
confidence, 150, 180, 228
conflict, 42, 73, 83, 84, 126, 224, 228, 229
conformity, 224
confusion, 31
connection, 2, 7, 9, 11, 17, 39, 64, 75, 84, 94, 109, 155, 156, 168, 175, 179, 213, 221, 240
connectivity, 115
conscience, 8, 76
consciousness, 2, 7, 14, 32, 53, 80, 125, 197, 234, 240
consensus, 50
conservation, 74, 141
consideration, 51, 172
contact, 97, 178
content, 80, 102, 205
context, 23, 26, 40, 62, 116, 136, 161, 168, 170, 238
control, 16, 29, 88
convention, 135
conversation, 54, 215, 244

conviction, 10
cooperation, 12, 14, 17, 19–21, 72, 74, 82, 89, 109, 112, 113, 126, 130, 131, 135, 146, 154, 196
coordination, 48, 52, 121
core, 14, 43, 50, 86, 111, 115, 157, 161, 225
corner, 79, 244
cornerstone, 23, 100, 165
cosmos, 2, 5–12, 14–16, 18, 19, 21–24, 33, 35, 36, 47, 54, 56, 58, 59, 61, 65, 66, 69, 73–75, 79, 80, 82, 84–86, 88, 94, 96–99, 103, 105, 112, 114, 115, 120, 124–126, 132, 143, 147, 149, 150, 155–158, 160, 161, 165, 167, 168, 175, 176, 194, 195, 199, 204, 209, 213, 221, 222, 224, 225, 231, 232, 235, 236, 239, 240, 244
council, 101
counseling, 96, 169, 176
couple, 101, 160, 161, 165
courage, 9, 29, 35, 43, 46, 58, 69, 70, 166, 194, 201, 215, 224, 232, 245
course, 8, 14, 33, 45, 180, 194, 199, 207, 216
court, 57, 135
coverage, 51
crackdown, 46
creation, 31, 60, 98, 109, 112, 130, 146, 148, 149, 201, 204
creative, 8, 27, 28, 32, 35, 36, 38, 41, 49, 55, 90, 98, 118, 122, 137, 151, 152, 174, 175,

193, 227, 245
creativity, 38, 64, 65, 81, 84, 112, 118, 119, 137, 144, 177, 185, 193, 228, 236, 239
credibility, 226
criticism, 156, 171
cross, 74, 81, 92, 96, 104, 111, 113, 115, 132
crowd, 45, 46
crowdfunding, 90
crucible, 15, 175
cry, 46, 157, 241
cuisine, 20, 93, 128, 129, 240
culmination, 46, 65
cultivation, 15, 159
culture, 13, 25, 36, 49, 74, 96, 104–107, 132, 141, 147, 149, 177–179, 188, 192, 196, 199–201, 205, 228, 231
curiosity, 5, 7, 14, 20, 27, 213, 221
curriculum, 14, 68, 97, 99, 114, 241
cycle, 13, 16, 24, 29, 211
Czechoslovakia, 47

Damian Hughes, 107
dance, 1, 20, 64, 143, 149, 151, 226, 228, 235, 237, 240
danger, 16
darkness, 194
data, 21, 26, 53, 75
date, 242
day, 20, 46, 51, 199, 235, 237–239, 242
death, 1
debunking, 72, 90, 106
decision, 74, 87, 101, 115, 119, 124, 125, 137–140, 149, 192, 196

dedication, 43, 45, 69, 73, 77, 150, 156, 179, 180, 196, 198, 227, 234, 244
defeat, 56, 233
defiance, 46, 201
degradation, 23
demand, 16, 34, 43–45, 58, 66, 69, 75, 76, 136, 205
democracy, 99, 101, 102
demonstration, 46
denial, 10, 31, 100, 137, 204
depletion, 22
depression, 180
depth, 167
design, 51, 201
desire, 2, 5, 7, 10, 12, 34, 65, 80, 121, 155, 161, 198, 214, 221, 226
despair, 187
desperation, 45
destiny, 5, 126, 146, 157
destruction, 22, 76
determination, 4, 8, 9, 11, 16, 29, 40, 45, 46, 50, 56, 65, 69, 70, 77, 82, 100, 115, 135, 160, 167, 171, 175, 176, 180, 189, 194, 197, 201, 207, 212, 214, 215, 220, 224, 227, 232, 239, 245
development, 14, 15, 22, 61, 79, 83, 232, 238
device, 109
dialogue, 20, 22, 26, 28, 35, 37, 39, 50, 52, 54, 58, 60, 64, 70, 71, 74, 82, 85, 87, 89, 92, 97, 100, 104, 107, 108, 119, 122–124, 126, 127, 130, 131, 135, 136, 143, 144, 148, 150, 151, 169,

174, 176, 188, 202, 212, 216, 224, 236, 238, 240
DiAngelo, 164
difference, 10, 12, 13, 15, 67, 82, 101, 119, 154, 189, 203, 215, 216, 220, 238, 239
dignity, 22, 44, 55, 67, 73, 89, 102, 131, 135, 162, 163, 166, 197, 203, 213, 241
dilemma, 2, 30, 40, 65, 225
dimension, 211
dinner, 175
diplomacy, 74, 127, 222
diplomat, 9
disability, 87
disadvantage, 89
disagreement, 38, 39, 176
disapproval, 153
discontent, 56, 65
discord, 73
discourse, 45, 79, 102, 212, 236
discovery, 6, 7, 14, 156, 224, 225, 230, 232
discrimination, 6, 7, 9–11, 16, 17, 23, 24, 26, 29–34, 37, 39, 40, 43, 44, 49, 53–57, 59–61, 65–72, 76, 77, 82–88, 92–94, 96, 98–100, 102–105, 107, 114, 123, 124, 133, 135–143, 147, 153, 154, 158, 159, 162, 163, 165, 167, 169, 171–173, 175, 187, 192, 194, 200, 204, 205, 211, 212, 215, 216, 221, 222, 228, 230–232, 236, 240, 244
discussion, 39, 123, 227
dish, 179

disillusionment, 180
dismantling, 6, 7, 19, 23, 25, 29, 54, 58, 61, 71, 113, 123, 125, 126, 136, 137, 141, 142, 146, 147, 157, 164, 168, 199, 230, 232, 234, 243, 244
disobedience, 8, 13, 16, 29, 44, 50, 65
display, 7, 201
dispute, 20
disruption, 89
dissemination, 24
dissent, 35, 42
distance, 75, 109, 115, 228
distribution, 138
distrust, 113, 122
diversity, 3, 4, 8–10, 13, 17, 19, 20, 35, 38, 60, 61, 68, 73–75, 82, 85, 93, 94, 96–98, 103, 104, 106, 107, 110–113, 115, 119, 121, 123, 126, 131, 132, 137, 139–143, 145, 147–149, 151, 154, 155, 157, 158, 160, 161, 167–170, 173, 176, 177, 195–197, 205, 216, 231, 234, 235, 239, 240, 244, 245
divide, 28, 32, 58, 113, 145
division, 17, 28–30
documentary, 200
dominance, 82
Donald Glover, 122
door, 157
doubt, 15, 158, 180, 189, 224, 225, 231
downfall, 17
Draclon, 98

Draclon, 98
dream, 140, 142, 152, 195, 215, 218, 225, 226, 245
drive, 114, 140, 152, 172, 180
driving, 4, 5, 16, 35, 43, 45, 72, 119, 140, 158, 160–163, 165, 166, 172, 185, 195, 220, 222, 225, 228
dust, 1
duty, 198, 245
dynamic, 171, 212

ear, 171
Earth, 1, 2, 18, 21, 52, 71, 76, 96, 107, 177
ease, 183
echo, 200
eclipse, 7
eco, 74
economic, 10, 11, 28–30, 40, 67, 74, 101, 138, 141, 173, 222, 233
education, 2, 7, 10, 12, 18, 21, 24–29, 31–33, 39, 44, 53, 58, 60, 61, 68, 72, 74, 76–78, 83, 86, 88–90, 92–94, 97, 99, 100, 102, 103, 105–107, 114–116, 119, 121, 130, 135, 137–139, 141, 175, 194, 205, 212, 213, 216, 221, 224, 235, 236, 238, 243, 245
effect, 2, 10, 11, 44, 54, 64, 72, 79, 108, 119, 122, 123, 176, 214, 220, 225, 232
effectiveness, 12, 41, 58, 62, 64, 108, 211, 222, 224

effort, 19, 39, 40, 44, 53, 65, 69, 77, 83, 96, 103, 107, 112, 135, 139, 159, 165, 176, 234
element, 152
elite, 29
else, 20
Elyn, 175
embodiment, 165
embrace, 15, 17, 85, 93, 107, 121, 131, 132, 143, 145, 149, 154, 157, 159, 161, 164, 166, 167, 170, 190, 192, 201, 215, 216, 225, 228, 231, 234, 244
Emma, 215
Emma González, 214
Emma, 215
emotion, 221
empathy, 2, 3, 6, 7, 9–11, 14, 15, 18–21, 23, 24, 26–28, 30, 32, 34, 36, 39, 42, 47, 49, 53, 55, 58, 59, 68, 73, 76–78, 80, 82, 84–88, 90, 92, 94, 97–99, 103, 106, 107, 109, 111, 112, 114, 122, 123, 131, 132, 137, 141–143, 145, 146, 150, 152, 154, 156, 159–161, 163, 164, 166, 171–173, 175, 176, 178, 192–194, 196, 205, 212, 213, 221, 234, 236–238, 241
emphasis, 14, 68, 145
employment, 8, 30–33, 35, 39, 44, 53, 60, 68, 86, 88, 89, 93–96, 102, 103, 107, 130, 137, 138, 141, 195, 222
empower, 13, 18, 27–30, 44, 60, 100, 101, 103, 116, 123,

150, 151, 167, 190, 194,
202, 216, 221, 245
empowerment, 2, 12, 23, 38, 40, 49,
116, 119, 139, 140, 199,
214, 233, 238, 244
encounter, 73, 75, 92, 96, 226, 228
encouragement, 109, 171, 184
end, 8, 13, 29, 56, 66, 67, 71, 135,
222, 234
endeavor, 33, 40, 72, 120, 142, 168,
227
energy, 1, 7, 46, 73, 75, 122, 152,
182, 183, 192, 219
enforce, 93
enforcement, 22, 46, 135, 172
engagement, 35, 40, 65, 100, 116,
121, 136, 174, 189, 190,
203
engineering, 144
enlightenment, 194
enrichment, 177
entertainment, 27, 104, 214
enthusiasm, 213
entity, 7, 8, 11–13, 26, 30–33,
45–47, 50, 57, 71, 74, 85,
88, 142, 143, 145, 158,
173, 174, 198, 199,
232–234
Envars, 28, 29
environment, 6, 17, 19, 22, 93, 103,
119, 139, 146, 151, 177,
203
epic, 65
equal, 2, 3, 8, 10, 11, 16, 17, 32, 39,
45, 48, 55, 57–59, 62, 68,
71, 72, 74, 93–96, 100,
102, 103, 130, 137–139,
141, 145, 152, 163, 171,
175, 177, 185, 197, 202,
204, 214, 232, 236
equality, 4, 6–13, 15–18, 21, 23, 25,
26, 28, 29, 33, 36, 37, 39,
43, 44, 47, 50, 53, 56,
58–62, 64–67, 69–71, 73,
75–86, 88, 90, 92–95,
99–105, 107, 110–112,
120–122, 124, 126,
130–132, 135–137,
140–143, 145–147,
150–152, 156–163,
165–168, 170, 171,
174–176, 184, 185,
189–191, 194–201,
203–206, 209–213, 215,
216, 218, 221, 222, 225,
226, 228, 230–245
equilibrium, 4
equity, 139, 171
era, 13, 25, 65, 143, 145, 147, 148,
150, 157, 164–166, 203
eradication, 84, 86, 138, 201
erasure, 60, 145–147
erosion, 29
escalation, 42
essay, 144
essence, 142, 201, 203, 242
establishment, 87, 98, 121, 150, 196,
235
esteem, 158, 228
evaluation, 126, 183
evening, 45
event, 1, 2, 18, 38, 45–47, 51, 52,
65–67, 149, 179, 240
evidence, 55, 136, 205
evolution, 225, 234
example, 16, 17, 19, 20, 24, 30, 39,
43–45, 47, 50, 83, 84, 98,
102, 104, 107, 110, 112,

122, 138, 150, 163, 165, 171, 172, 191–193, 196, 198, 200, 201, 204, 215, 220, 228
exception, 120, 151, 187, 213
exchange, 15, 20, 21, 68, 74, 82–84, 97–99, 104, 109, 113, 114, 120, 123, 131, 132, 135, 139, 146, 148, 154, 168, 169, 177–179, 197, 204, 240
excitement, 152
exclusion, 31, 88, 97, 167
exercise, 20, 100, 119, 182, 184
exhaustion, 162
exhibit, 142
exhibition, 85
existence, 1, 2, 5, 11, 14, 21, 89, 154, 164, 165, 194
expanse, 5, 7, 9, 11, 14, 112, 153, 155, 164, 177, 194
experience, 15, 20, 31, 39, 93, 96, 98, 143, 160, 168, 179, 187, 215, 216, 222, 225, 228, 234
expert, 136, 183
expertise, 37, 55, 96, 119, 140, 180, 185
exploit, 29
exploitation, 22, 23
exploration, 14, 21, 23, 43, 64, 74, 75, 127, 148, 166, 167
explore, 2, 5, 16, 19, 23, 26, 28, 40, 48, 56, 67, 73, 88, 90, 96, 99, 101, 105, 110, 112, 116, 124, 130, 132, 135, 138, 140, 142, 150, 151, 153, 155, 164, 168, 170, 173, 175, 177, 182, 184,

187, 191, 198–201, 204, 207, 209, 213, 216, 218, 228, 231, 232, 237, 242
exposure, 6, 73, 105, 172, 173, 221, 228
expression, 8, 38, 60, 61, 64, 118, 141, 144, 145, 151, 152, 162, 193, 234, 239, 241
extent, 4
eye, 17

fabric, 12, 113, 132, 155, 168, 225
facade, 10
face, 8, 16, 24, 29, 31, 34, 56, 58, 66, 69, 73, 76, 77, 88–90, 94, 96, 100, 102, 104, 107, 120, 138, 139, 154, 157, 160, 162, 165, 168, 169, 171, 176, 182–185, 187, 190, 191, 195, 204, 210, 214–216, 218–220, 224, 225, 227, 231, 233, 236, 244
factor, 219
failure, 191
fairness, 6, 101, 102, 127, 139, 140, 171
fall, 14
familiarity, 129
family, 6, 13, 164, 169–172, 175–177, 182, 219
fancy, 142
fantasy, 200
fascination, 7, 11
fashion, 201
fate, 180
fear, 8, 10, 29, 31, 59, 60, 73, 92, 96, 99, 105, 123, 146, 153,

157, 178, 180, 198, 201, 212
fearlessness, 201
feat, 56, 130, 179
feature, 202
federation, 101
feedback, 119
feeling, 7, 183
festival, 20, 38, 240
fi, 200
fiction, 25, 99, 200
field, 72, 113, 127, 138, 150, 214
fight, 2–4, 6–14, 16, 18, 21, 23–26, 28, 29, 32–36, 39, 43, 45, 47, 50, 53, 56, 57, 59–61, 65–67, 69–73, 76–78, 82, 86, 87, 89, 90, 92–94, 96, 97, 102, 104, 106, 107, 110–113, 115–117, 119, 120, 124, 135, 138, 140, 142, 143, 145, 150–152, 155–163, 167, 171, 172, 175–177, 184, 185, 187, 189–192, 194–206, 209–211, 215, 216, 219–222, 224, 225, 228, 232–236, 238–245
fighting, 16, 43, 58, 59, 77, 83, 103, 115, 121, 142, 155, 161, 171, 182, 189, 191, 200, 213, 214, 218, 222, 224, 239
figure, 31, 201
film, 174, 200
finding, 4, 10, 79, 83, 85, 89, 111, 120, 122, 168–170, 182, 184, 185, 190, 191, 196, 218–220, 224, 225, 227
fire, 6, 10, 21, 33, 40, 46, 66, 92, 175, 198, 214, 224, 245
firsthand, 6, 9, 11, 12, 84, 93, 94, 98, 119, 132, 143, 194
flame, 56
flaw, 231
flexibility, 185, 190, 228
flight, 142
flourish, 19, 74, 94, 157, 165
flow, 113
fluency, 85
focus, 72, 117, 145, 146, 193, 205, 215, 219, 232, 238, 243
food, 51, 128, 174, 179, 238
force, 4, 5, 8, 11, 16, 26, 43–45, 47, 64, 72, 76, 84, 109, 117, 120, 155, 157, 160–165, 194, 195, 210, 214, 218, 220–222, 232, 234
forefront, 45, 55, 59, 87, 124, 125, 130, 182, 210
form, 2, 14, 18, 29, 30, 49, 55, 64, 68, 72, 73, 81, 85, 96, 97, 124, 136, 155, 156, 161, 194, 200, 201, 233, 237, 239, 242
formation, 17, 19, 41, 83, 93, 97, 108, 110, 123, 195, 244
forum, 80
Foster, 119
foster, 5, 12, 15, 22, 26, 27, 32, 33, 39, 44, 47, 52, 53, 58, 72, 82–84, 93, 96–100, 104, 106, 109–112, 121–123, 131, 132, 135, 145, 146, 151, 163, 169, 175–178, 205, 212, 216, 234, 236–238, 244, 245
foundation, 6, 17, 19, 28, 38, 40, 48, 66, 73, 82, 84, 88, 109,

Index

110, 126, 127, 135, 141, 146, 171, 175, 199, 226, 235, 243
fragmentation, 229
framework, 57, 98, 126, 132–136, 216
freedom, 65, 66, 80, 100, 122, 141
friendship, 164
front, 34, 47, 54, 57, 60, 65, 85, 109, 124, 140, 193, 205
frustration, 45, 46, 187
fuel, 6, 26, 166, 172, 176, 205, 218, 220, 226, 232, 233
fulfillment, 160, 166
fun, 179
funding, 39, 139, 144, 152, 243
fundraising, 119
fusion, 1–5, 7, 8, 10–13, 30–34, 45–47, 50, 56–61, 67, 68, 71, 77, 85, 88, 142, 143, 158, 168–170, 194, 198, 199, 224
future, 9, 11, 13, 16–19, 21–23, 35, 36, 38, 45, 47, 56, 58, 59, 65–71, 73–75, 85, 86, 88, 90, 92, 94, 96, 104, 105, 107, 110, 112, 115, 124, 126, 131, 132, 135, 137, 141, 142, 146, 147, 149, 152, 155, 157, 161, 166–168, 171, 175, 179, 181, 185, 193, 195–199, 201–203, 206, 209, 212, 213, 216, 219, 222, 224, 226, 230, 235–237, 239, 241–245

galaxy, 9, 13, 16, 28, 41, 80, 90, 111, 122, 131, 142, 191, 197, 200, 225, 240, 241
Galaxy United, 101
gap, 24, 30, 32, 80, 114, 130, 132, 139, 141, 224
gas, 1, 46
gastronomy, 167
gathering, 39
gear, 46
gender, 23, 87, 110, 121, 141, 147, 163, 170, 211, 215, 233
generation, 9, 27, 28, 33, 61, 90, 103, 110, 114, 150–152, 165, 199, 202, 204, 235, 236, 241, 243, 244
gesture, 125
gift, 231
glimpse, 167
glow, 28
goal, 5, 34, 54, 58, 81, 82, 110, 115, 120, 138, 146, 165, 172, 179, 220, 222
gold, 28
González, 214
good, 198
governance, 101, 125, 126, 138, 140, 149
government, 8, 12, 28, 29, 31, 32, 41–43, 46, 48–57, 59, 60, 65, 67, 68, 76, 77, 85, 88, 89, 99, 125, 130, 131, 189, 194, 198, 209–211, 222
grace, 176, 237
graffiti, 64
grander, 2, 8
grant, 119, 137
gratitude, 185, 239
Greg M. Nielsen, 164
Gregory Sholette, 144
grief, 187

ground, 4, 20, 37, 39, 44, 83, 85, 89, 108, 111, 115, 119, 120, 122, 123, 127, 131, 172, 211, 227
groundbreaking, 31, 74, 86, 146, 152, 177
groundswell, 205
groundwork, 43, 53, 57, 65, 171
group, 8, 10, 29–31, 34, 46, 56, 77, 85, 92, 105, 111, 151, 200, 201, 224, 237
growth, 6, 12, 14, 25, 74, 75, 89, 121, 141, 156, 158, 159, 165, 172, 177, 184, 191, 218, 224, 225, 229, 231–234, 245
guarantee, 86, 101
guerrilla, 55
guest, 202
guidance, 18, 49, 67, 78, 109, 118, 150, 154, 175, 177, 190, 191, 213
guide, 36, 56, 73, 127, 150, 195, 209, 212, 213, 216

hall, 48, 58
hand, 40, 43, 53, 136, 166, 168, 215, 225
happiness, 133, 160
harassment, 51, 88
harm, 211
harmony, 13, 17, 19, 21, 31, 70, 73, 75, 82, 85, 87, 94, 98, 99, 113, 126, 131, 132, 144, 147, 154, 198
harness, 118, 137, 163, 226
hashtag, 72
hatred, 8, 13, 96, 228
haystack, 218

head, 53, 83, 86, 154, 189, 204, 222
healing, 83, 176, 230
health, 13, 49, 179, 180, 187–189, 192, 195, 244
healthcare, 29, 31, 32, 39, 53, 68, 74, 86, 89, 93, 102, 130, 137, 138, 141
hearing, 39
heart, 7, 10, 40, 45, 46, 66, 120, 147, 225, 237
heartbeat, 119
helium, 1
help, 2, 18, 67, 93, 94, 96, 99, 102, 112, 138, 139, 151, 154, 163, 169, 172, 188, 189, 219, 228, 229, 243
heritage, 4, 32, 60, 84, 85, 102, 145, 166–169, 221, 230
hero, 9, 13, 194, 195, 213, 214, 237, 244, 245
hesitancy, 122
hierarchy, 21
hiring, 21, 68, 103, 139
historian, 18
history, 2, 6–8, 10, 12, 14–19, 24–26, 33, 45, 62, 64, 67, 68, 76, 84, 85, 97, 106, 150, 167, 194, 199, 204, 205, 207, 214, 221, 224, 230, 235, 236, 244
hit, 200
hobby, 219
hold, 5, 17, 23, 28, 54, 130, 138, 146, 163, 166, 177, 199, 204, 205
homage, 201, 245
home, 2, 7, 9, 130, 131, 153, 176, 179
honor, 145, 158, 195, 196, 199,

201–203, 237, 239,
    241–244
hope, 6, 8, 11, 13, 15, 16, 35, 46, 69,
    71, 88, 92, 142, 152, 153,
    156, 159, 160, 162, 165,
    186, 191, 194, 201, 203,
    205, 210, 213, 214,
    218–222, 236–240, 244
host, 96, 97, 102, 125, 126
hostility, 105, 155, 215
housing, 31, 32, 53, 86, 88, 204
hub, 80, 114, 236
human, 25, 33, 36, 53, 55, 57, 59,
    67, 80, 85, 104, 130, 142,
    147, 149, 155, 161, 167,
    176, 188, 195, 205, 216,
    225, 228, 230
humanity, 31, 36, 44, 90, 92, 105,
    106, 142, 155, 161, 163,
    179, 205, 225, 240
humility, 75
humor, 28, 50, 53, 106, 107
hurdle, 109
hybridity, 167, 168
hydrogen, 1

idea, 8, 145, 149
idealism, 225–228
identification, 83
identity, 2, 4, 23, 38, 56, 60, 85, 121,
    138, 140, 141, 145,
    158–161, 166–168, 170,
    178, 189, 200, 203, 211,
    224, 228–232, 234, 244
ignorance, 2, 43, 59, 96, 99, 105,
    114, 146, 159
image, 142, 200, 201, 233
imagery, 81
imagination, 5, 112, 166, 222

immersion, 27
immigration, 21, 101
impact, 9, 13, 17, 18, 29, 35, 36, 41,
    47, 51, 52, 56, 57, 59, 62,
    69–71, 75, 81, 87, 101,
    105, 107, 110, 112, 120,
    135, 143–145, 157, 163,
    170–172, 175, 180, 183,
    193, 195–200, 202, 204,
    207, 212, 216, 220, 227,
    228, 230–232, 236,
    242–244
imperfection, 183
implement, 32, 55, 89
implementation, 83, 86, 89, 103,
    132, 135, 137, 178
importance, 7, 12, 14, 16–18, 22, 23,
    25, 27, 32, 34, 36–39, 49,
    50, 53, 54, 59, 61, 65, 66,
    70, 71, 76–79, 82, 83, 87,
    89, 90, 94, 99, 102, 103,
    108, 110, 111, 113, 122,
    124, 126, 135, 147–150,
    158–160, 168, 170,
    174–177, 182, 184, 185,
    189, 190, 192, 193, 196,
    200, 203, 204, 210–216,
    219, 220, 222, 224, 226,
    231–234, 236, 237, 240,
    241, 243
improvement, 185
in, 1, 2, 4–39, 42–83, 85–90, 92,
    94–127, 130–133,
    135–154, 156–180,
    182–185, 188–205, 209,
    210, 212–216, 218–245
inadequacy, 231
inception, 33
incident, 56

inclusion, 70, 96–98, 103, 104, 124, 132, 135, 136, 149, 196, 212, 231, 240
inclusiveness, 216
inclusivity, 17, 33, 50, 85, 86, 93–95, 100, 102, 112, 115, 119, 125, 131, 136, 142, 145, 148, 149, 151, 170, 196, 204, 205, 216, 226
indifference, 17, 27
individual, 2, 11, 12, 14, 24, 67, 76, 86, 95, 100, 102, 121, 158, 170, 180, 182, 190, 194, 195, 222, 224, 231, 238, 239, 244
individuality, 2, 8, 158–160, 231, 232
industry, 201
inequality, 6, 10, 11, 21, 23, 24, 28–30, 45, 53, 59, 68, 71, 89, 102, 136, 140, 141, 214, 216, 221, 222
infighting, 229
influence, 36, 47, 72, 98, 101, 108, 136, 138, 140, 160, 166, 170, 196, 199–201, 209, 214
information, 25, 32, 49, 76, 80, 100, 123, 206
initiative, 119, 152
injustice, 6, 7, 10, 11, 16, 17, 23, 29, 33, 37, 45, 46, 49, 50, 53, 56, 57, 65, 67, 69, 70, 80, 120, 123, 133, 142, 161, 162, 171, 175, 187, 194, 205, 210, 221, 224, 232, 237, 238, 241, 243
innovation, 109, 152, 168, 177
input, 136

insight, 132, 212
inspiration, 10, 13, 18, 24, 43, 46, 59, 67, 78, 88, 150, 152, 157, 160, 170, 176, 185, 191, 193, 197, 198, 200, 201, 214, 215, 220, 225, 230, 232, 235, 237, 238, 241, 243, 244
instance, 19, 20, 24, 103, 170, 171, 190, 241
institution, 2, 14, 15
integration, 27, 99, 137, 139
integrity, 111
intellect, 106
intelligence, 15, 75
interaction, 154, 179
intercommunity, 123
interconnectedness, 2, 14, 15, 22, 31, 72, 74, 77, 84, 104, 120, 123, 144–146, 213, 232, 240
interconnectivity, 3
interdependence, 74
interest, 137, 156
interference, 42
intergroup, 99
internalization, 228
interplay, 2
intersect, 11, 110, 170, 215
intersection, 167, 215
intersectionality, 60, 70, 72, 77, 78, 87, 111, 112, 121, 147, 149, 151, 152, 160, 170, 211, 212, 214–216, 232
intervention, 75
intimidation, 29, 51
intolerance, 200
introspection, 189, 225
investigation, 22

involve, 103, 125, 171
involvement, 171, 172
iron, 1
isolation, 77, 124, 154, 190, 215, 233
issue, 21, 22, 26, 30, 31, 52, 53, 81, 87, 88, 94, 113, 119, 124, 144, 163

Jamie, 172
Janelle Monáe, 214
Jaxon Blair, 143
job, 96, 103, 107
Johann, 164
journaling, 169
journey, 1, 2, 6–16, 26, 43, 47, 71, 75, 85, 90, 105, 115, 119, 126, 135, 140, 143, 150, 152, 153, 156–160, 164–166, 168, 170–172, 175, 176, 183, 185, 189–195, 198, 200, 202, 203, 213–216, 218–220, 222, 224–234
joy, 166, 176
judgment, 123, 201
justice, 2, 4, 6–13, 15, 16, 18, 22, 26, 28–30, 33, 34, 36, 37, 39, 43–45, 52, 54, 56–59, 62, 64–67, 69–73, 75–79, 81, 84–86, 88, 90, 92, 96, 98, 99, 102, 110, 111, 116, 120–122, 124, 126, 130, 137, 141, 144, 145, 150–152, 156, 158, 159, 161–163, 165–168, 170, 171, 175, 180, 184, 187, 189–191, 195–201, 203, 204, 206, 209, 211, 212, 215, 216, 221, 225, 226, 228, 230–237, 239–245

Kael, 56
Kara Jensen, 144
key, 18, 23, 28, 39, 40, 47–49, 52, 60, 62, 63, 76, 80, 82, 106, 107, 115, 117, 119, 127, 132, 133, 138, 180, 182, 190, 191, 196, 202, 204, 209, 213, 219, 235, 238, 240
kind, 155
King Jr., 164
kinship, 176
Kinxoria, 84
Kira, 46
Kira Vex, 46
Kivel, 164
knowledge, 2, 6, 7, 9, 10, 12, 14, 18–20, 23–26, 28, 40, 61, 74, 84, 97, 108, 110, 114, 119–121, 126, 127, 130, 148, 150, 173, 177, 185, 190, 193–197, 202, 204, 212, 213, 219, 221, 241

labor, 22, 23, 29
lack, 10, 11, 29, 31, 105, 113, 141
landmark, 236
landscape, 28, 124, 127, 130, 155, 162, 176
language, 24, 26, 79–81, 83, 85, 100, 109, 113, 118, 119, 122, 139, 142, 148, 174
laughter, 50, 176
law, 9, 46, 71, 130, 132–135, 172, 190, 204

lead, 46, 92, 97, 100, 153, 177, 187, 189, 192, 225, 228
leader, 8, 34, 46, 76, 180, 191, 192, 195, 199, 200
leadership, 9, 36, 48, 53, 56, 61, 65, 104, 139, 175, 179, 180, 189, 191–193
leap, 114
learning, 7, 12–16, 27, 30, 40, 74, 75, 83, 88, 108, 119, 132, 141, 145, 178, 184, 186, 191, 194, 203, 206, 232–234
legacy, 9, 13, 28, 33, 56, 65, 66, 69–71, 73, 75, 90, 115, 138, 145, 149, 150, 157, 161, 172, 193, 195–197, 199, 201–204, 206, 209, 221, 234, 235, 237, 239–245
legend, 201–203
legislation, 22, 32, 43, 55, 60, 71, 89, 101, 130, 135, 136, 139, 204, 236
lens, 3, 64
lesson, 17, 76, 77, 210–212, 231
level, 8, 23, 38, 64, 72, 80, 86, 97, 98, 113, 117, 121, 122, 130, 138, 142, 161, 173, 197
leverage, 30, 81, 108, 136
Levine, 164
liberation, 8, 13, 67, 71, 151, 158, 195, 198, 199, 203, 204, 222, 239, 244
liberty, 133
life, 3, 5–7, 12, 13, 15, 17, 25, 26, 42, 43, 56, 65, 69, 70, 74, 86, 88, 90, 102, 104, 105, 133, 145, 147, 149, 150, 156, 159, 162, 166, 167, 175, 176, 179, 182–184, 194, 195, 200, 202, 214, 221, 230, 231, 235, 237, 238, 240–245
lifeline, 219
lifetime, 196
light, 1, 9, 21, 22, 24, 26, 32, 43, 57, 114, 194, 205, 206, 236, 238
likelihood, 206
likeness, 201
Lila Rodriguez, 143
limit, 89
line, 198, 215
lineage, 86, 167
listening, 20, 39, 106, 123, 167, 171
literature, 49, 72, 74, 86, 105, 131, 149–151, 200, 201, 242
litigation, 55, 89
living, 22, 26, 27, 69, 144, 228, 243, 244
load, 180
lobbying, 43, 55, 60, 103, 136
locality, 39
location, 51, 109
longevity, 61
look, 92, 105, 117
Lorde, 164
loss, 85, 89
love, 5, 13, 153–157, 160–166, 172, 176, 177, 195, 197, 229–232
Luna Patel, 107
luxury, 182
Lyra Vega, 14

machine, 75
magic, 153

mainstream, 90, 205
majority, 26
maker, 216
makeup, 33
making, 15, 42, 51, 74, 79, 87, 90,
 101, 109, 110, 113–115,
 119, 124, 125, 137–140,
 149, 155, 174, 180, 185,
 189, 192, 196, 210, 211,
 219, 243
man, 104, 215
management, 183
managing, 168, 169, 183
maneuvering, 214
manner, 28
mantle, 11, 90, 198
marathon, 227
marginalization, 88, 147, 194, 224,
 228
mark, 11, 161, 196, 209
market, 96
Martin Luther, 164
Martin Luther King Jr., 44, 163
master, 86, 226
matter, 1, 13, 156, 196, 218
Maya, 171
meaning, 145, 164, 178
means, 8, 12, 26, 62, 65, 76, 102,
 120, 138, 147, 165–167,
 169, 179, 192, 216, 219,
 226, 227, 231, 234, 241,
 243
mechanism, 98
media, 25, 26, 30, 41, 43, 44, 48, 49,
 51, 53, 57, 58, 71, 72, 90,
 93, 98, 99, 102, 104, 105,
 120, 136, 143, 149, 151,
 189, 191, 197, 205
mediation, 50

meditation, 15, 169, 182, 184, 188,
 219, 225
medium, 84, 86, 144, 174, 203, 242
melding, 7
melting, 5
member, 135, 138, 171
meme, 52
memorial, 201
memory, 9, 13, 70, 167, 195,
 201–203, 239, 241–245
mentality, 106, 227
mentorship, 61, 121, 144, 150, 152,
 243
merchandise, 201
merging, 2
message, 5, 8, 13, 23, 24, 34, 47, 48,
 54, 56, 57, 64, 79–81, 90,
 119, 121, 122, 191, 195,
 200, 209, 211, 239, 242
messaging, 163
method, 125
Metz, 164
Michael, 215
midst, 59, 162, 182, 219, 220
milestone, 32, 235, 236
mind, 127, 180, 219
mindedness, 82, 106, 146, 154, 164,
 169, 172, 178
mindfulness, 15, 169, 182, 188, 189,
 225
mindset, 61, 74, 96, 106, 114, 183,
 184, 213, 216, 219, 226,
 227
mingling, 164
miscommunication, 31
misconception, 106
misinformation, 106
mission, 27, 71, 119, 189, 198, 204,
 214, 221, 245

misstep, 179
mistreatment, 66
mistrust, 51, 83, 212
misunderstanding, 59
mobility, 29
mobilization, 48, 52, 72, 80, 137, 234
mode, 19
model, 99, 125, 195, 230, 233
moment, 1, 5, 7, 10, 33, 45, 46, 56, 76, 188, 194, 204, 214, 215, 224
momentum, 29, 34, 42, 53, 61, 62, 122, 126, 136, 149, 226
monument, 201
morale, 171
morality, 14
mosaic, 146, 148, 239
motion, 16
motivation, 161, 175, 184
move, 46, 56, 126, 149, 170, 231
movement, 8, 12, 13, 15, 18, 23, 26, 28, 29, 33–35, 37, 43–45, 48–58, 60–62, 65, 66, 69, 76, 77, 81, 85, 87–90, 101, 102, 109–112, 116, 118–123, 142–147, 149, 156, 160, 163, 170–172, 180, 182, 190–193, 195, 196, 198–200, 205, 207, 209–212, 214, 220, 227, 232, 238, 239
multiculturalism, 146, 147, 149, 177–179
multilingualism, 83
multimedia, 80, 81, 97, 112
multitude, 21, 31, 147
mural, 201
Muralists, 200

museum, 70, 202, 235
music, 6, 20, 35, 49, 64, 72, 74, 86, 93, 118, 122, 131, 137, 149, 151, 167, 193, 200, 201, 205, 235, 237, 239, 240, 242, 245
myriad, 168, 177
mystery, 112, 213
myth, 8

naivety, 226
name, 243, 244
narrative, 15, 53, 106, 107, 154, 168, 233
nature, 4, 14, 18, 22, 29, 59, 66, 104, 113, 133, 138, 147, 151, 155, 164, 168, 170, 184, 186, 194, 214–216, 219, 221
navigation, 170
nebula, 5
necessity, 35, 77, 182, 212, 227
need, 6, 8, 28, 34, 36, 39, 42, 45, 48, 50, 54, 55, 70, 77, 78, 85, 87, 98, 105, 109, 112, 113, 125, 127, 133, 141, 144, 176, 180, 189, 197, 198, 222, 226, 238
needle, 218
negotiation, 44, 51, 127–130
neighborhood, 174
neighboring, 20, 66
network, 9, 37–39, 57, 86, 110, 113, 119–122, 169, 180, 182, 184, 190, 193, 219, 220, 222
networking, 96, 204
newfound, 7, 158
night, 5, 6, 194, 224

Index 269

noise, 114
non, 31, 32, 34, 60, 135, 139, 140, 188
nonviolence, 111
norm, 5, 21, 161
normalization, 154
notion, 27, 106, 123, 157, 162, 167
novel, 200
number, 51, 125, 197

objective, 50, 86, 123
obstacle, 57, 59, 83, 125, 154
occasion, 244
occurrence, 30
Octavia Butler, 214
office, 139
official, 33, 242
on, 1, 2, 5–11, 13–22, 24–33, 35–54, 56–59, 61, 64–66, 68, 70–72, 74–80, 82, 83, 85–89, 92, 93, 95, 97–103, 105, 107, 108, 110, 111, 114, 115, 120, 122, 123, 125, 126, 130–132, 135, 136, 140–147, 150, 151, 155, 157–159, 161, 163, 164, 166, 167, 170, 171, 173–177, 179, 180, 182–187, 189–205, 207, 209, 211, 212, 214–216, 218–222, 227, 228, 230–233, 235–245
one, 1, 2, 8, 11, 14, 23, 24, 26, 31, 37, 39, 46, 64, 71, 76, 77, 96, 99, 102, 103, 110, 111, 113, 120, 122, 127, 130, 138, 142, 145, 147, 148, 150, 151, 155–160, 165, 166, 168–170, 178, 180, 183, 185, 189, 190, 197, 198, 218, 219, 222, 225, 226, 228, 231, 232, 234, 244
op, 102
openness, 160
opinion, 63, 72, 98, 136, 172, 205, 210, 219
opportunity, 20, 37, 38, 56, 68, 119, 139, 148, 149, 166, 169, 172, 173, 191, 224, 235, 236
opposition, 162, 165, 184, 189
oppression, 2, 10, 16, 18, 21, 23, 24, 26, 29, 33, 34, 40–42, 46, 49, 53, 58, 61, 62, 64, 65, 71, 76, 77, 85, 89, 104, 110, 111, 121, 124, 133, 140, 142, 147, 151, 152, 156, 162, 187, 194, 205, 211, 214–216, 221, 224, 232, 236, 241, 243
optimism, 219
order, 1, 36, 37, 79, 90, 92, 133, 173, 192, 216, 219
organization, 44, 47, 66, 84, 99, 105, 144, 194, 243
organizing, 6, 11, 12, 27, 29, 32, 34, 40, 42–44, 48, 50, 52, 56, 58, 60, 65, 71, 72, 80, 87, 89, 90, 100, 109, 114, 115, 117, 136, 149, 151, 172, 179, 190, 197, 198, 202, 206
origin, 14, 55, 71, 73, 74, 93, 95, 102, 121, 122, 133, 135, 156, 176, 198, 203, 204
Orion, 14
other, 1, 2, 11, 15–17, 20, 23, 27, 34,

36, 37, 43, 44, 47, 51, 54,
57, 60, 67, 70–72, 77, 82,
83, 86, 89, 92–94, 97, 99,
103, 106–111, 114, 120,
121, 127, 140, 146, 148,
154, 156, 167, 168, 173,
178, 180, 182, 183, 185,
187, 193, 199, 204–206,
210, 215, 219, 225, 230,
233, 234
otherness, 158, 159
outfit, 201
outline, 52, 102
outlook, 180, 185
outrage, 56, 162
outreach, 8, 34, 51, 87, 100, 102,
119, 131, 206
outsider, 158, 224
ownership, 116, 119, 180
oxygen, 1

painter, 142
painting, 142
panel, 26, 43, 58, 236
paper, 102
paradigm, 222
part, 2, 14, 15, 36, 45, 71, 84, 96, 99,
102, 129, 146, 159, 166,
184, 185, 189, 191, 210,
213, 218, 220, 227, 238,
243
participation, 100, 102, 119,
137–139
partner, 160, 165
partnership, 165, 193
passage, 103, 204
passing, 9, 167, 236
passion, 2, 10, 11, 119, 160, 162,
165, 166, 176, 184, 190,

195, 225
past, 14, 16–19, 24, 67, 96, 166,
167, 185, 194, 221, 224
path, 6, 7, 11, 15, 17, 24, 88, 126,
138, 143, 147, 152, 153,
155, 156, 158–160, 165,
166, 168, 186, 194, 213,
215, 222, 224–227, 232,
234
patience, 38, 39, 85, 233
pattern, 16
Paul, 164
pay, 68, 103, 198, 201, 242, 245
peace, 19, 62, 64, 66, 74, 75, 126,
131
people, 43, 50, 64, 68–70, 76, 92,
115, 116, 142, 150, 159,
161, 162, 167, 175, 193,
201–203, 239, 240,
242–244
percentage, 138
perception, 31, 32, 87, 105, 160,
224, 231
perfection, 183, 184
performance, 64, 122, 137, 145, 242,
245
period, 132, 189
perpetuation, 29, 229
perpetuity, 152
perseverance, 10, 154, 155, 210, 233
persistence, 39, 61, 77, 78, 119, 210,
212, 233
person, 158, 239
personhood, 31, 32
perspective, 2, 4, 5, 10, 12, 15, 20,
23, 24, 92, 106, 121, 167,
170, 216, 230, 233, 234
Peter A. ", 164
petition, 172

phenomenon, 7
philosopher, 14, 16
philosophy, 6, 10, 12, 184
photography, 142
physics, 155
picture, 154, 219, 226
piece, 99, 142, 144, 239
pillar, 24
place, 1, 12, 14, 15, 34, 45, 47, 67,
    94, 126, 153, 158, 167,
    224, 230, 237
plan, 41, 48, 52, 86, 119, 122
plane, 14
planet, 1, 2, 7, 10–12, 15, 17, 19,
    28–30, 45, 69, 71, 79, 84,
    85, 94, 96, 98, 113, 130,
    131, 133, 175, 179, 194,
    235, 237
planning, 12, 41, 42, 48, 52
platform, 25, 30, 32, 44, 55, 58, 59,
    67, 80, 82, 97, 110, 112,
    114, 120, 124–126, 143,
    144, 149, 152, 160, 193,
    197, 234, 237, 240, 241,
    244
play, 30, 36, 45, 71, 72, 75, 82, 121,
    123, 130, 136, 141, 143,
    154, 167, 170, 180, 202,
    213, 224, 230, 237, 238,
    245
playing, 72, 113, 138, 222
plight, 26, 53, 197
poetry, 137, 193, 215, 240
point, 1, 12, 13, 36, 46, 56, 65, 83,
    87, 194, 224, 236
police, 29, 205
policy, 9, 43–45, 50–52, 60, 72, 87,
    93, 98, 99, 104, 135–138,
    140, 196, 214, 219, 222

policymaking, 47
pollination, 74
pooling, 103, 120, 180
pop, 199–201
population, 10, 26, 29, 31, 32, 42,
    45, 55, 57, 58, 61, 86, 99,
    121, 125
portion, 26
position, 12, 180, 189, 224
possibility, 154, 215
pot, 5
potency, 76
potential, 4, 5, 11, 22, 23, 30, 33, 35,
    42, 52, 54, 58, 59, 62, 64,
    65, 73, 75, 81, 84, 94, 95,
    119, 141, 158, 159, 161,
    165, 166, 170, 172, 175,
    177, 180, 194, 211, 227
potluck, 179
poverty, 29, 141
power, 2, 6, 8–16, 18, 21, 23–30,
    35–37, 39, 40, 43, 44,
    47–51, 53, 54, 57–61,
    63–67, 72, 73, 75–78,
    80–84, 86, 88–90, 92, 97,
    98, 107, 109–112, 114,
    115, 117–120, 122, 123,
    130, 132, 135–137, 141,
    144, 145, 148, 149, 151,
    154–157, 160–162, 165,
    166, 168, 170, 174, 175,
    177, 184, 185, 191,
    193–195, 200–203, 205,
    210, 212, 214, 215, 220,
    222, 223, 225–227, 229,
    231, 232, 234, 236,
    239–241
practice, 137, 188
precedent, 192, 196

prejudice, 2, 6–8, 10, 23, 24, 31, 32, 46, 53, 56, 69, 73, 83, 86, 88, 90, 92–94, 96–98, 102, 103, 107, 125, 126, 140, 143, 146, 153–159, 164–167, 169, 174, 195, 196, 201, 204, 221, 222, 224, 228–234, 240
preparation, 40
presence, 57, 75, 112, 174, 219
present, 6, 45, 47, 137, 152, 163, 167, 168, 182, 188, 226
preservation, 74, 75, 148, 154, 167, 180
press, 49, 51
pressure, 43, 49, 51, 54, 56, 72, 89, 110, 120, 137, 180, 205
price, 195
pride, 167
principle, 50, 116, 162
prism, 30
privilege, 6, 23, 72, 89, 140, 215, 216
problem, 4, 29, 30, 40
process, 2, 17, 30–32, 36, 50, 52, 59, 61, 67–69, 100, 101, 108, 119, 123, 127–129, 136, 137, 140, 156, 166, 170, 183, 185, 186, 204, 228–234
professional, 176, 182, 183, 195
profile, 42
profiling, 21, 23
program, 15, 85, 96, 132
progress, 9, 23, 33, 35, 45, 49, 59, 61, 70, 74, 77, 87, 88, 106, 107, 109, 119, 141, 150, 160, 179, 185, 197, 219, 225–227, 229, 233, 235, 236, 238, 240, 242, 244

progression, 29
project, 15, 99, 239
promise, 73, 74
promotion, 68, 86, 109, 136, 139
proof, 69, 195
propulsion, 75
prosperity, 74, 75, 222
protagonist, 14, 45, 200
protection, 22, 32, 74, 93, 135, 136
protest, 35, 41, 45, 49–52, 55, 64, 66, 201
public, 31, 32, 42–45, 48, 50, 51, 53, 55, 58, 59, 63, 71, 72, 76, 87, 93, 98, 102, 105, 119, 136, 137, 139, 174, 184, 189, 193, 197, 201, 203–205, 210, 212, 219, 234, 237–240
purpose, 7, 11–15, 47, 48, 50, 82, 120, 171, 192–195, 198, 225
pursuit, 9, 12, 15, 29, 36, 61, 62, 71, 77, 82, 90, 103, 104, 110, 122, 133, 148, 160, 161, 165, 184, 187, 189, 198, 212, 218, 226, 234, 244
pushback, 189

quality, 72, 139, 176
quest, 2, 5, 55, 69, 78, 88, 126, 148, 152, 209, 211, 215, 227
question, 6, 7, 10, 14, 25, 55, 75, 143, 161, 225, 226, 243
questioning, 35, 158, 221, 224, 230
quo, 2, 6, 7, 10, 12–14, 28, 29, 34, 35, 43–46, 50, 60, 61, 66, 73, 89, 90, 111, 115, 156, 161, 175, 194, 211, 222, 224, 234, 241, 243

quota, 125

race, 23, 88, 110, 147, 170, 215
racism, 45, 104, 121
rally, 8, 29, 56, 191
rallying, 46, 83, 157, 236, 241
range, 5, 14, 79, 81, 86, 101, 106, 116, 151, 210, 237
rarity, 11
rawness, 143
reach, 27, 54, 60, 64, 79, 80, 114, 115, 119–122, 132, 140, 143, 165, 234
realism, 225–228
reality, 10, 23, 29, 75, 80, 84, 140–143, 152
realization, 6, 33, 125, 158, 167, 221, 225
realm, 23, 47, 154, 196, 200, 214, 222
reassurance, 162
rebellion, 65
rebuilding, 67–69, 222
recognition, 2, 10, 11, 31, 32, 34, 60, 86, 89, 124, 133, 135, 149, 154, 165, 188, 202, 203, 225
reconciliation, 17, 68, 83
reconstruction, 67
record, 70
redefinition, 145
redemption, 17
reflection, 15, 35, 107, 118, 141, 158, 169, 180, 183, 189, 202, 220, 225, 228, 230, 232, 234–238
reform, 44, 45, 100
refuge, 46, 49, 123, 176
regime, 29, 46, 67, 220

registration, 100, 101
reign, 166, 168, 195
rejuvenation, 180
relationship, 20, 156, 157, 160, 161, 165
relaxation, 169
relevance, 16, 236
reliance, 75, 115
relic, 96
remembrance, 241
reminder, 9–11, 17, 33, 46, 66, 70, 71, 73, 76, 77, 88, 157, 159, 161, 166, 201, 203, 220, 225, 235–237, 239, 240, 242, 244
Rennan Jae, 142
repeal, 71, 89, 154
repository, 243
representation, 13, 30, 33, 35, 74, 93, 100, 101, 104, 105, 107, 124–126, 131, 138–140, 149, 196, 203, 214, 222, 230
representative, 9, 51, 102, 121, 179
repression, 77, 210
reputation, 189
research, 10, 25, 53, 86, 105, 107, 136, 214, 236, 243
residence, 133
resilience, 10, 11, 13, 15, 16, 35, 36, 38, 45, 46, 49, 57–59, 61, 69, 71, 76, 80, 85, 88, 115, 142, 156, 163, 165, 167–169, 171, 179, 185–191, 193, 195, 197, 199, 201, 210, 212, 218, 220, 222, 225, 227, 230–234, 237, 244
resistance, 8, 12, 13, 16, 18, 24, 27,

29, 30, 38, 39, 42, 44–46, 48–53, 56, 58, 65, 76–78, 86, 88, 90, 98, 110–112, 122, 137, 141, 156, 162, 191, 194, 206, 210–212, 222, 224–226
resolution, 20, 75, 126
resolve, 6, 8, 11, 34, 50, 56, 126, 131, 176, 180, 224
resonance, 65
resource, 73, 90, 108
respect, 17, 19–21, 66–68, 74, 75, 85–87, 92, 94, 95, 99, 102, 113, 114, 126, 127, 130, 131, 135, 140, 144, 145, 158, 166, 171, 172, 177, 178, 190, 192, 199, 203, 227, 241
response, 33, 46, 162, 188, 190, 211, 226
responsibility, 13, 22, 44, 74, 75, 171, 176, 179–181, 191, 192, 195, 199, 237, 241, 245
rest, 8, 58, 180, 182
result, 31, 196
revelation, 21
revolution, 9, 16, 45–47, 56, 65, 67, 161, 194
Rhea Patel, 143
rhetoric, 130
richness, 38, 60, 93, 96, 97, 111, 114, 126, 131, 147, 148, 157, 167, 173, 234, 240
right, 16, 32, 60, 66, 69, 77, 100, 101, 133, 137, 178, 195, 216
righteousness, 162
riot, 46

rise, 1, 2, 12–14, 70, 87, 88, 164
risk, 42, 162
road, 13, 88, 226
Robin, 164
role, 2, 16, 18, 19, 25–27, 30, 36, 43–45, 59, 68, 71, 72, 75, 76, 78, 82, 92, 103, 113–115, 121, 123, 126, 130–132, 136, 141–144, 148, 151, 154, 161–163, 167, 170, 172, 173, 175, 180, 182, 194, 202, 205, 212–216, 221, 222, 224, 227, 230, 233, 237, 238, 240, 244, 245
romance, 153–155, 160, 164, 195
room, 118
root, 10, 40, 59, 119, 184
Rosa Parks, 163
run, 126, 139

sacrifice, 198, 199
safety, 42, 43, 172, 198, 244
Safiya Umoja Noble, 144
Sagan, 213
Sarah A. Calderon, 144
satire, 28, 106, 107
say, 153
scalability, 119
scale, 13, 25, 30, 46, 54, 72, 80, 90, 108, 113, 131, 132, 143, 166, 240
scarcity, 73, 92
scenario, 29, 172
scheduling, 183
school, 92, 106, 172, 202, 243
sci-fi, 200
science, 25, 99, 127, 146, 200, 213
scrutiny, 31, 189

sculptor, 142
seat, 138–140, 222
secret, 56
section, 2, 40, 42, 175, 209, 241
segregation, 2, 29, 44, 163, 204
self, 4, 6, 7, 14, 15, 35, 60, 61, 100,
    107, 112, 135, 141, 143,
    156, 158, 160, 163,
    168–170, 180, 182–184,
    186, 187, 189, 190, 192,
    193, 219, 220, 224, 225,
    227–234
selflessness, 198
sense, 2–4, 6, 7, 11, 15, 20, 22, 23,
    25, 33, 34, 37, 38, 47–50,
    55, 56, 67, 68, 75, 80,
    82–84, 92, 93, 97, 100,
    104, 109, 113, 115, 121,
    129, 131, 145, 146, 150,
    158, 159, 161, 166–168,
    171, 173, 176, 179, 180,
    183, 191–195, 198, 201,
    205, 206, 213, 227–229,
    232, 233, 244
sensitivity, 100, 139, 178
sentient, 6, 73–75, 80, 94, 132, 133,
    135, 221, 222, 236
sentiment, 164
separation, 145
series, 56, 142, 144, 200, 239
serve, 16, 18, 36, 43, 59, 72, 73, 83,
    90, 110, 111, 117, 118,
    121, 129–131, 149, 175,
    185, 198, 201, 203–205,
    213, 219, 225, 237, 238,
    241–244
service, 171
set, 1, 6, 7, 16, 59, 67, 73, 79, 121,
    127, 132, 158, 177, 191,
    192, 194, 196
setback, 184, 185, 191, 228
setting, 42, 82, 182, 183, 219
sexism, 104, 121
sexuality, 215
shame, 158, 228
shape, 12, 13, 18, 28, 36, 69, 71, 75,
    126, 136, 138, 141, 145,
    149, 157, 167, 169, 209,
    215, 234
shaping, 12, 15, 23, 44, 68, 72, 100,
    141, 149, 170, 174, 175,
    180, 205, 213, 224
share, 14, 19, 20, 24, 25, 37, 47, 49,
    51, 54, 67, 68, 72, 81, 96,
    97, 104, 106, 108–110,
    114, 119–123, 143, 150,
    151, 160, 169, 173, 182,
    185, 194, 196, 197, 204,
    216, 219, 220, 227, 231,
    237, 240, 241, 245
sharing, 2, 7, 10, 12, 43, 58, 59, 80,
    82, 103, 108, 123, 124,
    131, 136, 140, 142, 148,
    159, 173, 180, 188, 196,
    206, 226, 233, 234
shift, 29, 35, 61, 63, 87, 96, 112,
    125, 160, 183, 184, 205,
    219, 222, 232, 241, 244
show, 39, 182, 200
sibling, 172
side, 2, 6, 12, 13, 21–23, 175
sight, 57, 142, 185, 189
sign, 188
significance, 17, 19, 36, 77, 78, 101,
    145, 147, 164, 169, 178,
    190, 210, 222, 231, 238
silence, 11, 17, 46, 188, 190
sit, 44, 48, 50, 51, 76, 211

situation, 185, 191
size, 218
skepticism, 38, 155, 160
skill, 183
skin, 28
skit, 52
sky, 5, 6, 194
social, 2, 4, 10–12, 15–18, 25–32,
 35–37, 39, 40, 43–45, 48,
 49, 51, 52, 54, 57, 58, 67,
 70–72, 74, 76, 77, 82, 85,
 88–90, 96, 97, 99, 102,
 109, 110, 112, 113, 115,
 119–121, 124, 125, 131,
 136, 138, 141, 143–145,
 147, 149, 151, 154, 157,
 160, 161, 163, 166, 168,
 170–174, 178, 184, 187,
 189, 191, 193, 197, 200,
 205, 214–216, 222, 225,
 226, 229, 232, 234,
 236–240, 242, 243
society, 2, 10–12, 17, 21, 29, 31,
 33–37, 43–45, 48, 52, 53,
 55, 58–61, 65, 67–69, 71,
 72, 77, 87–89, 93, 94, 96,
 98, 100, 102, 105–107,
 124, 126, 130, 135,
 137–141, 147, 155, 161,
 162, 166, 172–177,
 179–181, 195, 196, 198,
 199, 204, 205, 209–211,
 216, 222, 224, 228–230,
 232, 233, 235, 238, 240,
 243, 244
socio, 130
sociology, 6, 10, 214
solace, 15, 169, 175, 180, 215, 219,
 225

solidarity, 6, 11, 27, 30, 34, 37, 38,
 45, 47–49, 53, 54, 56, 60,
 66, 72, 77, 78, 82–84, 89,
 97–99, 102, 103,
 108–111, 120, 122–124,
 140, 142, 150, 159, 160,
 172, 173, 176, 193, 195,
 204, 216, 220, 222, 224,
 227, 234, 244
solitude, 215
solution, 29, 94, 132
solving, 4
song, 200, 202
soul, 7, 10, 84
source, 158, 168, 176, 238
South Africa, 30
space, 1, 2, 9, 10, 28, 58, 60, 69, 72,
 75, 80, 108, 109, 114, 115,
 119, 121, 153, 169, 171,
 176, 180, 201, 209, 236,
 240
spark, 16, 27, 45, 46, 54, 56, 66, 122,
 143, 194, 237
speaking, 11, 43, 71, 173
species, 1, 2, 5, 6, 8–10, 12–14, 16,
 19–25, 28–30, 48, 74, 77,
 79–81, 86, 88, 94–97, 99,
 102–105, 111, 113, 125,
 126, 130–133, 140–142,
 144, 147, 154–157, 160,
 164–166, 168, 169, 176,
 179, 196, 211, 222, 231,
 236, 239, 241, 244
speciesism, 104
specific, 26, 38, 48, 81, 104, 105,
 112, 119, 120, 136, 139,
 173, 182, 192, 228, 242
spectacle, 237
spirit, 11, 33, 36, 59, 67, 70, 122,

155, 161, 195, 197,
200–202, 206, 213, 214,
218, 236, 238
spirituality, 167
spotlight, 53
sprint, 227
square, 45, 51
stability, 74, 131, 198
stage, 1, 28, 54, 56, 59, 143
stand, 6, 8, 11, 59, 70, 76, 77, 83,
   161, 165, 173, 175, 196,
   221, 244
star, 194, 205
stardust, 11, 194, 221
stargazing, 7, 213
start, 119, 127, 228
state, 16, 33
statement, 57, 156
statue, 201
status, 2, 6–8, 10, 12–14, 28, 29, 31,
   34, 35, 43–46, 50, 60, 61,
   66–68, 73, 77, 89, 90, 111,
   115, 156, 161, 168, 175,
   194, 211, 222, 224, 234,
   241, 243
step, 8, 25, 36, 48, 53, 67, 94, 120,
   122, 143, 145, 155, 158,
   168, 171, 172, 185, 226,
   228, 230, 231
stereotype, 19
stigma, 188, 189
story, 1, 7, 9, 11, 13, 17, 30, 31, 45,
   59, 67, 69, 70, 81, 90, 92,
   99, 142, 155–157,
   159–161, 165, 168, 191,
   194–197, 199–203, 225,
   230, 232, 234, 237, 240,
   241, 245
storytelling, 6, 18, 30, 59, 80, 81,

112, 122, 143, 173, 175,
193, 205, 214, 220, 230,
234, 236
stranger, 45, 215
strategy, 32, 44, 49, 97, 103, 107,
   109, 119, 122, 138, 169,
   183, 190
streaming, 205
street, 12, 55, 58, 64, 118, 214
strength, 4, 13, 15, 40, 59, 66, 76,
   108, 110, 123, 157–161,
   169, 171, 180, 184, 189,
   193, 199, 201, 214, 220,
   222, 225, 227, 230–232,
   235, 241, 244
strengthening, 34, 50, 93, 109, 120,
   132, 176, 192
stress, 188
strike, 4, 176, 182, 183, 226
strip, 178
structure, 28, 29, 53, 115, 182
struggle, 10, 11, 16, 19, 24, 30, 33,
   34, 36, 43, 56, 58, 60–62,
   65–67, 70, 71, 73, 77, 79,
   80, 83, 87, 89, 92, 94, 96,
   102, 110–112, 120–122,
   124, 130, 132, 135, 137,
   150, 151, 156, 161, 162,
   167, 176, 180, 184, 185,
   191, 195, 199–205,
   209–212, 214, 218, 219,
   222, 224, 225, 231, 232,
   235–238, 241–243, 245
student, 14
study, 12, 14, 17, 221
stun, 46
style, 24, 144, 192, 193, 201, 241
subsection, 6, 14, 16, 19, 23, 26, 28,
   37, 45, 48, 53, 56, 59, 61,

62, 67, 69, 73, 76, 78, 79, 82, 88, 90, 94, 96, 99, 102, 105, 110, 112, 115, 124, 127, 130, 132, 135, 140, 142, 145, 147, 150, 153, 158, 160, 164, 168, 170, 173, 175, 177, 179, 182, 184, 187, 189, 191, 198, 201, 204, 207, 213, 216, 218, 224, 228, 231, 232, 242
success, 15, 41, 47–49, 53, 58, 66, 107, 110, 139, 151, 160, 163, 170, 185, 193, 196, 198, 229, 235
suffering, 198
suit, 8, 226
sum, 7, 227
summary, 15, 146
summer, 45
superiority, 168
supernovae, 1
support, 8, 9, 24, 29, 30, 32, 37–40, 42–44, 46, 48–52, 54–58, 66, 72, 76, 77, 86, 87, 93, 96, 105, 109, 111, 115, 117–123, 136, 139, 140, 150, 152, 154, 158, 162, 163, 165, 169–172, 175–177, 180, 182–184, 186, 188–193, 196, 197, 201, 203–205, 219, 220, 222, 224, 227, 230, 232, 234, 238, 240, 243
suppression, 12, 29, 50
surface, 23
surveillance, 49, 51, 88
suspicion, 59
sustainability, 101, 180, 182, 190, 192
symbol, 11, 35, 46, 69, 71, 142, 156, 158, 194, 201, 239, 240
sympathy, 27, 58, 211
symphony, 1
system, 8, 41, 53, 55, 79, 100, 125, 182, 183, 190, 191, 221

t, 2, 6, 7, 9, 112, 180, 241
table, 138–140, 158, 175, 222
taboo, 153, 195
tackle, 15, 87, 185, 197, 215
tactic, 42
tale, 17, 155, 194
talent, 35, 96, 149
tapestry, 2, 3, 5, 16, 24, 121, 147, 153, 167, 175, 177, 194, 221
task, 12, 48, 67, 130, 135, 179, 216
teaching, 83, 103, 106, 141, 241
team, 40–42, 48, 50, 53, 55, 57, 80, 113, 114, 198, 220
technology, 17, 25, 72, 75, 80, 81, 109, 113–115, 143, 145, 146, 151, 152, 191, 205, 206
technopathy, 28
teenager, 46
telepathy, 19
teleportation, 109
television, 200
tenacity, 214
tension, 176
term, 36, 51, 74, 96, 135, 163, 189, 190, 192, 226, 233
termination, 68
terrain, 225
testament, 11, 28, 57, 59, 67, 115, 154, 155, 157, 161, 175,

Index 279

194, 195, 220, 222, 234, 236
the United States, 30, 44, 163
theater, 17, 118, 151, 174, 240
theme, 16, 161
theory, 27
therapy, 169, 219
thinking, 4, 26, 28, 41–43, 48, 61, 90, 106, 216, 227, 237
thirst, 6, 12, 213
thought, 55, 80, 81, 143, 237
threat, 31, 88, 106, 180
thrive, 8, 33, 36, 70, 86, 96, 124, 141, 142, 147, 148, 165, 179, 198, 222, 241, 245
Thromidons, 17
time, 1, 2, 8, 10, 14, 15, 27, 39, 57, 75, 77, 114, 117, 132, 158, 163, 165, 169, 171, 176, 182–185, 189, 191, 209, 210, 212, 213, 218, 219, 225, 226, 230, 235–238
timeline, 119
tipping, 56
tolerance, 141
toll, 13, 158, 176, 179, 180, 187, 189, 190, 195, 198, 244
tomorrow, 245
tool, 19, 25, 27, 28, 36, 50, 55, 58, 62, 76, 80, 83, 94, 103, 106, 136, 137, 142, 193, 239
toolbox, 65
torch, 9, 152, 195, 197, 203, 214, 241
tourism, 93
town, 48, 58, 139
traction, 35, 65, 118
training, 15, 49, 94, 100, 118, 139

trait, 218
trajectory, 180
transformation, 7, 9, 43, 44, 72, 114, 158, 184, 196, 232, 234
translation, 24, 75, 109
transmission, 171
transparency, 51, 127, 190, 192, 193
travel, 5, 21, 42, 75, 83, 93, 109, 114, 164, 168
treatment, 21, 31, 54, 55, 59, 60, 71, 87, 92, 94, 96, 173, 204
tribute, 198, 200, 239, 242
trick, 39
trigger, 43
trip, 5
triumph, 8, 13, 65, 80, 155, 157, 165, 195, 196, 200, 214, 220, 222, 239
trust, 19, 21, 38, 39, 51, 74, 83, 108, 110, 123, 127, 129, 132, 165, 174, 185, 192
truth, 17, 83, 190
tug, 224
turbulence, 176
turn, 19, 152, 154, 220
turning, 12, 13, 36, 46, 65, 87, 194, 224

uncertainty, 75, 198, 225, 227, 228
underrepresentation, 138
understanding, 2–4, 6, 7, 10–12, 14, 15, 17–21, 24–28, 31–34, 36, 37, 39, 40, 42, 47–49, 53, 58–60, 68, 73–75, 81–85, 87, 90, 92–94, 96–101, 104–106, 108, 111, 113–115, 122–124, 127, 130–132, 135, 137, 139, 141, 142, 145, 146,

149–151, 154–157,
 159–170, 173, 176–179,
 184, 186, 194, 197, 202,
 205, 212, 213, 215, 216,
 221, 224, 225, 230–232,
 234, 238, 240, 245
undertaking, 126
unfamiliar, 31, 73, 98, 154
unfamiliarity, 92, 100
union, 2, 160
uniqueness, 4, 158, 218, 233, 234,
 239
unison, 114
unity, 4–7, 9, 12, 17, 31, 33, 34,
 36–39, 46–50, 53, 57, 59,
 60, 66, 68–70, 75, 76, 78,
 80, 84–87, 89, 92, 93, 97,
 98, 104, 106, 107, 110,
 112, 113, 120, 122, 123,
 131, 140, 142, 145–147,
 149, 154, 158–160, 166,
 168, 170, 173–179,
 192–197, 200, 209, 210,
 214, 222, 227, 234, 236,
 237, 239, 244
universality, 179
universe, 1–9, 11–15, 20, 21,
 23–26, 28, 36, 39, 43, 46,
 53, 65–67, 69–75, 78, 84,
 86, 88, 92, 94, 107, 110,
 112–114, 120–122, 124,
 130–132, 135, 138,
 140–142, 144–150, 152,
 153, 155–161, 164–167,
 172, 175, 177, 179, 185,
 189, 194, 196–200, 203,
 204, 206, 213, 215, 221,
 222, 224, 232, 234–240,
 243–245

unknown, 10, 25, 59, 73, 75, 92, 96,
 99, 153, 154, 164, 178
upbringing, 3
uprising, 8, 12, 13, 28, 40–42,
 45–48, 58, 59, 66, 67, 69,
 71, 76, 77, 79, 88, 191,
 194, 198, 222, 235, 236,
 242, 244
urge, 188, 232
urgency, 55, 206
use, 38, 43, 49, 72, 97, 112, 118,
 140, 144, 145, 151, 193,
 205, 237
utopia, 8, 9, 13, 107, 140, 145, 152,
 195, 197, 222, 241, 245

validation, 169
value, 31, 38, 61, 78, 82, 87, 88, 93,
 140, 148, 155, 156, 160,
 162, 179, 194
variety, 167
vastness, 6, 10, 24, 75, 114, 213
Vega, 14
Velan-7, 2, 48
Veridian, 4
vibrancy, 193
victory, 11, 71, 204
view, 167
vigilance, 87, 180, 204, 241
violence, 8, 12, 44, 46, 50, 58, 62, 76,
 77, 88, 97, 111, 154, 187,
 198, 210, 211
visibility, 51, 101, 104, 159
vision, 8, 9, 11, 13, 37, 47, 48, 69,
 73, 74, 84, 121, 140–142,
 149, 156, 172, 185, 195,
 197, 198, 201, 214, 222,
 226, 227, 233, 237, 243
visit, 10

Index 281

visual, 49, 57, 80, 86, 118, 122, 149, 151, 200, 201, 203, 237, 240, 242, 245
voice, 12, 35, 46, 47, 100, 102, 110, 115, 119, 121, 139, 200, 204, 210, 218, 222, 231
volunteer, 102, 171, 238
volunteering, 27, 171
Vorta, 10
voter, 100, 101
voting, 8, 99–102, 125, 204, 222
vow, 10
vulnerability, 180, 189, 220, 225

wage, 139
wake, 196, 241
wakeup, 21
walk, 142
war, 224
warning, 16
warp, 114
water, 51
wave, 43, 66, 70, 175
way, 4, 8, 21, 25, 28, 33, 45, 47, 48, 53, 63, 65, 69, 74, 75, 81, 83, 103, 105, 111, 112, 115, 120, 132, 137, 142, 146, 147, 149, 153–157, 161–163, 166, 167, 174, 175, 179, 184, 195, 196, 199–202, 218, 219, 222, 224, 225, 242–244
weakness, 188, 232
wealth, 7
weapon, 50, 222
web, 11, 14, 40, 130, 190
weight, 13, 176, 179, 180, 189, 195
welfare, 74

well, 4, 15, 42, 49, 74, 86, 89, 109, 130, 133, 161, 162, 165, 169, 172, 174, 175, 180, 182–184, 187–190, 192, 193, 198, 218, 219, 228, 231, 235
whole, 121, 145, 164, 216, 239
wildfire, 46, 56, 58
will, 2, 6, 11, 16, 19, 23, 40, 48, 66, 67, 73–76, 92, 94, 96, 105, 110, 112, 115, 130, 132, 135, 138, 150, 155, 170, 173, 175, 177, 182, 184, 187, 191, 197, 203, 207, 209, 213, 216, 218, 228, 232, 241, 242, 244
William Morrow Paperbacks, 163
willingness, 35, 38, 75, 126, 154, 164, 169, 178, 190, 191, 199, 228, 232
win, 111
window, 167
wisdom, 7, 14, 15, 19, 25, 84, 194, 227
woman, 104, 215
wonder, 7, 112, 213, 221
word, 51, 143
work, 6, 11, 15, 18, 20–23, 32, 38, 43, 55, 67–72, 81, 83, 84, 94, 96, 98, 100, 103, 110, 128, 131, 140–142, 144, 150, 152, 161, 162, 171, 172, 176, 177, 182, 183, 185, 189, 196, 197, 199–201, 203, 204, 214, 216, 220, 228–230, 235, 236, 238, 242, 243, 245
workforce, 94, 139
working, 5, 22, 27, 37, 43, 50, 74,

87, 89, 103, 110, 121, 123, 125, 136, 140, 142, 146, 148, 160, 163, 181, 199, 203, 204, 206, 212, 214, 215, 220, 227, 233, 243
workplace, 68, 94–96, 103, 139, 204, 215
workshop, 85
world, 3, 5, 9, 13, 19, 20, 25, 29, 30, 45, 64, 65, 99, 101, 105, 107, 115, 136, 140, 144, 153, 161, 162, 165, 166, 170, 171, 186, 194–197, 200, 201, 203, 214–216, 222, 225–228
worldview, 15, 166
worth, 34, 102, 125, 126, 156, 158, 162, 165, 189, 228, 233
writing, 18

wrong, 191

Xalara Zenn, 107
Xandra, 214
Xandra Renn, 214
xenolinguists, 79
xenophobia, 8, 10, 96–100, 103, 143, 167, 195, 196, 222

year, 235, 242, 244
yearning, 7, 45
youth, 6, 30, 150, 243

Zara, 142, 165, 171
Zara Kael, 142
Zara Ramos, 107
Zaraa, 160, 161
Zaraa Kallik, 160
Zaraa Kallik's, 160
Zor, 53–55, 65, 210–212